A Memoir of
Lying, Stealing,
Writing, and
Healing

THE
MANY
LIVES
OF
MAMA
LOVE

~

LARA LOVE
HARDIN

SIMON & SCHUSTER

New York London Toronto Sydney New Delhi

Simon & Schuster
1230 Avenue of the Americas
New York, NY 10020

Interior design by Lewelin Polanco

Manufactured in the United States of America

ISBN 978-1-9821-9766-7

For my boys—Dylan, Cody, Ty, and Kaden—
my forever Loves through these many lives

contents

THE
MANY
LIVES
OF
MAMA
LOVE

chapter 1

AS NEEDED
FOR PAIN

Reading was my first addiction. When I tell people this today, they laugh and nod as if they understand, as if they too are part of a secret book-addict society whose greatest crime is staying up late, a flashlight under the covers, compulsively reading page after page.

The strange thing is, no one ever asks me what my *second* addiction is. I mean, someone who loved to read could never be a real addict, could they? The kind of addict who steals from their family, betrays the people they love, commits felonies, implodes their life because the finding and using and finding more consumes every ounce of who they used to be. No one ever loses their job because they read too much. There are no book club interventions. The prisons aren't full of people who stole to fund their Kindle habit.

The truth is I've only ever had one addiction. The white whale of addictions: escape. From as far back as I can remember there has always been a better place than wherever I am. A better me than whoever I was. Books helped me escape when I was young. Not just

because of my precocious angsty-ness and early onset existential crises; they were literal escape.

Most of my early childhood memories are just stories told to me decades later. Stories of violence and starvation and abandonment.

I do remember every teacher, though, from kindergarten through high school. I remember the first multisyllabic word I read in school: *policeman.* I was so proud of myself as I sounded out the letters. In first grade I read *Gone with the Wind*—twice. It was over a thousand pages. I didn't understand Rhett Butler or Scarlett O'Hara or the Civil War, but I savored the endless tiny print pages of word after word. I savored the escape. The longer the book the better.

The only clear memories I have besides school after the age of ten are of moments of crisis. My brothers stealing my stepfather's Pinto and sinking it in Walden Pond. The police bringing my sister home for public drunkenness. My aunt Janice arriving from San Francisco in the middle of the night, her face swollen and unrecognizable—a mix of red, black, and blue. My brothers and sister dancing around my stepfather's finger that they found on the front lawn after my mom rushed him bleeding to the hospital. It was a lawn mower accident of some sort, and it was the only time I remember my siblings expressing joy. I didn't know why they hated my stepfather so much, or what made him pack up one day and leave for good.

I don't have a single memory of eating dinner at home with my family. I don't recall any vacations. If I try to remember my childhood, there is only a vague sense of fear, of unease. I have no clear picture of anything concrete or symbolic representing home, and with two of my siblings dying young, I don't have anyone left to fill in the blanks. I only see myself alone in my room, reading. And not in a meet-cute, flashlight-under-the-covers, love-affair-with-books kind of way.

When I talk about my childhood book addiction, I'm talking about a desperate grip on the pages, reading the same books over and over,

never having enough pages to fill the void. When I read, I could pretend I was someone else. I was Harriet the Spy, Nancy Drew, Lucy in Narnia. I was Scarlett O'Hara declaring she would never go hungry again. I was a teenager visiting California for the first time, meeting the boy of her dreams, and fighting all night to keep the distant family's orange grove from freezing in a cold spell. I was a feisty woman who didn't need a man until she desperately needed him in every Nora Roberts book ever written. Because we moved from Maynard to Concord, I also read Alcott, Thoreau, Hawthorne, and Emerson. I read Tolstoy and Dostoevsky but found Russian relationships to be far more confusing than the ones in Nora Roberts's worlds. I loved happy endings, characters who had clear motivations for doing what they did. I read books like a peeping Tom, and I stalked all these lives that weren't mine. Even the sad people in books had moments of joy and redemption that I envied.

Eventually the reading turned to writing. I started writing short stories in high school and they got me the attention I hungered for. I always loved school. I played varsity lacrosse and field hockey. I could be friends with the cool kids and the smart kids and the sporty kids and even the stoner kids although I didn't like to get stoned. I could cross social lines seamlessly and be whoever people needed me to be. I'd like to say it was a gift born of my curiosity about people, but in truth it was more of a response to trauma. I wanted to be loved. I wanted to feel safe. So I needed every single person I met to like me, and if I could make them love and need me, even better. After school I went home with different friends and did homework at their kitchen table and joined their family for dinner. At each home I could pretend I was exactly who they thought I must be. Everyone's parents loved me, except my own.

I was the first person in my family to get into college. I took out loans and put myself through undergrad and graduate school three

thousand miles away. I reinvented myself in California. I moved into the dorms at UC Santa Cruz and wore tie-dye shirts and played Ultimate Frisbee. I hung tapestries in my dorm room and slept with my resident adviser. Then I slept with his best friend. No one could believe, with my long beach-blond hair and my flowing hippie scarves, that I grew up in Massachusetts. The first week of college I tried mushrooms, and cocaine, and LSD. They were passed around like candy during orientation week. Who I was before college was quickly tucked away on a shelf. That Lara was over, and I was officially a carefree peace-and-love California surfer girl.

I majored in creative writing, because that meant I could keep reading, keep writing, and keep escaping. I thought I could outrun whatever afflicted my family, and I swore I would never be like any of them. I thought education equaled inoculation, and if I just kept being the good girl with the good grades who said the right things and played the right parts, my life would not end in *Anna Karenina* tragedy.

But you can't outrun yourself, and eventually books and writing didn't give me the escape I still craved. I turned to sex, and food, and money when I had it, and more sex when I didn't. And then it was opiates; Vicodin for a long, semi-manageable time, and then heroin. I was addicted to all those things and none of those things.

Escape was always my real addiction, the one true high. Books were just my gateway drug. Sex just got me pregnant. Food just made me puffy. Vicodin just helped me pretend I was happy.

The heroin, though, that gave me everything I had ever wanted—peace, joy, escape.

Until it didn't.

And everything I knew and everyone I loved was gone.

STAYCATION

The key to committing a crime is the same as it is for doing anything you're unsure of—confidence. With my head held high and a straight fake-it-till-you-make-it attitude, I walk into the Seaside Inn Resort and Spa like I belong there. I haven't showered in three days and my hair is in an unkempt topknot, but I put on my sunglasses and do my best impression of Miranda Priestly in *The Devil Wears Prada* as I saunter through the revolving door.

I stumble a little because I haven't eaten much in the last three days, and the revolutions give me vertigo. Kaden's chubby toddler hand is held tightly in mine, and he's wearing his favorite Spider-Man onesie. Our dog, Chase, is in the back seat of the car waiting with the valet. I don't have any money to tip the valet when we leave, but I'll worry about that later.

"Aren't you excited for a little vacation?" I say to Kaden. "Your brothers love the Seaside Inn, and they are going to meet up with us after school."

Kaden does a little Spider-Man wiggle and holds my hand tighter.

"They even have a hot tub," I say a little too loudly. I'm desperately trying to pass as nonchalant. The power is turned off at our house so we can't stay home with no heat and no electricity. Plus, my next-door neighbors saw me greet the mailman and take their mail along with my own, which I played off as a mistake and handed to them when they ran out of their house. But I know they know.

I'll worry about that later.

I spent the morning on my computer buying online Best Western gift cards with a credit card I had stolen from an unlocked car at back-to-school night two days ago. Then I prepaid this hotel using the gift cards. I have to show ID to check in, but I'm hoping the gift cards aren't connected to the stolen credit card. The woman had a ton of credit cards in her purse, so fingers crossed she hasn't noticed one missing.

I only took the one card, which is safely in the pocket of my sweat-pants, so I feel inordinately virtuous. I did use it to buy gas and lunch for Kaden, plus some snacks for the boys when they get here, but I kept my head down in case there were cameras at the store.

"Checking in?" the clerk asks.

"Yes," I say.

"Last name?"

I hesitate for just a second too long, and he tilts his head to the right slightly. He can't be over twenty-five, and he peers at me expectantly from behind wire-rimmed glasses. I can tell he's wearing them to look older, to look professional. I know that game, and I smile brightly at him and take a deep breath.

"Love," I say, "Lara Love."

"If I could just see your ID, please."

I let go of Kaden's hand and reach into my pocket to pull out my driver's license. I leave the credit card with another mom's name on it in my pocket.

He takes my license and then starts tapping away on his computer. I pick Kaden up in my arms and rest him against the marble counter.

The tapping continues, marked with occasional pauses while he squints at his screen. The squinting confirms to me that the glasses are just for show, and for some reason this makes me feel better.

"There are giant goldfish in the koi pond here," I say to Kaden.

The clerk smiles at me, and I smile back. "I got married here," I explain to him. "A long time ago—twelve years ago actually. My first husband."

He nods and continues tapping.

I have to stop myself from saying more. I can't act like I'm nervous. That's the first thing that will give you away. "Boy, has it changed around here."

I need to shut up, but if we can't stay here I don't know where we'll go. I'm dodging the repo men who are coming for my car, dodging a neighbor who knows I took a check from him and used it at the grocery store. I can't take Kaden home when we have no food and no electricity. If only we can get in our room, then I can take a breath and figure out what to do next.

Then it will be just like we're on vacation.

The clerk finally stops tapping. "It looks like you're all prepaid for the room for a week. I'll just need the plate number for your parking pass and a credit card for incidentals."

My grip on Kaden tightens. *Shit, shit, shit.* I completely forgot that part of resort check-in. I have to think on my feet. I don't have a working credit card.

"Will you charge the card?" I ask. "My sister's joining me here and I left my purse in her car. I happen to have her card, though. Long story. But I don't want to charge anything to her. This trip is my treat, so can I switch the card later?"

"We'll just authorize the card, but you can use a different card if there's a balance when you check out."

"What sister?" asks Kaden.

I smile at him but ignore the question. My sister died twenty years ago, but I can't think about that right now. I just need to get us to our room. I pull out the card and hand it to the clerk. He swipes it without even looking at the name, and I realize I've made up the sister lie for no reason.

"There's not a lot of people here right now; we're before the holiday rush, so I've upgraded you."

I don't register what holiday he's talking about, but then I remember it was just Halloween so he must be talking about Thanksgiving. "Thanks so much, that's very kind. My sister will love it here. She's visiting from the East Coast."

I really need to stop talking.

"And we're a polling place, so in a couple of days there will be a lot of activity in our main ballroom for the presidential election, but your room is far away."

"Oh great, I love to vote."

He just blinks at me a few times too many and says nothing.

"We love Obama," I add unnecessarily, looking down at Kaden for acknowledgment.

Kaden has no comment on the election, and after an awkward pause, the clerk hands me a set of key cards in a little envelope. "Two keys enough?"

I nod and watch as he writes the room number on the outside. He pulls out a little map of the resort. "You're here," he says, and marks the lobby with an X. "If you drive around to the right side here, you can park right behind your suite. Room service is until ten p.m., and the hot tub is really close for Spider-Man. And the koi are here."

I study the line he's drawn with an arrow to our room as if it's an

algebra problem I'm going to be tested on. "Wonderful, and thanks so much for the upgrade."

"Ready, buddy?" I ask Kaden.

"I want a baby sister," he says.

"I think three older brothers is enough," I say with a laugh. I roll my eyes at the clerk before we turn to walk out, but then remember I'm still wearing my sunglasses.

I really need to get it together.

My car is still out front, and the valet looks at me expectantly. "I don't have any cash on me," I say, "but I'll catch you before we go out to dinner."

"No problem," he says.

Only it is a problem, one of many big problems.

We park and walk into the hotel through an open courtyard. Our suite is located on the ground floor and is decorated with seashell lamps and large abstract paintings that I think are supposed to look like ocean waves. Despite its name, the Seaside Inn is a good twenty-minute walk to the nearby state beach, with Highway 1 running between the hotel and the shore. The suite is large, and there's a bedroom with two beds and a large living room with a beige foldout couch. There's also a sliding door that opens to the back where I've parked, which makes it easier to sneak in the dog and unload our bags, toys, snacks, and dog food. Once everything is inside, I hang the DO NOT DISTURB sign, double-lock the door, and pull the curtain closed in front of the slider. Only then do I lie down on the bed and take a deep breath. I still have to figure out the credit card situation and tip the valet, but for now we are here. We are safe.

And I can pretend everything happening outside of this room is far, far away from me. Not long ago, I could vacation at a resort like this for real, with my own credit card and ID and plenty of cash to tip everyone. In the past year, my life has collapsed.

I turn on PBS for Kaden and give him a Fruit Roll-Up, and as *Sesame Street* plays I grab my purse, walk into the bathroom, and lock the door.

I carefully unfold the tarnished piece of foil and study its surface. It's marred with black scorch marks and tiny remnants of black tar heroin. There's nothing here really, but it's worth a shot. I grab a lighter and a straw, and I hold the flame under the bottom of the foil and pray that something on the surface bubbles into smoke. I just need a little bit to get me through until my husband, DJ, gets here with more.

I had told him I would handle the hotel if he handled the drugs. "Go provide," I had joked, "while I get shelter."

But now, sitting in this bathroom, my joke doesn't feel that funny. And the tinfoil yields nothing but parched soot.

I open the door to check on Kaden. "You okay, baby guy?"

He smiles at me, his baby teeth covered in red Fruit Roll-Up, and points at Big Bird. "I know," I say, "I love him too! I'll be out in a sec, okay?"

He turns back to the television, and I close the bathroom door and sit on the marble floor. I dump my entire purse out and carefully move all the items—hairbrush, which I haven't used in a while, wallet, empty pill bottle, grocery store receipt—to the side in their own pile. Then I carefully pick through the dust and bottom-of-purse debris until I find some small brown chips. I carefully use the pad of my index finger to blot them up and then gently scrape them onto the foil. I do this over and over until every last crumb rests on the foil. This time, when I put the flame under the foil, the top slightly boils and smoke rises. I quickly inhale it through the straw and hold my breath as long as possible. I don't know if I'm smoking heroin or food crumbs or lint, but I feel the anxiety slowly leave my chest.

Anxiety for me has always felt like being in trouble, and with one big exhale, for a few brief shiny-foil moments, I feel all my troubles float away.

~

No villain ever thinks of herself as a villain, and certainly in the story I told about my life, I was always the good guy. Everything I did, I told myself, was for my children. In my mind, my crimes had no victims, or if they did, the victims were corporate entities so vast they were as formless as air. I couldn't think about the woman whose card I had used to check into the Seaside Inn, because I knew her. She was a crunchy, granola-type mom with five children all in a Montessori school. We weren't close, except in the way mom friends are who only say hi to each other at school events or birthday parties or commiserating in the pickup line after school. I didn't know her story, or what she did for a living besides being a mom, or what she feared or what her struggles were. In my mind, she had to be someone well off, oblivious to suffering, untouched by heartache or struggle. Just another perfect mom living a perfect life, parenting perfectly in her perfect house with her perfect partner.

She probably did Pilates, made her own yogurt, and had deep, meaningful conversations with her close circle of friends.

I didn't hate her; I just wished I could be her.

~

DJ doesn't get to the hotel until almost nine. Kaden is asleep in the bedroom when he comes in.

"Nice place," he says.

"Did you get it?"

"Who takes care of you?" he asks.

"You?" I say weakly.

"That's right. I sold some stuff from the house and hooked us up." His pupils are tiny pinpricks, so I know he used before he came here. I feel jealous, and I'm anxious for the small talk to stop so I can get to

it. I don't ask what he sold because I don't want to know. I just hope it wasn't anything that belonged to our children. I have three boys from my first marriage, he has a boy and a girl from his first marriage, and together we share Kaden Love Jackson—the second-marriage baby glue that holds us all together. We are a blended family, sharing custody and coparenting with our exes: we don't believe in saying "step" children or "half" siblings.

Six children ages three to seventeen who depend on me.

I don't tell DJ about the stolen credit card, because he's just set down a golf-ball-size lump of black tar heroin. "Wow," I say. "Did you sell your car?"

He shakes his head and pulls out a fresh sheet of tinfoil. He breaks off a small piece of heroin and hands it to me along with a strip of foil. I get up quickly to check that Kaden is still sleeping in the other room and then softly close the door between the bedroom and the living room.

"Did the boys come after school?" DJ asks.

"No. Cody had basketball and Dylan was with friends and Ty said he had a lot of homework."

"So Bryan and Darcy wouldn't let them?"

"No, they just had teenage things to do. It's a school night for them." I know I sound defensive, but it's easier for me to believe my boys are busy than face the truth: I'm chaos right now, and they have chosen to stay at their dad's.

"I mean, it's the same with Hailey and Logan."

DJ blows smoke in my face. "It's her week with them, but the boys were going to spend time with you."

I can't believe we are going to have a coparenting fight right now. I haven't told DJ that Bryan informed me he is keeping the boys for the foreseeable future because they told him I wasn't getting them to school on time, or picking them up on time, and that I was making

dinner really late at night, if I made it at all. "Handle your business," is all he said to me, which is Bryan-speak for "Get your shit together, because I know something is wrong but I don't really want to know what." I never would have told Bryan anyway, but it would have been nice to have been asked if I was okay.

I'm suddenly so angry at DJ I want to throw something at him, but I don't want to wake Kaden. "You know," I say, "this hotel is where Bryan and I had our wedding." It's not a lamp to the face, but it will still cut him.

"Great. Did you have your honeymoon night in this room?"

"Maybe."

In truth, our wedding night was spent in a top-floor suite on the other side of the hotel. Our friends had covered the bed in rose petals, but we were so tired we'd just brushed them off and gone to sleep. Dylan was a year old, and I was pregnant with Cody at the time, so I wasn't up for a wild night unless it involved a foot massage and more wedding cake. But those are the last things I would tell my current husband right now.

After we smoke, DJ immediately nods off on the couch and begins to snore. I check the locks on the doors and peer out the back window to make sure the car is still there. Opiates never make me sleepy. They give me a boost of energy and life. They make me feel capable and normal.

The credit card is still in my pocket, so I pull it out and read the name: Carol Clark. For some reason the alliteration makes me weepy, and I send a silent apology to Carol wherever she is.

Then I call Bryan.

"Hey," I say. "Sorry to call so late."

"No problem," he says. "What's up?"

"We're having a little staycation at the Seaside Inn. Just a break before the holiday madness, you know?"

Bryan says nothing.

"Could the boys come by after school tomorrow for swimming and dinner? The pool is heated and there's a hot tub. I'll bring them back to your house right after dinner."

Still more silence.

"Please, I really miss them. I know things have been a bit crazy, but all is good now, really."

"Are you sure?"

"I promise. Everything with me is back to normal." I stare down at the half-melted lump on the tinfoil. When we were married, I had told Bryan I had a problem with Vicodin. *I took three pills every day this week and they make me so happy,* I had said. *I think I have a problem. I might need help. Please throw them away for me. I can't do it.*

He had just shrugged and put them on the top shelf of the linen closet. *"It's no big deal, everyone takes them."* Later that week, after watching out the window all night waiting for him to come home, I had dragged a chair over to the closet and retrieved the bottle. Five years later we were long divorced, and my three pills a day had become sixty.

I look over at DJ snoring and say the thing on my mind to Bryan. "It's no big deal, everyone goes through a hard time now and then."

He doesn't get the reference.

~

I wake up to the hotel phone ringing loudly. Its tone is shrill and jarring. DJ is not in the bed next to the one Kaden and I are sleeping in, and I fumble with the receiver when I answer.

"Hello?" My voice comes out dry and croaking. I'm dehydrated and my head hurts.

"Ms. Love?"

"Yes?"

14

"There is a problem with your credit card that we need to speak to you about." The woman's voice is too sharp for my brain.

"It's my sister's card."

"Well, it's been reported stolen, so we need to speak to your sister."

"She's asleep right now."

"Well, we need you both to come to the front desk immediately."

I look around the room frantically. "Okay, just give us a few minutes and I'm sure we can sort this out. There's obviously been an error with the bank. I'll give you another card, and my sister can call the bank with you."

Her tone softens. "Well, okay, that would be great. I'll be here, and I'll see you in a few."

"Fifteen minutes tops," I say. "My baby is sleeping so I need to get him up."

"Oh, I'm so sorry, of course . . ."

"It's okay, it's not your fault. We'll be there as soon as possible. We're supposed to be on a staycation." I laugh softly and hang up.

I run into the living room, but DJ isn't there either, and when I look out the back window his car is gone. I try his cell but he doesn't answer.

Now what? I go into the bathroom and splash water on my face. My eyes are red-rimmed and my face is pale. I quickly pinch my cheeks to give them color and hurriedly throw my sweats and T-shirt on. I open the slider and let the dog out to pee and then put him in the back of my SUV. I roll down the front passenger window and run back into the suite grabbing everything I can carry and then run back out to toss it through the window. I do this several times, just loosely piling up toys and food and Kaden's books and our clothing on the floor and the passenger seat. I toss our empty tote bags on top of the pile then run back inside. DJ must have taken all the heroin because I can't find anything but the used foil and my lighter and straw. I throw

them in my purse and strap it across my body. Kaden is still sleeping, both arms stretched above his head and his cheeks rosy pink. I gently lift him from the bed and carry him to his car seat. He wakes up when I strap him in.

"Hot tub now?" he asks. "Fish?"

"Soon, baby," I say. "We're going to go play at the park first."

I close the back door and get in the driver's seat. I don't have time to worry if DJ will come back before I get ahold of him. I throw the car in reverse and peel out of the lot. As I'm driving back toward the lobby I see a serious-looking man and woman in black suits walking toward my room. They look like security, and their heads whip around to watch as I speed past.

"No park, I want to see the fish." Kaden starts to cry in his car seat, and I know a full-blown three-year-old tantrum is brewing. "Fish!" he screams and begins to kick his feet against the back of the passenger seat.

I turn onto the highway but don't know where I'm going. Kaden is crying harder, and I want to cry with him. We're both tired and hungry and want comfort. I get off the freeway at the exit to our house but instead of going home I drive to Willowbrook Park. It's Kaden's favorite, and I'm hoping a turn on the swings will distract him.

I need to take him to see some fish.

I need to find DJ.

I need to call Bryan and tell him there's been a change of plans.

I need so many things I can't think straight, but mostly I need to smoke some heroin because I'm already starting to feel a bit nauseous and uncomfortable. Every mom from our neighborhood goes to Willowbrook with their children, and I definitely don't want to see anyone I know. Not looking like this. Not feeling like this.

I pull up next to the park but don't turn off the car. Kaden is suddenly quiet, distracted by all the kids playing.

I startle when my cell rings, but quickly see it's DJ. "Where are you?" I say instead of hello.

"I went to get some stuff from the house."

"Is the power still off?"

"Well, it's not going to magically turn itself on."

"I had to leave the hotel," I whisper into the phone. "We're at Willowbrook. They found out the card was stolen. I ran out the back. And I need to . . . you know . . . you took the stuff."

"Yeah, sorry. I'm just around the corner, I'll be right there."

My whispering has caught Kaden's attention, so I smile at him in the rearview mirror. "Want to go on the swings?" I ask brightly. "We'll have a picnic."

All I have is chips and Fruit Roll-Ups and juice boxes, but that will have to be enough. I try to push all the clothes and toys down onto the floor so if anyone I know walks by they won't think I'm messy and homeless.

I'm so messy and homeless.

DJ's truck rolls up in a couple of minutes, and he is lit up and happy. He swings Kaden out of his car seat while surreptitiously handing me the ball of heroin. "Handle your business while we play," he says.

What is it with men telling me to handle my business?

I get in the back seat and hang towels in the windows so I can't be seen while I smoke. The dog starts to whine so I know he needs to be walked.

I have to make a plan but can't until I get my mind right. I need to get the power on at home. I need to call Bryan so that he doesn't bring the boys to the hotel later. I need everything to go back to the way it was a year ago. I was clean and sober and running a successful business, and I wasn't stealing and lying and running from hotel security.

After my fifth inhale, I decide I'm going to report my purse stolen—that will explain my ID being used with a stolen credit card. This idea

feels ingenious, and as soon as I have a plan I relax. I will also call PG&E and pretend I've just moved into our house as a renter and need to set up new service. They won't bill me for a month. I can't believe I haven't thought of this before.

High on the heroin, I pull the towel down and look outside—it's beautiful. The grass is green and the sky is blue and children are laughing and playing. I'll tell Bryan that he can drop the boys at the house after school. I know I'll need some groceries before they get there, but as I see all the blankets spread on the green, green grass and all the diaper bags and backpacks and purses lying unattended on those blankets while parents chase their toddlers around the park, I know I can get grocery money easily.

In this moment, anything and everything feels possible. I don't want to stay at a hotel, I want to go home. My home with Kaden's giant playroom, where my boys have their bedrooms with matching bedroom sets, and the dog has room to run, and my king-size bed is comfortable and warm.

Kaden and I will bake cookies and start getting ready for Thanksgiving by making construction paper turkeys after tracing his beautiful little hand on the thick brown paper and cutting carefully around the lines. I'll pull out the glue sticks and stickers that he loves, and we'll watch his favorite Disney movie, *Mulan*, and I'll make popcorn with butter and salt, and we'll both take baths and come out clean.

It will be cozy and soft and all the good things.

My boys will come home, and I will talk about college applications with Dylan, and basketball with Cody, and Ty will tell me about the latest books he's reading and all about the magical worlds where the stories take place.

In this moment I know everything is going to be okay, it's all going to work out. I will fix all the things I have broken.

I just need to go home.

chapter 3

CUL-DE-SACS
AND
SQUAD CARS

H ide the drugs!"
DJ thrusts a piece of tinfoil and a small baggie made of
Saran Wrap filled with white powder into my hand and runs out of
our bedroom. I'm still trying to register what sounds like a million fists
pounding on the front door. I don't know if it's cocaine or meth in the
wrap. I have never asked. I look around our bedroom, which lacks a
secret hidey-hole to stash drugs when the police come. This isn't a
crack house or a drug den; it's an overpriced two-story home on a cul-
de-sac in Aptos, California.

I look around our room, the tinfoil held awkwardly in my hand like
a butler holding out a silver tray. I hear loud voices downstairs.

Kaden is down there. Now that the power is back on, I had just
gotten him settled in the living room in front of the big screen to
watch his favorite show, *Wonder Pets!* We lined up all his stuffed an-
imals around him in a circle. We sing the theme song all day every

19

day—it's about teamwork and saving a baby penguin that's in trouble. It's sappy but not as bad as the purple dinosaur song that was the soundtrack when my three older boys were toddlers.

I could use the Wonder Pets right now because I'm in trouble. I'm not surprised the police are here, but I'm also not prepared.

I pull open DJ's sock drawer and throw the tinfoil in the back. In our bathroom, I pull out the top drawer of the vanity and throw the small baggie in the back, behind the toothpaste and eye drops and dental floss.

These drugs have lived in our home for almost a year, and like bad houseguests, they have taken over everything. I should have evicted them. Instead I welcomed them, and now it's too late.

DJ calls my name from downstairs. I walk out of my room and down the hall.

To the left is Kaden's room—my sweet baby with the pudgy cheeks and the white-blond curls who loves stickers and dogs and who can only fall asleep at night if I lightly run my fingernails up and down his arm.

Straight ahead is the room Ty and Cody share. To the right is the room my stepchildren, Hailey and Logan, share. Dylan's room is downstairs.

We are a confusing group at back-to-school nights and sporting events. My ex-husband and his wife. My current husband's ex-wife and her partner. My current husband and me. Kaden is the only constant, the child who doesn't share time at another house. We like to think we are progressive parents who put the needs of our children over our own needs and wants. But that's a hard truth to justify considering I've just hidden illegal drugs in my bedroom. Considering I've failed them all.

I have tried to be the mom I never had. I've tried to show up. Let them know they are loved. I have the house and the SUV. I volunteer in the classroom and only occasionally argue with refs at junior high basketball games. I've tried so hard to play the part of the perfect

mother. But trying to be the perfect mother makes it really hard to admit when you have a problem.

Perfect mothers don't do drugs.

And perfect mothers don't get arrested.

~

I pause at the top of the stairs and look down. Two sheriff's deputies in uniform are staring up at me.

Like Scarlett O'Hara at her first ball, I descend the stairs slowly. Only I am no debutante and neither of these men are Rhett Butler.

I see the past year in a flash, and I realize that every single choice has led to this moment. I can't pretend I didn't know it was coming. I used to imagine what I would do if they came for me. I'd put a ladder out my back window that I could climb down, Kaden in my arms, and escape into the woods behind our yard. I never put the ladder up, though. Maybe I didn't want to escape. Or maybe I just knew I had no one and nowhere to run to.

I still had enough self-awareness to know that this person I had become was not me. I didn't hurt people. I didn't steal. I didn't lie. I didn't push away friends and family. I didn't cheat on my husband. I didn't neglect my children. I didn't do hard drugs. I didn't commit crimes. Only I did. I do.

And I am so tired. I don't eat. I rarely drink water. I have been living on Reese's Peanut Butter Cups, Coca-Cola, and heroin smoke. My clothes are hanging off me. I finally found the perfect diet to lose the extra baby weight, but an unfortunate side effect of the addiction diet is there's no one left in your life to admire your new physique. Plus, it turns your skin gray. From the neck down I look fantastic, but my face looks like I'm pushing eighty instead of forty. A few months ago, when a worried friend asked me how I had lost so much weight, I said I'd read *The Secret* and was visualizing myself skinny. I thought

it was genius at the time, but that's another symptom of addiction—thinking you're smarter than you really are. I promised her I was okay, and I thought she believed me.

I have been pretending I'm okay for so long that I don't even know what *okay* means.

I go to sleep every night swearing I will fix everything tomorrow. I will end this marriage. I will get clean. I will stop trying to hustle through the day like the perfect cul-de-sac housewife I thought I wanted to be.

Tomorrow I would face the fact that all our money was gone, school fees were unpaid, the mortgage was behind, the car was about to get repossessed, my business was in shambles. But yesterday I had to steal to buy groceries, gas, and the drugs that would get me through today so I could fix everything *tomorrow*.

Lather. Rinse. Repeat.

As I take each tentative step down those stairs—see the handcuffs the deputy has out for me, hear the *Wonder Pets!* theme song playing louder and louder—I know I've run out of tomorrows. And part of me is relieved. But then I lock eyes with Kaden, who has looked away from his show, from his stuffed animal family, and I can see his worry. He knows this is not normal.

"Turn around," says one of the sheriff's deputies, yanking an arm and spinning me so it's behind my back.

Kaden stands up at the loud voice.

"It's okay," I say as the handcuffs snap on. "Watch your show. I promise it's going to be okay." My voice cracks when I tell this lie. I give him a big fake smile.

The deputy starts to push me toward our family room. I see Kaden's lip quivering. "Please," I beg, "please just watch your show."

He takes a step toward me. "No," I yell, harsher than I mean to. The Wonder Pets start singing again, and he sits back down.

The other deputy goes upstairs, and DJ follows me to the family room. They have not handcuffed him. We sit next to each other on the couch. I watch him surreptitiously pull a tiny baggie out of his pocket and tuck it in the back of the couch. He's stuffed drugs down with the loose change, pencils, bouncy balls, and all the other couch detritus of suburban life.

The deputy asks us, "What is my partner going to find upstairs?"

I think about the drugs I have just poorly hidden. I also think about the neighbors' mail and credit cards that I've stuffed in a drawer in my closet. I don't answer, and neither does DJ, because we have watched every episode of *Law & Order*. I just stare at the back wall of the family room. It's a dark blue accent wall. When we moved into this house, with down payment help from my mother-in-law, I let the kids choose what color they wanted for each of their rooms. I decided on the cream walls in the family room except for this accent wall. I felt so happy to be someone who had an accent wall in her home. This house wasn't in my name but it was my house—it was the first house I had ever come close to sort of owning. And this accent wall had always made me feel like I was an adult who had her shit together. This accent wall was a lie.

The deputy glares at us while riffling through our papers on the coffee table. Past-due notices and permission slips and postcards from the dentist reminding us it's time for a teeth cleaning. The deputy upstairs shouts, and I know he's found the drugs.

Suddenly there are more deputies in the house. I hear the front door open and close, and DJ is handcuffed, and they are reading us our rights.

My shoulders ache from the cuffs, and I can't make sense of what's happening in the chaos. I remember reading about spontaneous combustion when I was in middle school. How people can be going about their life, and suddenly they just implode and turn into a pile of ash on

the ground. I was obsessed with this idea when I was thirteen. How a person could be there one minute and gone the next. How every problem, worry, math test, etc. could all disappear in an instant.

As a kid, spontaneous combustion didn't scare me—I was fascinated by the possibility. It gave me hope.

~

I hear loud voices in the living room and awkwardly try to stand up without using my arms.

"My son . . ." I plead.

"Do you understand the rights I have explained?"

DJ nods.

"Why don't you tell me what else we're going to find? Things will go easier on you if you tell me ahead of time. If you talk to me."

DJ shakes his head no again, and I'm not sure what to say. I don't know what he means by go easier.

"Are we under arrest?" I ask. "Can I call someone to pick up my son, please?"

The other deputy is in the room now, holding the drugs. "We've got Child Protective Services here." He gives me a dirty look.

"Please, can't I call a family member to come get him? We have family who can be here in five minutes."

"It's too late for that."

"Please . . ." I start to cry now and have no way to wipe my eyes.

"Are you going to talk to us? It will make it easier on your baby if you do."

"We aren't saying anything, this is all bullshit!" DJ says angrily.

My whole body is shaking, and I just want to get to Kaden. The deputy matches DJ's anger and roughly grabs my elbow as I stand. "Let's go, then." He pulls me back toward the front door.

Five strangers are gathered at the bottom of the stairs and through

my open front door I see nothing but police cars in front of the house. Kaden runs to me when I get to the door. He is crying and holding his arms out for me to pick him up, but I can't comfort him with my hands cuffed behind my back. I drop to my knees and his arms go around me.

"Mommmyyyy . . ." He is crying and burrowing his face into my neck. A man and a woman in dark suits are talking to the deputies. Child Protective Services.

"I love you, baby," I cry. "These people are friends. It's okay, they are going to take you somewhere for a while, but it's okay, it's okay . . ."

He gets hysterical and tries to climb on me, his arms around my neck. "I don't want to go. Please, Mommy, please."

At that moment I split into two pieces. One is me floating on the ceiling and watching Kaden crying and pleading with the other me as strangers pry his arms from my body and pull him out the door.

Kaden is there. And then Kaden is gone.

I wish I could stay on the ceiling. I wish I could spontaneously combust. I wish I could go back in time and do everything differently.

DJ and I are pulled outside. Our neighbors stand in front of their houses. Our cul-de-sac is full of police cars.

All I can think is *I did this. This is what I have done.*

chapter 4

THE
SALLY PORT

The back of the police car smells like rust and vomit. DJ and I don't say a word, and our hands are still cuffed behind our backs. I look down as we make the turn around the cul-de-sac. I know my neighbors are all outside, but I don't want to see them. The deputy doesn't say a word but glances at us in the rearview mirror periodically. DJ's right knee moves up and down rapidly, and every few minutes he blows out a big gust of air as if he has just run a sprint.

We drive past the Montessori school before getting on the freeway. The same school where at desperate moments over the last few months I would drive to at 8 a.m., even though my kids no longer went there, knowing that moms always leave their purses in their unlocked cars at private schools. Once they went inside, I would steal any cash I could find or a credit card if they didn't have cash. And then I would slip back into my white SUV, perfect soccer mom camouflage, and tell myself that I was only using the money to feed my children. I never

followed that virtuous thought all the way through to the truth behind it: I needed to steal money for food because I spent all my own money on drugs. It was so much easier to tell myself that I was only hurting the credit card companies, and that twenty dollars here or there meant nothing to these other parents.

I duck my head in case anyone I know is driving in front of the school or stopped at the light and might see me in the back of a police car. DJ sees me do this.

"Fuck them," he says. He always gets angry when he's defensive, when he feels like he's being attacked.

~

The police car doesn't pull into the jail parking lot but the county courthouse across the street. There's a steep driveway that goes under the walkway between the side of the building that holds six or seven courtrooms and the side that holds the offices of the tax assessor, the county recorder, and the district attorney. I've never noticed this driveway before, or the underground area that traverses the whole complex. I dated an assistant DA back in college who showed me all around these buildings, but we never came down here.

"Welcome to the tombs," the deputy says over his shoulder.

"Why are we at the courthouse?" asks DJ.

"You're going to talk to some detectives, they have some questions for you."

"We're not talking to anyone."

I don't say anything as DJ and the deputy glare at each other.

"You're not going to talk to the detectives?"

Another deputy walks out of the tombs and up to the car as the driver lowers the window. "What's the problem?"

"He says he doesn't want to answer any questions."

"What about her?" The deputy nods at me.

28

"She's not answering questions either," says DJ.

Normally, as a good feminist, I would tell DJ I can speak for myself, but in this case I can't speak. Even though it's a bright sunny day outside, it is dark and eerie under the courthouse. I don't like this place they call the tombs, and I definitely don't want to go inside. The deputies and DJ argue, and I open my mouth to finally speak, but nothing comes out.

"It will be easier for you if you talk to the detectives."

"Like I said at the house, we're not talking without our attorney."

DJ sounds important when he says this, and confident, but as far as I know we don't have an attorney.

The deputy from the tombs shrugs and steps away from the car. "Take them over to the jail and book 'em."

DJ smiles like he's won something. Until recently he was a mortgage broker, so that smarmy look comes easily to him.

It's a one-minute drive over to the county jail. The deputy pulls up to the side of the building. "I'm going to take you in one at a time. Do not make eye contact or talk to anyone in the sally port. There are cameras everywhere. We will see if you drop anything. We will see if you send a signal to anyone."

I have no idea what a sally port is and who or what we would be signaling. He takes DJ out of the back seat on the driver's side first and then in through some double doors. They are tinted so I can't see what's on the other side. I swivel my head around looking for who I'm not supposed to signal or make eye contact with. All I see are police cars from all the different cities that make up this county—Watsonville, Santa Cruz, Capitola—but Aptos isn't incorporated, it's a village technically, so it's under the domain of the sheriff. The other police cars are empty. I stare out the front window and then, one by one, I see three women poke their heads around the side of the building and then step out in front of me. They are wearing green pants and

white shirts—like they are nurses or doctors. One of the women waves to me, but I can't wave back. She has huge brown eyes and long, thick brown hair pulled into a high ponytail. The other two glance over at me then look away. They are wearing some kind of black hairnet and are discussing something intensely. All three women crouch down and look under the cars and then bolt upright and back around the building when the double doors slide open.

The high ponytail woman pokes her head out one more time, grinning, and waves at me again as the deputy walks over to open the passenger-side back door. It's not easy getting out without being able to use my arms. I'm weak and definitely haven't been doing my squats, but I manage to stand and when I stumble a little, the deputy grabs my bicep tightly. Too tightly.

He drags me stumbling toward the double doors, and they open automatically. We step inside and they quickly close behind us. There's another set of double doors. I wait for them to open but they don't. We stand there awkwardly.

After a few minutes pass I take a deep breath. "Can you tell me where my son is, where they took him?"

He ignores me.

"Please," I beg, and my voice catches on the word.

For the first time he looks right in my eyes and growls, "You will never see him again."

I start to cry. "Please, just tell me where he is, tell me if he's okay."

He slowly looks me up and down. My hair is still a rat's nest piled on top of my head. I'm wearing an old T-shirt, loose sweatshirt, and baggy pajama bottoms. I know my eyes are red and swollen from crying. A look of disgust comes over his face. "He is better off without you. You should not be anyone's mother."

He gives my bicep a hard squeeze as he says this, and then the double doors open and he pushes me inside.

I want to push back but I don't. I want to scream in protest, but all I can see in my mind is Kaden reaching out for me as he was taken away. Dylan, Cody, and Ty will be out of school by now. They must know what's happened. The deputy's words echo in my head. *I will never see Kaden again. I will never see any of my boys again. I should not be anyone's mother.*

I know what he says is true, and I hang my head. A tsunami of shame and grief and guilt and loss washes over me, and then there is nothing but numbness.

I am grateful for the numbness.

I am nobody's mother.

I am nothing.

~

I get my picture taken and press each finger into black ink and onto a little card, and then I am locked in a cold cell the size of a changing room at Target. There's a little window in the door and a pay phone on the wall and a bench in one corner. I sit on the bench and move my wrists in circles now that I am out of the handcuffs.

Nothing happens for what feels like hours, and once in a while I peek out the window and see deputies come and go. If I tilt my head to the right, I can barely see another door with a small window and what I think is DJ's face pressed against it. I stare at the pay phone. I don't know who I'm supposed to call—who I could call.

I shiver. It's been roughly twelve hours since I last smoked heroin, and I'm about to start detoxing. I've never detoxed from heroin, but I've quit pills a million times so I think it will probably feel the same. Cold shivers, body aches, runny nose—basically the flu on steroids. I have a strong constitution, though, so I've always been able to hold my liquor, take twenty Vicodin and sound normal, detox, and not get too ravaged. I come from a long line of hardy Scandinavian women. I

31

am descended from women who survived because they didn't pass out in front of a Viking.

I finally stand and pick up the pay phone. I don't have money, so I press zero for the operator.

"I need to place a collect call," I say. I tell her the phone number and my name, and after a few minutes I hear the muted sound of a phone ringing.

No one answers.

"Can you try again?" I ask the operator. "She just doesn't recognize the number."

I hear the far-off sound of a phone ringing again and then, finally, it stops.

"Hello?"

My mom has always answered the phone as if the house was on fire around her.

"I have a collect call from Lara Love," the operator says. "Do you accept the charges?"

There is a long pause before she answers.

"Yes, I accept."

I wait a few seconds for the operator to hang up although I don't know how collect calls work. Maybe she has to stay on to keep us connected. I would listen to collect calls if I had her job. I mean, how could you not?

"Mom?"

"Hold on," my mom says. I can hear her fumbling and then the click of a lighter and a long drag on a Marlboro. I feel the same old annoyance at her smoking that I have felt since I was a kid. But then I remember where I am: no place to judge.

"Mom . . ." My voice cracks, and I feel the tears start all over again.

"I don't have any money," she says. "Your bail is two hundred and fifty thousand dollars."

"What?"

"DJ's mom called me. You know I don't have that kind of money. Oh, Lara, this must be a mistake. Carol said there was a gun in the back of your car."

"What are you talking about?"

"You have gun charges against you. And drugs and robbery and . . ." Her voice fades off, and I don't know what to say.

"We don't have any guns, that's wrong." I listen as she takes a long drag again and blows it heavily into the phone. "What about Kaden?" I ask. "Did she say anything to you about Kaden, about where he is? Or the other boys?"

"No."

"Can you please call her back and ask her? I'm sure she's talking to DJ. And then I'll call you back."

"I can't deal with this tonight, Lara. It's too much. There's nothing I can do. This must be DJ's fault."

"It's not, Mom. This is all my fault." I start to cry again. The little holding cell echoes with my sobs and a high-pitched wail that comes from somewhere deep inside me. I try to say "Mom" again, but I am choking on my tears and snot. I try to get it together, but I can't.

My mom doesn't say a word, or if she does I can no longer hear her. I hang up and slide down the wall to the floor. I'm grateful she can't call me back. Grateful no one can reach me in this place. I lift my forehead a few inches and then bring it down hard against the cement floor.

I do this a few more times and although it hurts, I'm too weak to do any real damage so I just lie on the floor and do something I haven't done since I was a kid. I pray.

The same prayer that's probably been said a billion times in every little holding cell in every jail throughout the world.

"Help," I pray. "Please help . . ."

~

I am still curled up on the floor hours later when the door opens. A female guard brings in an older woman who is obviously drunk. She's wearing a sparkly cocktail dress, and her eyes are watery, and her mascara is smeared in such a way that each eye looks like a smiley face. I stand up, thinking the guard must be taking me out if she's bringing this woman in but she shuts the door quickly, and the woman and I are both left in this tiny room.

"Hi," she says brightly.

I sit down on the bench and press myself as far against the back wall as I can and keep my eyes down.

The woman sighs loudly and then immediately picks up the pay phone.

"Hello? Hello?" she yells into the receiver. "Hello?"

"You have to dial zero," I say. "And then give the operator the number for a collect call."

The woman smiles at me and sways a little bit on her heels. I look down again so she can be messy-drunk with a little privacy. She tells the operator the number and slurs her name. Helen comes out as Schmelen, so she says it again and then kicks off her shoes while she waits.

"Johnnie, it's me Schmelen, Johnnieeeeee! I was at the Hindquarter and I had a couple of cocktails before schdinner and maybe one glass of schwine, and they pulled me over and said I was schweaving in traffic. I'm at the schnail."

Helen goes silent while Johnnie responds, and she tries to put her shoes back on but ends up kicking one so that it rolls over and lands near my foot.

"I am not a drunk driver who drives drunk," Helen screams into the phone. "Come get me right now, this is ridiculumous!"

Helen slams the phone down and bends over to grab her shoe. She plops down on the bench next to me. "Why is it so cold in here?"

I shrug. I have never been good at small talk.

Helen looks me up and down, pauses on my swollen eyes. "So whass happened to you?"

I don't know how to answer this question.

"Is this your first time in the schnail?"

I nod.

"Me too, and it's so ridiculust, I am not drunk. I just went out to dinner with some of my girlfriends."

The whole cell smells like alcohol, but I'm not going to point out the obvious, so I just nod again.

"So what happened to you?"

"I was arrested at home. They wouldn't let me call someone to pick up my three-year-old son. I have no idea where he is."

Helen is immediately outraged on my behalf. "That's ridiculous, they shouldn't not do that—why can't you call someone and say that?"

I start to cry again, and Helen pats my back a few times. "We'll be out of here soon, and you can get your son, and I can get my car back. Can you believe they had it towed? Do the police have nothing better to dos? It's outragulous, and I need my car!"

I smile weakly at her.

"There you go. See, it's all not going to be not okay."

I can't even unwrap her double negative, but I close my eyes and pretend she's right for a minute.

The door opens and it's the same female deputy who brought in Helen. "Love, let's go!"

"See," says Helen. "You can go get your son now. Good lucks to you!"

I give Helen a little wave and walk out the door. I know I'm not being released but I don't want to ruin her happy-drunk vibe with the truth.

~

The deputy walks me into a small room. Shelves line the walls, and there are stacks of maroon clothing organized by size. It's like a small sad thrift store. She hands me a shirt and a pair of pants. Then she opens a drawer and pulls out a gray sports bra and a pair of giant green underwear and hands them to me. "Take everything off and put your things in this bag." She hands me a used brown paper bag and I look around to see where I'm supposed to change. "Go ahead, take everything off."

I'm awkwardly holding the new clothes and the brown bag and there's nothing to set anything down on. "Here?" I ask.

She gives me a weird look and nods.

I drop the brown bag and set the pile of jail clothes on the floor. I start to turn around but the deputy stops me.

"Face forward, remove all your clothes and put them in the bag."

I pull off my sweatshirt and T-shirt at the same time. I'm not wearing a bra. I put them in the bag. The guard stares at me. I slide my sweatpants down but leave my socks on. I wasn't wearing shoes when they arrested me.

"Take off the socks too."

I take those off and put them and my sweats in the bag. I don't fold anything—just shove it inside the bag. I am freezing now. I've lost so much weight in the last year that my hip bones and collarbones protrude and I actually have a six-pack. I don't work out, but without any body fat it looks like I do. I bend over to pick up the maroon pants but the deputy stops me.

"Squat down," she says.

"What?"

"Squat down. Knees out."

I do what she says.

"Stand up, turn around, and then bend over pulling your ass cheeks apart."

I do it, and she doesn't say anything, so I just stay bent over. For some reason I think of Helen. I hope she doesn't have to do this. She will definitely fall.

"Okay, get dressed."

I quickly pull on the giant underwear, pull the sports bra over my head, and step into the maroon pants and shirt.

"Put the T-shirt on first."

I didn't realize that under the stiff maroon pullover was a brown cotton T-shirt. I put that on instead. "You have to put the red on when you leave your cell. This is your ID card. Keep it with you and make sure you have it every time you leave your cell."

I look at her blankly.

"Now put your red shirt on." I do as she says and then put my ID card in the front pocket without looking at it.

She hands me a pair of slip-on woven sandals. "Put these on and follow me." I slide on the sandals and look at my toenails sticking out and cringe—I have definitely deprioritized mani-pedis during my criminal phase. Who knew jail would be open toe?

She picks up my bag of clothes with gloved hands and carries it under one arm. I walk behind her, back out to the main part of the jail. She hands the bag to another deputy behind the front desk. "Love," she says.

He laughs. "What?"

"Last name is Love." She shrugs. He takes a black Magic Marker and writes my last name on the bag and throws it on the counter behind him. I see there's another bag marked Jackson. DJ must have already done all of this.

"Let's go."

I follow her through a series of locked doors. They get buzzed open and closed from somewhere else. Each door we walk through slams shut behind me, and there's a loud grating noise as it locks. I startle every time.

"Follow the yellow line," she says, pointing to a painted line on the slate-gray floor. I walk along the line down hallways that lead through two more sets of loud, locking doors. Finally, we enter a large circular room. In the center of the room are steps leading up to a raised pavilion of some kind. There are two guards behind glass windows in front of what looks like computer monitors. I look around and see that the circular room is more like a hexagon, with a thick door and window on each section. There's a clock on the wall—it's 2 a.m. I wonder where Kaden is sleeping. It's been twelve hours since he was taken. How did he get to sleep? I imagine him all alone. I imagine strangers hurting him. A cold terror engulfs me. I frantically look around. I have to get out of here. I have to get to him.

Behind one of the windows DJ is waving to me. "No communication with other inmates. No signals, no signs, nothing," the deputy yells, waving at DJ to back away from the window.

A male guard steps out of the pavilion and hands what looks like a yoga mat and a sheet and blanket to the deputy. "Here you go. We don't have any mugs or hygiene. We'll get them in the morning. He turns his head and yells into his shoulder, "Opening G!"

My escort deputy grabs the mat from him and shoves it into my arms. "Let's go," she says, and we walk over to one side of the hexagon. The door groans loudly as it opens. "Welcome to G block," she says, and pushes me inside.

~

I am in a large semicircular room. There are faint lights on the ceiling and to my right a stairway leads to a long balcony with six doors. Right under the balcony is a lower level with another six doors. Between those doors and me is what looks like a school cafeteria—a cluster of small tables bolted to the floor. Between the cafeteria tables and the closed doors are about ten bunk beds, forming a perimeter around the entire room.

I look behind me, but the deputy is gone. I have no idea what I'm supposed to do. I can't tell if there are people in the beds or not—if there are, they aren't moving. I take a few steps forward and then freeze.

"Hey." I hear a muffled voice coming from somewhere in front of me and look around in the dark. I can't see anyone, but I hear the voice again. "Hey!"

I walk through the group of tables and stop in front of the ring of bunk beds. The bunk to my left is empty—just a bare metal grate. I throw my skinny yoga mat mattress on top and see that the mat fits into the frame perfectly. I throw the thin sheet and blanket on top as well. I have no idea if this is my assigned bed.

"Hey!"

The voice sounds closer but still muffled. I walk between the bunk beds and stop in front of the row of doors. Each door has a small square window three-quarters of the way up, and I scan back and forth until I see a woman's face in the door to my left.

Her face fills the entire square, and I can see that she's saying something, but it's too muffled to hear. I walk closer.

She gives me a little wave and then points her finger down. I don't know if she's the welcome wagon or what. Is she going to tell me where to sleep? I look down on the ground in front of me where I think she's pointing but don't see anything. She points again and raises her eyebrows at me and then waves me closer.

I get a little closer and she points down at my waist. I have no idea what she wants but I definitely do not want to take my clothes off again. I shake my head at her, but she just points down again. She holds a finger to her lips telling me to be quiet. I am so confused. I take another step and reach my hand out to the door, thinking she wants me to open it. I turn the knob and pull but it doesn't budge. I try again.

She immediately starts to laugh, and suddenly her voice isn't muffled. It's loud. I look around me and I see other faces pressed to the windows. "Try mine next," someone yells.

More laughter. I'm embarrassed but have no idea what I've done. The girl in the window laughs and flips me off. I return to my bunk.

"Come open my door," yells another voice, and there's more laughter.

"Shut the fuck up," a voice yells from one of the top bunks across the room. I look around and see about ten women sitting up in various bunks—all looking at me. Some are laughing.

I didn't know then that the bunk beds are called the freeway—where the lower class of inmates sleep. Those with no connections, no street cred, and first-timers like me who are unknown and automatically suspect. I don't know that the Black girls, the Bible thumpers, the homeless transients, and the harmless mentally ill are also kept out here. Jail is a class system, and a study in racial segregation worthy of the South in the 1950s. There are rules I don't know. A system I can't comprehend. A hustle I have never learned. A power structure that is somewhere between an adolescent sleepover party and being jumped into a gang.

I quickly lie down in my bunk and pull the blanket over my head. I have no idea that my one little gesture—trying to open a locked cell door—told everyone in G block all they needed to know about me.

I have never been to jail before and I've brought nothing in—meaning there's no stash of drugs packed in my vagina that I could

use to establish myself, work my hustle, flex my power, or be invited to move into one of the locked-door cells that had more privacy.

Under the blanket, my mind runs through the last twelve hours, starting with the knock on the door and ending with the woman in the cell flipping me off. Maybe I am dead, and this is my bespoke hell.

chapter 5

COUNTRY MUSIC HELL

Hank Williams Jr. is in my house.

My head is pounding, and I'm not sure if I'm awake or asleep. I reach my arm out to my right to see if Kaden has climbed into bed again, and my hand hits cold cement.

Cold cement.

I sit up wildly, a scream building in the back of my throat, and the top of my head scrapes across hard metal.

I imagine Kaden waking up somewhere with strangers. I worry again that someone has hurt him in the night, and there is a thickness in my throat that I can't swallow away.

I slowly look around G block.

To my left is a woman sitting up in the bottom of another bunk bed. She has long, stringy brown hair. She's slowly licking a green Jolly Rancher and staring at me from behind the brown curtain of her hair. Her eyes glitter with hatred.

In front of all the cafeteria tables and right below the side of the stairway, there is a television mounted on the wall. In front of it four women are singing along to a country music video and performing a synchronized dance routine.

I look around to see if there's some kind of brochure or instructions about what I should do next. I have to pee, but I have no idea where I'm supposed to do that. Apart from the girl with the Jolly Rancher, nobody looks my way as I sit up in bed.

I feel lost. *How did I get so lost?*

I stare at the country music video. It's a man sitting on a barstool singing to a bartender about breaking parole.

The four women are singing along at the top of their lungs with their arms locked together and shuffling right and then left with some complicated crossover foot movement in the middle. Three women on the top-tier balcony start clapping and yelling "yeehaw!" They join in on the chorus about jacking keys and crashing a car.

A guard opens the main door into G block, and the women on the balcony start dancing and then singing even louder. As he walks across the floor below, they scream the lyrics at him.

"That's enough. Quiet down!" he yells, but the girls just sing louder and do a weaving do-si-do with each other.

The final lyrics are about going back to the pen to see friends.

The guard doesn't yell again, just shakes his head while the song finishes. He walks in front of the bottom row of doors and peeks in each window if the door is closed. He opens one door and snarls at the woman inside, "No covering the window. Take it down!" He points to a postcard in the window. I can't see the picture on her side, but on the white side that faces out red block letters say: WISH YOU WERE HERE.

My tears start again, so I lie back down and turn toward the wall.

My mind races, wondering if Kaden thinks we are gone forever, that we've just given him away or that he's been stolen. He's at that age where he turns his head away if a stranger talks to him. He can only fall asleep if someone lightly scratches his arm.

I can't endure these thoughts, so I sit back up in my bunk.

The woman with the Jolly Rancher is still staring at me, and she slowly pulls it out of her mouth and holds it up to show me the sharp point she's fashioned. She angles it toward me.

Over and over, she air-shanks me with her little green sticky shiv.

~

I stay in my bed all day. I don't eat when they bring food in on trays for breakfast. I don't eat lunch either. No one speaks to me. I turn my back to the room and face the cement wall.

Eventually, I have to get up to pee. I can only hold it so long. I do a long, slow walk around the room, trying to be cool, but really I'm just looking for the bathroom. The other girls stop talking when I walk by them, and then they whisper and stare. I am sure they are talking about me. At its core, addiction is an extreme form of self-obsession. We addicts are pathologically self-absorbed, self-serving, selfish, and all the other self- words. The drug is our secret lover, our treasured best friend, and our primary relationship. We live in service to that relationship, and it drives and colors every interaction we have. Are you a friend or foe to my using? Will you help me or thwart me? Like any compulsion, the rituals of using are a solace. How could anyone else ever understand our terminal uniqueness?

So of course I think they are talking about me—matching the running commentary in my own mind.

I listen to snatches of conversation as I walk: Apparently, Jolly Rancher hasn't showered in four days, and a group of girls—the ones

who were dancing on the top tier—are planning an intervention. They are going to force-shower her while one girl keeps lookout. I have always been good at eavesdropping and reading lips, and I can usually see schemes unfolding. I am a master at subtext and plot and body language, so I know the stringy-haired girl is about to get a very violent and cold washing.

Even though I am freezing, many of the girls have stripped down to their sports bras. I pick up that the non-showered girl also didn't turn in her old clothes for new ones in the last two clothing exchanges. This, along with a general lack of personal hygiene, has made her the biggest problem in G block.

I don't dare walk up the stairs to the top tier. I don't know if that's allowed, but I do notice there's a mop bucket at the bottom of the stairs. One girl with short brown hair, styled like Victoria Beckham, sees me looking at the bucket.

"We used to have a big container of bleach next to that," she says, "but someone did something stupid and got the bleach thrown in her face."

I'm not sure how to reply. Is she threatening me? I don't meet her eyes and instead stare at the large black spider tattooed on her throat. The spider's legs wrap around to the back of her neck, and when she smiles, it looks like two of the legs are moving toward her face from under her chin. Is she the one who threw the bleach?

These women don't look particularly scary or violent, but I have no idea if I'm surrounded by killers and bleach throwers. Really the only person who sort of threatened me did so with a piece of candy. One girl who looks to be about six months pregnant is playing cards with two other women, who could pass for twins. What happens when she has her baby? Will the baby be in some sort of baby jail, or will CPS take the baby away as soon as it's born?

I smile back at the spider-face girl and nod knowingly about people who do stupid things and get bleach thrown in their face.

I also notice a hot pot of water on a small table next to the mop bucket. Not boiling water apparently, but hot enough that two girls who smuggled in some contraband real coffee into the unit are using the corner of a bedsheet as a filter to make some fresh brew.

I come to a row of phones on the wall. I know I should call my mom back since I just hung up on her yesterday. But these aren't pay phones, so I just stand in front of them looking stupid. I pick up a receiver and hold it to my ear.

"You need to dial your S number to make a call. Do you have minutes?"

It's spider girl being helpful again, but I smile and shrug like she's speaking a foreign language.

"On your ID card."

I pull the card out of my shirt pocket. There's a number on it below my picture. I dial it into the phone and follow the recorded instructions for placing a collect call.

My mom answers right away but takes a long time to accept the charges. I imagine she's grasping for her cigarettes and lighter. There's no privacy in the room so I whisper into the phone when she says hello.

"Hi."

She says hello back and then asks if I know how much the charges might be. "I don't have a lot of money," she adds.

"I know. I'll be quick. Have you talked to Carol or anyone?"

"I spoke to Carol again this morning. Your bail is still set at two hundred and fifty thousand dollars. For each of you."

"What? That doesn't make sense."

"Carol is pretty furious. Lala, what did you do?" She hasn't used my childhood nickname in a long time.

"I can't really talk about that now," I say. I don't want to talk in front of everyone, and I don't want to start crying.

"Carol said the felony charges add up to twenty-seven years in prison. I don't have money for an attorney, you know that. I don't know what to do." She starts to cry a little.

I can't deal with her tears. All I want to do is hang up and get back in bed.

"Call me back later if you can. I'll see what else I can find out."

"Mom . . ." I stop speaking for a second and swallow the lump in my throat. I take a big breath. "Did she say where Kaden is?" I don't ask her about my older boys because I know they're with their dad.

My mom is silent now except for her own big inhale of nicotine.

"No, she has no idea."

I need to get off the phone and back to my cement wall. I cannot cry in front of all these women. "I love you, Mom, and I'm so sorry . . ."

"Oh, Lara . . ."

She starts to say more but I hang up. My eyes are swimming with tears, and I stumble my way back to bed.

Twenty-seven years.

I start doing the math in my head. Kaden would be almost thirty-one, Ty forty, Cody forty-three, Dylan forty-four. This cannot be real. I didn't kill anyone. My boys are going to grow up without me. I have lost them all.

~

When a new guard comes in the afternoon and hands me a clear plastic bag, I inspect it closely. There's a roll of toilet paper, a toothbrush, a small, unmarked tube of what I'm guessing is toothpaste, a tiny bar of soap, and a plastic razor. I pull the razor out and twist and pull the top apart to see if there's an actual razor in there that I can use but there's not. There's also a small pen and a few pages of notepaper in

the bag. The pen is just the plastic inside of a pen, and it's hard to hold or write with. I try anyway.

I write my boys' names across the top of a sheet of paper. *Dylan. Cody. Ty. Kaden.* I rub my finger across their names slowly. The last seventeen years play across my mind. Birthday parties and karate lessons and baseball games and basketball tournaments and school plays and vacations. I tried so hard to be who they needed me to be. I tried to be the right kind of mother. But I've just failed. I've failed them and I've failed at life.

> *Dear Boys,*
>
> *I'm so sorry.*
> *I love you more than anything in the whole wide world.*
> *I pray that addiction never gets ahold of you.*
> *Always take care of each other.*
> *I love you so much.*
>
> *Mom*

I have decided to end my life. It feels like the best decision I have made in a long time. I want that sweet relief. I can't take another moment of not knowing where Kaden is, of thinking I won't see my boys again until they are grown men. I am freezing cold, and my head aches, and I feel like I won't ever sleep again. Every part of my body hurts, but the pain in my mind is the most unbearable.

I read the letter again. My spark has gone out. Even in the day-to-day misery of addiction, there was a little spark that kept me going.

Now I feel no inner strength or spark or flicker of anything resembling hope. I am a black hole that has swallowed all the light, and I

want a quick end to my dark life. It sounds dramatic, but it doesn't feel dramatic. It just feels right.

As I form my suicide plan, a peace washes over me. My mind stops racing, my nausea goes away, even the chills and headache disappear. I float on a calm black lake of no thought.

I fold the note carefully and tuck it under my pillow. Someone will find it after I'm dead, and my boys will know I thought of them, that in my last moments I had nothing but love for them. When I imagine their lives without me, it feels better, easier for them to have a dead mom than a prison mom.

After everyone is asleep I'm going to walk up the stairs and hang myself from the top railing with my bedsheet.

At 10 p.m. the guard comes in and yells "Lights out!" I am wide awake when he comes back at eleven and again at midnight. I figure out the routine. He walks around the freeway, peeks in all the locked-door windows, then walks upstairs and checks all those rooms. It takes about five minutes every time he makes his rounds. After the 1 a.m. check, I wait a few minutes until after he leaves and then I sit up in bed. I slowly wrap the sheet around my neck, tying it in what I hope are six strong knots.

I can still hear some girls whispering, so I lie back down to wait until it's quiet. I tell myself that I will be gone within the hour, and a little thrill courses through me. I've never been overly afraid of death—have always thought of it as this next big adventure where the mysteries of the universe will be revealed. I don't believe in heaven or hell. I believe we are all energy coming back lifetime after lifetime until we learn what we need to learn.

I need to take a mulligan on this lifetime.

The only thing that ever scared me about death was the idea of my boys missing me, hurting because I was gone. But I'm already gone, so I believe this will be easier for them, cleaner.

I lie in my bunk and try to remember the first time I took an opi-ate. I had knee surgery in high school after tearing a ligament playing lacrosse, but I don't remember taking anything for pain after surgery, although I must have. The fact that I don't remember the pills means I took them as prescribed, and they simply did their job.

In my second year of graduate school I tore the same ligament. I was skipping down a hallway and the previously repaired ligament simply gave out. It required surgery, even though I was four months pregnant with Dylan, and when they hooked me up to a morphine pump I refused to press the button. The orthopedic surgeon and my ob-gyn both assured me it wouldn't hurt the baby. The nurses tried to get me to push the button, but I wouldn't.

I do remember the first time I took a pain pill when I wasn't in pain. I was in Visalia, California. I was not married to Dylan's father; in fact, we had only spent a few weeks together for what was supposed to be a summer fling before I found out I was pregnant. I had a baby daddy before baby daddies were a thing.

Bryan and I barely knew each other; we were both twenty-four-year-old wannabe writers and broke. His family was meeting their grandchild and me for the first time. I had just finished graduate school, was carrying an extra forty pounds of baby weight on my sleep-deprived body, and not feeling like my best self.

And while I was madly in love with my baby, I was distant with his dad. Bryan had cheated on me during the pregnancy, and I was hurt and guarded with him. I wanted so badly to create the family I never had, but I had no skills to do that. Our relationship was supposed to just be a one-night stand, but I had fallen in love with the possibility of being loved. And on the night we had drunkenly conceived, a beau-tiful curly-haired toddler had appeared in my dreams. I was filled with a love I had never experienced before, and when I woke up, hungover, I ached for that little boy in my dream. I missed him desperately.

When I found out a few weeks later that I was pregnant, I knew instantly I would have the baby and that he would be a boy.

Bryan's dad and grandfather adored the baby, and they proudly took a photo of four generations of men carrying the Love surname. It was beautiful, and my family-starved soul was happy my son would have this Love legacy. He would have a family. But I felt like Oliver Twist with his hands out begging for food. The Loves were skeptical and suspicious of me, and worried for Bryan that because we were not married, I could eventually take the baby from all of them.

On the second day of our visit, I used the master bathroom and there on the counter was a giant prescription bottle of Percocet. Hundreds of pills. I read the label: TAKE 1–2 PILLS EVERY FOUR HOURS OR AS NEEDED FOR PAIN.

I had no ominous music playing in the background. No precognition of what this tiny pill could do. It was 1991, and the opioid crisis wasn't yet a crisis.

I opened the top and shook out a pill. With a palmful of water from the sink, I swallowed it, dried off my chin with a bath towel, and steeled myself for another dinner with a family who gave me smiles that didn't quite reach their eyes.

Twenty minutes later I felt a rush of warmth and joy and happiness flow through my body. My anxiety evaporated. I told funny stories. I showed intense interest in their vending machine business. The Percocet opened my heart, and I saw a million loving family dinners just like this one. For the first time ever, I really felt like I belonged somewhere.

I had taken that pill as needed for pain and my pain had gone away.

The next day, as we said our goodbyes and promised to see each other again soon, I still felt the warmth and glow from that one pill.

And from the forty pills I had hidden in my purse.

~

As I lay in the dark waiting for everyone to fall asleep, I think about redemption, about second chances, and while I believe in them, I know that this time they are not for me. Redemption is for the good, and deep down I have always known that I am bad.

chapter 6

MAKEOVER

I am stepping off a cliff and falling, falling, falling toward something with teeth. I wave my arms in the air, knowing instantly that this is a horrible mistake. I didn't mean to step off the edge. I flail and flap and try to reverse course and even though I am screaming the only sound is the scraping and gnashing of giant teeth that rush toward me from below. I am blinded as a giant spotlight rises out of the teeth and hits me straight in the eyes.

I jerk upright, startled, and clamp down on a scream.

The scraping sound is tall stacks of chairs being moved across the floor. The lights are on, and a guard is yelling, "Breakfast, ladies, rise and shine." An overhead light blares right in my eyes, and as I turn my head away the entire top sheet of my bed moves with me.

It takes a minute for me to realize what's happening. Chairs. Guards. Breakfast.

A sheet tied in six knots around my neck.

I quickly lie back down in my bunk and pull the blanket over my head. How could I have fallen asleep? The last thing I remember is waiting for the girls to stop talking. I claw desperately at the knots around my neck, afraid someone might have seen them when I sat up.

I am mortified. Embarrassed.

I am ashamed that I am still alive.

~

It takes me five minutes to undo all the knots, but it feels like hours. I am sure that when I come out from under my blanket all of G block will be staring at me. Of course, everyone is eating and not looking at the new girl hiding under a blanket on the freeway. It doesn't cross my mind that I have a suicide note under my pillow, and I should ask for help—I am just angry that I have to endure another twelve or sixteen hours of living until I can try again. I've detoxed from opiates before, and there's no way I should have fallen asleep. It doesn't feel like a miracle, it feels like punishment. I am shivering and my entire body is aching, so I will also have to endure the worst of detoxing during this long day of being alive.

~

"S-201761!"

The guard is yelling some random numbers, but everyone ignores him. "S-201761, get ready for court in ten!"

Each syllable feels like a nail to my head and I close my eyes and hope he stops. I don't know why he has to scream; everyone is quiet in G block. The country music videos haven't even started up.

"Love!"

My eyes fly open, and I raise my hand like I'm about to answer a question in school. One of the girls eating at a table sees me and snorts out a laugh.

"You have court in ten. Get ready!" With that the guard walks out of G block.

I don't understand what he means, but I slowly get out of my bunk.

The girl who snorted looks at me. "Is Love your last name?"

I nod.

"That number he called out is your S-number—it's on your ID card. If your name is Love there's no way he's gonna yell that out if he can help it." She laughs. "Better learn your number, because that's your name now, and you need to bring your ID with you whenever you leave G."

"He said I have court?" The girl just shrugs and goes back to her breakfast.

"Hey, I'm Nina." A small girl, not even five feet tall, with a short brown bob that seems strangely freshly styled, stands up from the table. "They take you to your court dates in the morning, but you could be in the tombs all day. You might want to eat something and like, fix your hair or something." She waves vaguely at my face and hair, and I'm instantly embarrassed.

~

I find the door to the communal bathroom for the freeway dwellers, and two girls standing in the corner together scurry out without saying a word to me. Later I will find out that this is the one part of G block where the cameras can't see you if you live on the freeway. This corner is where girls will go to fight or squash a potential fight, to share their drugs, or to plot and plan.

There is a semblance of a mirror above the sink. The toilet is out in the open. The locked-door cells each have a toilet and sink in them. Going to the bathroom in public is one of the joys of incarceration. I have the bladder of a sloth, so I can go days without using the bathroom. And there's no water to drink that I know of, so I feel weak and

dehydrated. I tell myself I just have to get through the day, and then I can finish what I started last night.

I look at myself in the mirror. My hair has been up in a bun since my arrest and I'm afraid to try to take it down. I don't have a comb or brush. The mirror is made of murky metal, not glass, and it shows a warped version of my face that probably looks better than I actually do right now. My eyes are red and painful and watering constantly from the detox. I lean over the sink and splash water on my face. Even this minimal exertion leaves me exhausted. I pat water on my tangled hair.

I don't know what else to do.

A girl walks in the bathroom and I startle.

"Hey," she says.

"Hey."

"You done with the mirror?"

I nod yes and go over to the toilet. I really do need to pee; even sloths have their limits. She is carrying a cup and a pack of colored pencils. I watch as she takes out a black pencil, dips it in the cup, then uses the pencil as eyeliner. She then takes out a red pencil and dips it and then draws circles on each cheek and rubs them with her fingers. She dips the pencil again and it becomes lip liner. She takes out a pink pencil and dips it and that becomes lipstick. She then takes the white pencil, dips it in the cup, and uses it to whiten up the corners of each eye.

I'm still on the toilet. I'm done peeing, but I'm transfixed by her makeover. Plus, it's just a nice place to rest.

"You have court?" she asks when she's finished.

I nod yes.

"Me too. Do you want me to do your makeup? No offense, but you are looking a little ragged."

I wipe and pull up my pants. "Sure, thanks," I say and walk over

to the sink. She steps away while I wash my hands. There's nothing to dry them with so I wipe them on my pants.

"Let me get some more hot water." She walks out of the communal bathroom, leaving her pack of colored pencils, and comes back a minute later with the cup. "You need really hot water for the pencil color, so I have to get it out of the hot pot, not the sink."

I nod like this makes perfect sense to me.

"So what do you want?"

"Umm, maybe just some color on my cheeks."

She laughs. "Yeah, you're looking a little gray. Meth?"

"No."

"H?"

I nod.

"What's your name?"

"Lara."

"Is your last name really Love?"

I nod again.

She laughs at this. "I'm Kiki or Little K," she says. "Hold still. I don't have any mascara, they're out in commissary, but this is better than nothing. There are always lots of homeboys in the tombs, so you gotta look good on court day."

I nod like I know this already.

"When did you get picked up?" she asks.

"Yesterday."

"That's weird you have court already; it usually takes at least a few days. Has Classification been to see you yet?"

I have no idea what she's talking about, but I'm trying to be cool during my makeover, so I just say no and shrug. She doesn't ask me what I was arrested for, and I don't offer any information or think to ask her anything.

"Let me just do a little something with those eyes." Kiki dips various pencils in and out of the cup of hot water and works on my eyes. "Just a little brown in the creases will help and I'm going to use the white to take away all the red. You'll feel better in a couple of days. Detoxing off H is the worst. I'll make you a hot water bottle when you get back, it will help with the chills. We save all the OJ containers and fill them from the hot pot. Helps with cramps—although we're all synced up in here so there's a shortage once a month—and it helps with the heroin detox. The meth heads just sleep for two weeks with their detox. Lucky bitches."

I take in all this information and look at myself in the mirror. I look much better than I did a few minutes ago. "Thanks," I say. "Thanks so much!"

Kiki packs up her pencils and walks to the bathroom door. "This your first time?" she asks.

I nod.

"Don't worry. The first few days are the roughest. It will get better."

My eyes start to well up from her kindness, but I blink the tears away so I don't mess up her work.

"But stay away from Daddy. She likes to make it rough for the newbies. She'll roll you up if she doesn't like you."

I don't know who Daddy is—I only know Nina and Spider Girl and now Kiki—and I don't know what it means to get rolled up, but I'm not going to ask.

Kiki is young and blond and tall and looks like she could be a model if prison clothes were a fashion line. "How old are you?" I ask.

"I'm nineteen."

"Wow," I say. She's only a couple of years older than Dylan.

"I know," she says. "But I've been in and out of here like ten times already, not to mention juvie. How old are you?"

"Forty-one," I say.

"Wow," she says back.

"I know . . ."

"You'll probably be out by the weekend, don't worry." She gives me a big smile, and I offer a weak one in return. We walk out of the bathroom together, and I hope the colored pencil makeup will stay on my face through the day. I'm vain enough to want to look my best for my death.

~

The tombs are as grim as their name suggests. Myself, Kiki, and another girl whose name I didn't know are taken out of G and marched down the yellow line. I don't know the layout of the jail, but it has lots of twists and turns and what seems like different wings. We are taken into a large room where a female guard puts handcuffs on us. This time my hands are cuffed in front, which, while bad, is still better than before. The cuffs are tight and dig into my wrists. Two shackles with a chain connecting them are snapped around my ankles.

We are loaded into a van divided into two sections by a metal grate. Kiki tells me that usually the men are in the other section. She's disappointed to find it empty after spending so much time on her makeup.

Once we're in the tombs, a new set of guards takes over. Kiki and the other woman are put in a holding cell under the courthouse and I am put in a separate one. I have no idea where I'm going or what will happen. The room is all cement except for a sink and toilet—there is a built-in bench along one side of the room and a clock on the wall that says it's 8 a.m.

I should be dead.

I can't pace because of the shackles, so I just sit on the bench and

wait, my legs shaking from the detox. I grab the roll of toilet paper and wipe my runny nose awkwardly, grateful again that my handcuffs are in the front this time. There's a vent midway up the wall that I can hear voices through. It's Kiki and the other woman, but I can't make out what they're saying.

I watch the clock. Nine a.m. Ten a.m. Eleven a.m. Three hours feels like three days. I think this must be how people go crazy. Left alone with their own thoughts and a ticking clock. I start humming the country music songs I've already learned in a day. Anything to keep my mind off where I am. Noon. One. Have they forgotten I'm in here? I hobble over to the small window in the door and put my face against it. All I can see is a corridor in both directions. No people. The voices in the vent stopped hours ago so I imagine Kiki is back in G already.

I go back to the bench and lay on my side, trying to tuck my knees against my chest to keep warm. Every cell of my body hurts. It's like a toothache when you don't know exactly what tooth it is—a dull aching and then a deep pain that flares up for no reason and then returns to the relentless throb of ill-defined agony. I am both restless and exhausted.

Right before 2 p.m. the door opens, and I quickly sit up. A guard comes in and hands me a paper bag.

"Lunch," she says.

"Do you know how much longer I'm going to be in here?"

"Emergency CPS court works on its own schedule," she says cryptically and shuts the door.

My heart starts racing. I don't know if this means Kaden will be in court. If he sees me, he will want to be with me and I can't bear the thought of him thinking I don't want to hold him, that I'm rejecting him in some way. I desperately want to see him and know that he's okay.

I look in the bag and see a sandwich of some kind and an apple.

I have no appetite for food and no energy to wrestle a sandwich out of a bag in handcuffs. I toss it to the end of the bench and start to lie down again when the door opens.

"Love, let's go."

I stumble a little when I stand and shuffle my way to the door. I am led down a hallway to where a male guard stands outside another door. Next to him is DJ.

"Up against the wall," the guard says.

I stand next to DJ and my mouth is too dry to say anything. He looks just as haggard as me, and really pissed off.

"Are you okay?" he whispers.

I shake my head, and my eyes fill with tears.

"No talking," the guard yells.

"This is my wife," DJ growls.

"I don't care. No communicating!"

I watch as he and DJ stare each other down. DJ's eyes are red-rimmed, and he has two days of stubble on his face. He looks like a different man. Harder. Meaner. Angrier.

"This is bullshit," he mumbles.

The guard opens the door and leads us into the courtroom. There is a female judge and I quickly scan the room.

No Kaden. No Dylan, Cody, or Ty. Nobody that I recognize.

The guard leads us to a row of chairs on the side of the room, where the jury would sit if it were a trial. He makes DJ sit at one end of the row and me at the other. He again tells us no communication of any kind. After the guard walks away, I can see DJ in my peripheral vision trying to get my attention, but despite my many pending felony charges that suggest the contrary, I have always been a rule follower. I keep my eyes down and obey the rule. DJ mutters "Bullshit" again under his breath, and I can sense the anger coming off him without even looking.

I keep my eyes down but shake my head slightly. I want my idiot husband to shut the fuck up. This is family court. We are being judged as parents, and right now the only thing he is conveying is white-privileged asshole with some rage problems.

I know I am one green Jolly Rancher away from looking just like the crazy unwashed girl, and all my pencil makeup is gone now, but I quickly try to smooth my hair back, and put on my best PTA-mom face. My neck is sore from the bedsheet knots, and I'm hoping there are no marks.

~

In front of the judge are two big tables. There's a man and woman at one of the tables, and two women at the other. Behind them in the general seats of the court are a handful of people I don't recognize. All are in suits of some kind so I figure they must be court people. One man seems to be staring at me intently.

The judge reads off a case number and the woman seated next to the man at the table walks up to a little podium in front of the judge.

"In the matter of Kaden Love Jackson, the minor child, in protective custody . . ."

I lean forward, trying to hear what they are saying.

"Protective custody . . . age three years and eleven months . . . emergency foster care . . . multiple serious felony charges . . . trash in house . . . serious neglect . . . left all alone . . . drugs . . . recommend removal."

A lot of the details she gives are false—our house was not full of trash, he was not left alone—but it doesn't matter at this point. I am not a good mother simply because I'm wearing shackles and the uniform of the county jail. The attorney goes on and on about my failures as a mother. There's not a mother I know who hasn't been

mom-shamed in one way or another—it goes with the territory. This is the Olympics of mom-shaming, though, and I look down at my lap, my cheeks burning. I know I would throw myself in front of a bus to save each one of my boys. I would sacrifice my life for theirs, but I couldn't stop using drugs for them. I don't know how to reconcile those two truths.

The simpler answer is most likely: I am not a good mother. I am a horrible mother. I must love drugs more than I love my children. There's no other reason for why I am here—for why I didn't spend the morning making lunches and driving carpool.

I deserve to be mom-shamed.

DJ starts to yell that it's not true and the bailiff threatens to pull him out of the courtroom. I kind of hope they do.

It's all going so fast I don't understand what's being decided. Another woman walks up and says she's the attorney for the minor child.

Kaden has an attorney.

"And the other minor children?" the judge asks, shuffling through paperwork as if she's lost something. I hold my breath, not knowing if Dylan, Cody, and Ty were also taken. Or Hailey and Logan.

"They were not at home when the defendants were arrested and are in the care of a custodial parent so are not subject to CPS proceedings."

The judge nods and looks up from the file.

"Your Honor, the defendant's ex-husband and his wife are currently getting emergency foster care certification and are willing to foster the minor child. We recommend this placement for a minor child with siblings pending a home inspection that is happening this afternoon."

I lift my head quickly, imploring the judge with my eyes to approve this. A bailiff walks over and hands DJ and me each a manila envelope

full of documents. I can't open it and look at the papers with my hand-cuffs, but I sit upright and try to look like a good mother.

Finally, the judge looks over at DJ and me. "The court is approving the CPS removal of Kaden Love Jackson and orders reunification ser-vices pending completion of all the requirements of CPS within one year given the age of the minor child."

A woman from the other table stands.

"Your Honor, given that the minor child will be four years old in one month and the parents are in custody, we'd like to ask for the longer time period for reunification services. If we were a month out from here there would be two years to reunify before parenting rights are forfeited."

"But we are not a month out. I'm afraid the time period is based on the age of the child at time of removal."

I have no idea what any of this means. My mind is only focused on one thing: Kaden is going to get to be with his brothers, not strangers. He won't be afraid. He won't be hurt. He won't be alone.

I take my first full deep breath in two days. When I exhale, it is shaky, and tears start to roll down my face. I quickly try to wipe them away and catch the eye of the man sitting in the back seats still staring at me. He gives me a little nod, but I look away. The bailiff brings over a tissue and I take it gratefully.

I wipe my eyes and sneak a look at DJ. I can tell he is not happy that his son is going to be living with my ex-husband. He is glaring at Kaden's attorney. I will him with my mind to look at the big picture—to see why this is such good news.

~

The guard opens the door and waves for us to come out. I look around the courtroom and meet the eyes of the judge.

"The clock is ticking," she says. "Good luck."

When we get out in the hallway DJ says, "That was fucking bullshit, they can't take our son away. Forfeiting parental rights, what the fuck?"

"No talking!" the guard barks.

"This is good, Kaden will be okay," I say. "Bryan will take care of him. He'll be with his brothers!"

The female guard brings me to another holding cell and locks me in. I sit on the bench, my manila envelope in my hands, and I stare at the clock. With each pass of the second hand, I feel the pressure building in my chest, behind my eyes, until finally I can't hold it any longer.

I cry for all the stupid, stupid decisions that got me to this place. I cry for whoever I once was and for who I have now become.

I cry because I'm grateful for Bryan stepping up to save Kaden.

I cry because I'm in handcuffs, and even if I could read the papers that determine my son's future, I don't want to read them. I can't face whatever words are on these pages, so I cry because I'm a coward.

I cry for everything I threw away. I cry because I have never felt so alone and lost.

I cry for my four boys and for how thoroughly I have changed the trajectory of their childhoods, of their lives.

At home I have pictures of every birthday party, every vacation, every visit to the zoo and the beach and Halloween costumes and Easter egg hunts and Christmas mornings. When somebody once asked me why I kept so many printed pictures I jokingly said, "It's so when they are adults I can prove to them they had a happy childhood."

None of those pictures will matter anymore. My arrest changes everything. The future and the past.

Mostly I cry because it's all my fault. There is no one else to blame. There is no one I hate more in this world than the ugly woman I see in the distorted mirror above the sink in this holding cell. She deserves

nothing but pain and punishment. There is nothing the court can do to me worse than what I will do to myself. I don't need a trial. I have already judged myself guilty. I have already been sentenced.

When I am done crying, I feel wrung out. The front of my shirt is wet with snot and tears, and my whole body shakes. But my mind is finally quiet. There are no more thoughts left to think.

There is only the sound of the ticking clock.

chapter 7

LOST GIRLS

The first time I stole something I was thirteen years old. I had passed my velour tracksuit, Dorothy Hamill–haircut phase and went straight into my awkward phase—long Farrah Fawcett–style flipped bangs, breasts that developed way before I knew how to handle the attention they garnered, and crippling self-consciousness. I was obsessed with clothes, not fashion. I was obsessed with any clothes that weren't my clothes. My mom was too busy to shop for me, so she would just give me some of her clothes whenever I begged her to go shopping. I wanted to dress like Brooke Shields in *The Blue Lagoon*—flowing beachy-boho white dresses—but in reality I was dressed more like Dolly Parton in *9 to 5*. My mom was into the power suits and shoulder pads of the eighties.

My Aunt Jodee was only ten years older than me, and while I was self-consciously peering out at the world from behind my blond bangs, she was a hippie who didn't care what people thought of her. She had been living on her own in California since the age of sixteen

and although I saw her only once every few years, I worshipped everything about her. I wanted to be her. And I coveted every piece of clothing she owned. Faded denim jeans and lacy tank tops and layered T-shirts with an arm full of bangle bracelets.

And so, on one visit to see her I stole her favorite pair of jeans. I grabbed them from a bench in the back of the VW van she was living out of and stuffed them in my suitcase. When she couldn't find them the next day and started looking everywhere for them, I helped her look. When I went back to Massachusetts I pulled them out of the bottom of my suitcase and put them on. All the women on my mom's side are tiny, so they fit perfectly. Once in a while I would think of her tearing apart her van looking for the jeans, but then I would just put the thought aside. I wore the jeans every single day, along with the white lacy top I had also stolen from her. In them, I felt like I was somebody else, and it was the best feeling in the world.

I remember this story while I'm riding in the van back to G. Maybe I was just born a criminal. Was it in my blood all along— was I destined to be bad? Could I trace a line from my aunt's jeans, to my neighbors' mail, to facing twenty-seven years in prison? These thoughts exhaust me.

~

I have missed dinner, but there's about ten girls still sitting at the tables when I walk back in. Kiki, Nina, and others whose names I don't know.

"Vivian thought you got out," says Kiki. She nods over to a woman with long brown hair parted in the middle and giant round eyes, the one who had beckoned me over to her door on my first night. Her skin is smooth and so pale against her brown hair it almost looks translucent. She looks like a Breck shampoo girl from the seventies.

"No," I say, "I'm not getting out."

"You have Marigonda?" another woman asks.

"Who?"

"Judge Marigonda?"

"No," I say. "My judge was a woman, Judge Guy."

The women all gasp.

"You had family court in Watsonville?"

"Emergency CPS court in Santa Cruz."

The women all exchange looks that I don't understand.

"Did you do something to your child?" The woman who asks this stands up. She's short and squat and has a completely buzzed haircut. She looks like what I imagine the Buddha would look like if he were in G. "Did you hurt a kid?" She growls this at me.

"Daddy, come on . . ." says Kiki.

I don't know how to answer this question, and everybody stares quietly at me. I look around the tables. "When I was arrested . . . they took my son, he's almost four . . . I didn't hurt him . . . they just wouldn't let me call someone . . ." I swallow. "And now they're saying my charges add up to twenty-seven years in prison." My body starts to shiver again, and I hang my head. Let them beat me. I don't care anymore.

There is silence for a minute and then all the women start talking at once.

"Those fuckers . . ."

"They just want a case so they can get paid. They wouldn't let my mom take José and now he calls a total stranger Mami."

"They have three of mine."

Nina gets up, walks over, and hugs me. "Why don't you lie down? We'll make you a hot water bottle. Little K told us you were detoxing from the shit. You want some ramen?"

I shake my head and let her pull me over to my bunk. I stand there while she straightens the sheet and blanket. She lifts my pillow and I

see the letter to my boys underneath, but she ignores it and sets the pillow back on top of it.

"Take off your reds, it will be more comfortable." She points to my cover shirt I'm wearing over my T-shirt and then grabs the manila envelope out of my hand and sets it at the edge of my bed. I pull the shirt off over my head. She folds it and puts it on top of the envelope.

"You're skinny, girl. You're going to have to start eating."

I'm still shivering when I get into bed. Little K comes over with a plastic soda bottle full of water from the hot pot and tucks it in next to my chest then walks back over to the tables.

The warmth feels so good that I just clutch it and stare out at the other women.

"Hey, Love," says Vivian.

"Yeah?"

"How much time did they give you?"

"Time for what?"

"To reunify—to get your son back."

"Oh," I say. "One year."

The other women are quiet except for Nina who mutters, "Oh fuck . . ."

I lie in bed and watch country music videos until the water bottle cools. Nina comes over to check on me. "You know," she says, "I was gang-raped by some guys I thought were my homeboys and got pregnant and my family was so ashamed they kicked me out of the house. I didn't have anywhere to live so CPS took my son. That's when I started doing the meth. He's almost six now."

Nina doesn't look older than twenty-two, and still has the fullness of her own babyhood in her cheeks. "That's not right," I say. "Did they catch the guys who did it?"

She looks at me funny.

"Where you from, girl?"

"Aptos."

Nina laughs. "Hey girls, this one here is reppin' Aptos."

Everybody laughs, but it's not a mean laughter, so I laugh also. "PTA gang," I say weakly and then I freeze for a minute, worrying this might be offensive.

Nina laughs harder. "That's right, Aptos, whaaattt!? Fuckin' PTA gang, that's good."

I smile.

"Leah over there is six months pregnant. She gets a double pad to sleep on and extra milk."

Leah waves at me and pats her stomach. I don't know where she will have her baby and what will happen after. I don't know if they let babies in here. I imagine Kaden in this room with me. I would give anything to snuggle him in this bunk bed.

"Nina?"

"Yeah?"

"Where do I shower?"

She points over to a curtain next to the main window that has a view of the guard center. "In there, but wear your shoes."

"How do I get a towel?"

"They didn't give you one?"

"No, just this." I hold up the bag with the toothbrush and comb and tiny pen and disassembled razor.

"You get a cup and a spork?"

"What's a spork?"

"It's like if a spoon and a fork had a baby. Half round with tiny little prongs so you can't stab anyone with it."

I shake my head. She doesn't say anything about the razor.

"Hey, Daddy," she yells.

"What's up?"

"CO didn't give homegirl here any towel, cup, spork, or hygiene."

Daddy slowly gets up and walks over to the window. She bangs on it a few times and waves the guard in. As soon as the door opens, a few women get up and start dancing to the music.

Daddy talks to him for a few minutes, looks over at me, and then back at the guard. I can't hear what they are saying. He shrugs and walks out.

"What's with the dancing?" I ask.

"They play it all day for punishment. They have the remote control to the TV out there," says Nina, flicking her head toward the guard pavilion thing. "We pretend to love it so they don't get one up on us, ya know?"

I nod. "Like they did to the POWs."

"Say what?"

"Prisoners of war. I don't know what war, but I remember hearing that music was used as a weapon of torture."

"Wow," says Nina. "That sounds right, only we turn it back on them. And besides, it's not so bad once you listen to it. These songs got some good stories. At first we faked liking it, but now I think everyone kind of likes it. Don't tell the po-po."

The door opens again, and the guard hands Daddy a bunch of stuff. Nina runs over and takes it out of Daddy's arms and brings it over to me. A plastic cup with a spork in it, a travel-size shampoo bottle, another tiny soap, and a scratchy towel. She dumps it all at the end of the bed.

"Thanks," I say.

All of a sudden there's a scream from the bunk across from me. It's Jolly Rancher Girl looking better than she did yesterday. The shower intervention must have happened while I was at court.

"My milk is gone, my milk is gone." She starts ripping up her bed and looking around the room. "Somebody stole my milk." She runs

over to Vivian. "What are you going to do about this—somebody stole my milk!"

Vivian doesn't take her eye off the video for a good minute. The girl just stands there getting more and more agitated and then she runs over to the hot pot and comes back with her cup. "I don't have any milk!" she screams, slamming the cup down on the table so that black liquid splashes out of the top.

Vivian finally looks away from the TV, reaches a hand out, and slides the cup so it's in front of her. Then she lifts her T-shirt, pulls out a breast, and squirts milk into the coffee cup.

Jolly Rancher Girl grabs the cup and walks back to her bunk.

Nina looks at me. "They took Vivian's baby girl straight from the delivery room." She shrugs and then walks away.

~

It's almost 8 p.m. now, and I pray Kaden is with his brothers. What if Bryan and Darcy didn't get emergency certified? I can't take not knowing so I get up from bed and walk over to the pay phone.

I don't want to talk to my boys, and I desperately want to talk to them. I make a collect call to Bryan's house. Dylan answers. I wait for the pause while he accepts the charges.

"D?"

"Mom?"

I don't know what to say to my seventeen-year-old. It's awkward and weird. "Are you okay?" I ask.

"Yeah, are you?"

"I'm okay," I lie. "Is Kaden with you?"

"Yeah, he's here."

"Is he okay?"

"He seems fine. He keeps saying he slept in a cat bed. He says you got him lost."

"I'm so sorry, D, I'm so sorry!"

"It's okay, Mom."

"I love you so much, Dylan. Please tell your brothers I love them and give Kaden kisses from me. Please tell him I love him, and I'll see him soon. Please tell him it's all going to be okay. I'm sorry, I'm so, so sorry!"

I don't know what more to say to him. We have never been so awkward. My firstborn, the child who made me a mother, the love of my life, really. "I only have a couple of minutes to talk, but I'm just . . . sorry." There is silence on the other end.

"Just take care of yourself, Mom. Just get better."

"Bye, I love you."

"Bye," he says.

After I hang up, I realize he didn't say he loved me.

I get back into bed. I'm grateful that no one can call me in jail. It means I only have to speak to people if I call them. There's a kind of freedom in that. I won't know what's happening in the outside world. In here I just need to focus on taking a shower and getting back into bed. Everything is stripped down to the basics.

The shower is only a trickle, but the warm water feels good. I've always preferred crying in water—the ocean, a bathtub, showers—and as the tears start to come my knees buckle. I sit on the shower floor, the same one that Nina said to make sure I wore my sandals in, but I don't care. I curl up in a ball and let the water run over my head like a baptism. I think about the note under my pillow. I think about my plan to hang myself.

And then I hear Dylan's voice asking me to get better.

Fuck. I'm not going to kill myself.

I can't imagine how I'm going to get through what's ahead of me, but there's no escaping it. I think of Kaden believing I lost him, and about how I only have a year to get him back.

And while technically I haven't lost my older boys and there's no threat hanging over my right to be their mother, I don't know if I will ever really get them back. Are they all lost to me?

Am I lost to them?

~

In jail, I am surrounded by girls so young their faces could break your heart. Girls who will ask me to explain to them exactly when in your cycle you can get pregnant. Girls who have children, lots of children, but will look at me blankly when I say the word *ovulation*. Girls who are full of shame because, like Nina, they have been gang-raped, jumped into a gang, beaten up, beaten down. These are the ride-or-die girls. These are the lost girls, the forgotten girls, the girls whose faces wear scars because they picked at them while staying awake for days with their meth dealer boyfriends, their ride-or-die men, who forget them the minute they get locked up, the minute they go down for crimes that aren't their own. The hungry girls who think love is a punch to the face, a knife to the neck, a "hold this bag for me and give it to my guy when he comes over and show him some love" girls. When the doors get kicked in, these girls get locked up. So tough on the outside, but inside they are scared and alone and desperate for things they have no name for.

Everyone I've met so far in G is a lost girl—Kiki, Nina, Jolly Rancher, Vivian, Leah, Spider Girl, even Daddy. I'm a lost girl, too, but as I climb back into bed and clutch my makeshift hot water bottle I feel just a little bit found.

~

I am pulled out of G for criminal court a few days later, on Monday. I've been given a public defender, Elizabeth, who is very pregnant. I take her extreme pregnancy as a hopeful sign that they think things

might get resolved quickly. I spend another full day alone in the tombs for a fifteen-minute court appearance. The assistant district attorney glares at me like I kicked his puppy then smiles at the judge as the case gets a continuance. DJ has his own public defender.

I'm quickly getting the routine of G down: 5 a.m. breakfast, 12 p.m. lunch, 5 p.m. dinner. Every day is one long country music song broken up with intermissions of gray, tasteless mystery food. Saturday is a tuna and egg salad sandwich; that's the party meal everyone looks forward to. Otherwise it is a slab of unknown meat between two pieces of white bread. At dinner, the same slab is breaded and served alongside canned vegetables, usually green beans. Breakfast can only be described as scrambled egg soup. The apples that come with lunch are bruised and mealy. Occasionally there's an orange, and that is cause for a citrus celebration. There is orange juggling and competitions to see who can peel it in the fewest strips. There is something about the smell of oranges that brings a bit of joy to G.

After a couple of weeks, most of my detox symptoms are gone except for the insomnia. I've always been a light sleeper, so being on the freeway means that every hour, if I do happen to fall asleep, I'm woken up when the guard makes his rounds. It's no wonder that the freeway girls are crazy. We also have a front-row seat to everything that happens in G in the middle of the night. And all the guards who make *extra* rounds.

The guards control our visits, our meals, our mail, and our access to commissary, which means paper and pens and stamps to stay in contact with the outside world. They control whether we get soap and shampoo and any sort of comfort item.

If you look at any list of the red flags for domestic violence you will find this jail's operating manual. Embarrassing or putting you down; looking at you or acting in ways that scare you; controlling who you see, where you go, or what you do; keeping you or discouraging you

from seeing your friends or families; taking your money or refusing to give you money for expenses; preventing you from making your own decisions; telling you that you are a bad parent or threatening to harm or take away your children; preventing you from working or attending school; blaming you for the abuse, or acting like it's not really happening; destroying your property or threatening to hurt you; intimidating you with guns, knives, or other weapons; pressuring you to have sex when you don't want to or do things sexually you're not comfortable with.

Check. Check. And check.

The result is a unit full of traumatized and triggered women. And the guards have no idea just how similar they are to the men that, one way or another, landed these women in G block.

~

There is a small cement courtyard attached to G—about the size of a racquetball court, and we walk around it like it's a track. Some of the girls waiting for transfers to prison are working out in hopes they will get chosen for fire camp. California uses inmates to fight wildfires and gives them two dollars a day. "It's better than being locked up," says Grace, one of the girls already sentenced and waiting for the prison bus to pick her up. "And two dollars is better than no dollars."

I don't want to think about going to prison, but if I do I try to imagine myself fighting fires. It does seem better than being locked in a cell. I join the girls walking in circles in the courtyard. I try to do a push-up but my arms are too weak to support me. There is a set of about six steps that lead to nowhere in one corner of the courtyard and because it's out of view of the cameras, girls go up to the top step and smoke contraband cigarettes. The cigarettes, like everything illegal in G, arrive in two ways: packed in the vagina of a girl who knew she was getting remanded or tucked inside one of the "special meals"

that come from the kitchen. The kitchen is run by inmates in Blaine Street—the minimum-security unit for nonviolent offenders who have already been sentenced. It abuts the main jail but isn't connected. The girls who work in the kitchen walk on their own over to the main jail, and I realize these were the girls I saw when I was brought into the sally port. Everyone wants to serve their sentence at Blaine Street with its backyard and bathtubs and rooms rather than cells. It also has its own kitchen and a gym. The Blaine Street residents are responsible for working all over the main jail. They clean the lobby, they clean the offices, they cook the food, they prepare the trays, they do the outside landscaping. They have four communal dayrooms each with their own television. They get to control their own remotes.

The equivalent men's version of Blaine Street is the Rountree Medium Facility. Unlike Blaine, it is a good ten miles or more from the main jail. The nonviolent men are taken to the main jail every morning and they deliver supplies and then serve the meals to each block. They are the inmate trustees, and they wear a special beige uniform that identifies them.

If an inmate requests a special diet because of a food allergy or religious preference, these meals are marked with a specific name. And these special meals are the vessels for messages and contraband to and from anywhere in the jail. Drugs wrapped in plastic are sent in the middle of sandwiches with a name attached so the special-meal person knows who to deliver it to. Cigarettes come in this way, as do kites, which are tiny folded-up notes or information for a specific person or the unit in general. An inmate getting his tray in solitary can pass a message to the trustee who can slip it in a special meal going to a unit where that person can hand it to the recipient. It's an underground information and commerce system as busy as the internet and more reliable than Amazon. No special-meal person would dare not pass on the information or drugs.

It is my fourth week in G when I get my first kite. A quiet vegan girl who battered her boyfriend walks by my table and drops it on my tray. It's from DJ and has my initials in tiny letters in the corner. It's only a few sentences, telling me he loves me and that he's going to get us out of here. He addresses it "Dear Homegirl." I read it and flush it down the toilet. The guards do random searches of everyone's bunks, and you don't want to get caught with a kite.

I think about this note all afternoon. It feels weird that he's using the term "homegirl" considering he's been a mortgage broker for most of his adult life, and he grew up in Los Gatos—a wealthy Silicon Valley suburb. I guess he's adapting to his surroundings, but it feels strange and unsettling.

Soon, I learn the third way that kites and contraband get in the jail. I am awake one night when the guard comes in to do the 3 a.m. rounds. At first I think I'm dreaming because I smell McDonald's fries. I watch as the guard walks around the freeway and close my eyes when the flashlight passes over me so he doesn't know I'm awake. I track him as he peers in all the door windows of the lower tier and then walks upstairs. He's carrying a McDonald's bag, so I know I'm not crazy. I can't see him on the upper tier, but I hear a door open and then shut. When he walks downstairs twenty minutes later, the bag is not in his hands. I don't know whose room he went to and what was traded, but after a month in jail I know that the guards don't give anything for free.

~

Once a week you can leave G block to go to a twelve-step meeting in a small classroom in the jail. I decide to go during my fifth week. I'm nervous. Not because it's a recovery meeting but because I'm afraid I'm going to see someone I know. Before my relapse that landed me in jail, I had been in recovery for six years. I met DJ in recovery.

I had also volunteered on the Hospitals and Institutions Committee within Santa Cruz County's Narcotics Anonymous group. The H&I committee was responsible for recruiting and training people to bring meetings into the jail. I have to weigh my desire to get out of G and away from country music for an hour against my fear of being seen in my reds as a criminal, a relapser, a twelve-step failure, and a cautionary tale. I can't listen to another song about backyard barbecues, so I line up with five others to attend the meeting. H block is also a female unit, so twelve-step and religious meetings are the only time the two units mixed. G is a de facto tribe and we felt we were superior to H block. In reality we were exactly the same, but there was competition over which unit was better looking, had more street cred, and had less snitches. I don't understand what the competition is about, but it feels exactly like my high school rivalry between Brookline and Newton. Since you couldn't tell where one city ended and the other began, it was a silly, pointless rivalry that still felt super important.

I line up in my reds with my ID card in my hand and walk the yellow line to the meeting room. The guard unlocks the door and we all pile inside. Two women in street clothes are at the front of the room. I look up and see Cheryl, a friend I knew from recovery. I steel myself and smile and walk up to her.

"Hi, Cheryl," I say.

She seems surprised to see me. "Oh my god, Lara, hi . . ."

I make a move to hug her and she jumps back. "We're not allowed to hug you," she says. I know this, of course. I trained her in my home on a Saturday morning while the boys watched cartoons. I served her donuts and coffee at my dining room table. I went over every rule she had to follow to bring meetings into the jail.

I feel my face flush in embarrassment. I turn quickly, retreat to

the back of the room, and sit down. I am suddenly angry. Angry at Cheryl. Angry at everyone in this room.

But mostly I'm angry at recovery—the program, the community, the platitudes, the higher power, the false anonymity, and the hollow applause. NA was full of the worst gossips in the world and bored people looking for drama to replace the using. It was a dangerous combination. I spend the rest of the meeting with my eyes closed, litigating every minute I spent in NA and vowing not to go there again twenty-seven years from now when I get out of prison. That would show them.

If I hadn't voluntarily gone into recovery, I wouldn't have met DJ. If I hadn't met DJ, I would have never smoked heroin. If I had never smoked heroin, I would never have stolen credit cards. If I had never used a stolen credit card, I would have never been arrested for identity theft. If I had never been arrested, I would never be in jail at this stupid meeting.

This loop replays itself in my head during the walk back to G.

I don't care that my circular logic is flawed. I don't care that if I had never gone into recovery and married DJ, I wouldn't have Kaden. I'm angry, and I don't know what to do about it other than rerunning this loop.

Back in G, there are still two hours before lights out at ten. I pace restlessly around the freeway. I walk to the phones, but I don't know who to call. Most of the women are playing a card game I don't understand. Others are making spreads in the hot pot, which involves ramen noodles and then a mix of other items squirreled away from meal trays or ordered from the commissary. Hot Cheetos are a favorite addition to spreads. There are a thousand creative ways that one pot of warm water can be used in jail, and every day I marvel at the culinary creativity.

Kiki sees me pacing and asks me what's wrong. I shrug and wave my arms around me to encompass G, the jail, the universe. She understands. Everyone in G understands.

"Grace left a book when she went to Chowchilla, do you want it?"

"What is it?" I ask.

"I don't know. Does it matter?"

It doesn't matter. I can't think of the last time I read a book. There was never time in mom life to read, and certainly there wasn't time in my addict life. I had ordered several parenting books a couple of weeks before I was arrested, but I had ordered them with a stolen credit card.

"Okay, I'll take it, thanks."

She goes into her room on the top tier and comes back down with a paperback. I am praying it's not historical fiction or some kind of heaving-bosoms romance novel. When she hands it to me I read the title: *The Power of Now.*

I don't know who Eckhart Tolle is, but I like self-help books, and if there was ever a time and place for a self-help book it's now. I thank Kiki and take the book over to my bunk.

I open it and read the first line. "I have little use for the past and rarely think about it . . ."

I'm instantly intrigued. If this book says don't think about the past, then I'm all for it. I have just spent the last hour reliving the past. I have spent every night here reliving my arrest. The past is *all* I think about, except for when I take a break to agonize over the future.

I read until lights out, and I read first thing in the morning. I finish the book in twenty-four hours and start reading it again. I want all the things Tolle describes. I want a higher good, I want to end drama, I want to transform suffering, I want to find the space between my thoughts and soothe my pain body. I want enlightenment and peace. I want to be in the now and not in fear and anxiety and regret. I want

to end psychological time. I want wholeness. I want to live in truth—spiritual truth, emotional truth, psychological truth.

Give me all the truths.

~

I read *The Power of Now* over and over, and I strive to live by its advice. Whenever I'm in fear of the future I take deep, cleansing breaths and remind myself that in this moment I am okay. Tolle says that pain only feeds on pain, not joy, so I try to find joyful moments, things to be grateful for right now.

When Thanksgiving comes, I try to be grateful there's an ice cream cup on my tray and not focus on the fact that it is the first holiday I have ever spent without my children.

The book offers a kind of freedom I have never felt before—freedom from my restless, worried mind. I've spent my entire life waiting for the next bad thing to happen, and now that it has I remind myself I'm still here. I'm surviving. As heavy as life is in jail, I actually feel lighter.

The next time I go to court and the prosecuting attorney glares at me, I don't lower my eyes. I look at him, and I stay in the power of the now, and I send him love and light. I stay present in the courtroom, and I try to find the life beneath this life, the self that is thinking about itself.

In the tombs, I practice deep whole-body breathing and try to meditate to let the endless, useless hours pass after a ten-minute court appearance. Everything is just a continuance. It's so hard to be in jail not knowing how long you will be there. It is psychological-time mind fuckery, so I try to ask myself, *What would Eckhart do?* And then I take a deep breath and try to stop my racing thoughts.

Tolle says waiting is just a state of mind that we need to snap out of—but he's never spent time in the tombs.

I am sitting in the tombs deep breathing, trying to be joyfully present, when the door opens. I go to stand, grateful to get back to G, but it's the guard bringing in another woman. Unlike mine, her uniform is striped, green and white. She walks in and sits on the bench next to me.

I have never been in the tombs with another person in my cell. It's unsettling.

"Hi," she says.

"Hi."

She stares at me for a minute, and then pushes her hair back from her face. "I'm Gina."

"Lara," I say.

She stares straight ahead in silence after that, and I don't know what to say. "How are you?" seems too rhetorical and mundane for such a dire moment.

After about ten minutes, Gina starts to cry. I grab the roll of toilet paper and hand it to her.

"Are you okay?" I finally ask. It's a ridiculous question, but I must say something.

"I killed my daughter. I didn't mean to. Oh God, I didn't mean to." She starts to sob and I am at once shocked and a little scared. Her tears are heart-wrenching, though, and I feel my own eyes well up.

"It'll be okay," I say. "It'll be okay."

She shakes her head at me. "I miss her so much. I didn't mean it. I don't even remember doing it."

I had heard some of the girls in G talking about a woman in O— the medical unit—who had killed her three-year-old daughter by smothering her in a hotel room. Gina is the woman from O.

As she cries, I realize I'm not afraid to be in a locked room with a murderer. Her anguish and sorrow are real and relatable. In an instant

I am grateful. My children are alive. They are safe. They are with someone who won't hurt them.

I try to stay present with her as she cries. I send her compassion in my mind. Every few minutes I murmur to her, "It will be okay. It will be okay."

We are two mothers sitting on a bench in shackles.

We both know I'm lying.

The truth is great, but sometimes lies are all you have to get you through.

Sorry, Eckhart Tolle.

chapter 8

MAMA LOVE

It's safe to say that when you go from husband and wife to code-fendants, the romance is over. DJ is angrier and more belligerent every time we go to court. I get it, the tombs are the worst, but he's not helping us any by acting exactly like the prosecution is portraying us.

DJ and I met in recovery. He got his third DUI before I met him, and his mom had gotten him a high-powered attorney who negotiated five months at the Camp Recovery Center rather than jail. She even moved in a special mattress for him. They say that dating in recovery is like fishing in polluted waters, but when your whole world is recovery, who else are you going to date?

My first marriage was over before it really took off. We were young and broke, and I had three boys in less than five years straight out of graduate school. Stressful under the best of circumstances. I was pregnant with Cody during my wedding and Dylan walked me down the aisle. I knew Bryan and I weren't right for each other, and I'm sure he knew it, too, but we didn't have the language to discuss it or work

through it. I had doubts even before we got married, but it seemed easier to say yes than to break up.

When he cheated on me I tried to forgive him, but at the same time I disconnected from him emotionally. I was trying to protect myself from getting hurt and trying desperately to stay with him so our boys would have parents who were together. It was hard to do both things at the same time.

He cheated again. And again.

I knew that to stay would mean staring out the window night after night, wondering where he was. I knew that to stay would mean giving up on ever being loved.

Bryan Love wasn't a bad guy. He just didn't love me.

So I said goodbye to him and moved with two toddlers and a baby into the bottom level of a friend's house surrounded by redwoods.

We shared custody.

I was twenty-eight years old and I was in grief, but every other weekend when the boys went to their dad's house, I went out on the town.

I started dating a musician.

I became the life of the party.

I pretended to become the motherfucking happiest woman alive.

~

DJ and I had sat on the lawn of his rehab and talked about white picket fences and how we both wanted a nice, boring life. He had two young children from his first marriage. I had been a single mom for almost a decade at this point. He left the recovery center every day to work as a mortgage broker, and when he was done serving his time at the Camp he would whisk me away on magical weekends to fancy hotels and lake houses. One time I got off work and went home to find he had redecorated my entire bedroom. I had a new comforter and

throw pillows and it felt like being taken care of. It felt like a grand gesture. He was over-the-top and he swept me off my feet in a way that I craved.

Sure, he had gotten in legal trouble for drinking and driving three times and had cheated on his first wife while in rehab—but those throw pillows!

When I accidentally got pregnant with Kaden, DJ got me a ring, and we eloped to Hawaii. Part of me wished I could experience a marriage ceremony without morning sickness, but I pushed that aside and said "I do" under a palm tree with a volcano looming above us. This was going to be the suburban soccer mom life I wanted. All the bad stuff was in our past.

We bought a business—a pet cemetery (of all things), with down payment help from his mother.

We bought a home in a cul-de-sac in Aptos.

When Kaden was born, our new neighbors brought over meals. Their children became our children's best friends. It was perfectly perfect.

And when Kaden was two months old, DJ had to go to rehab in New Mexico because he had started smoking heroin. I took care of all my boys and my two stepchildren and ran our business while he was gone.

And I was miserable when he came back because I couldn't get over the betrayal of him using. I loved fully until someone hurt me, and then I just pretended to love while remaining vigilant for the next bout of pain. I didn't have the skill set to work things out. I didn't know how to talk something through or express my deepest feelings. My own emotions embarrassed me so I kept them private. Vulnerable wasn't a look I was willing to wear.

DJ was miserable too. He had his own demons, his own fears, and we just danced around each other, not willing to look below the

surface. So we smiled and fronted and pretended it was all exactly what we wanted. He started smoking heroin again in secret. I started taking pills in secret. We both denied it and tried to catch each other in the act.

One day I came home from work, and he was waiting at the door with a drug test in his hand. I was outraged that he would suspect me. And angry.

"I don't have to pee right now."

"Pee in this cup when you can then," he demands, pulling the cup from a store-bought drug-test kit and stomping away.

"You're the one who relapsed and went to rehab, leaving me with a two-month-old, five kids, and a business!" I throw this at him to see if it makes him back off, but it doesn't work.

Outwardly I am mad, but inside I am terrified. The pills are my secret and I need them. They give me my suburban superpowers. In my mind, this is better than all the other moms in their workout wear carrying water bottles full of vodka water. Or sitting at the park drinking chardonnay from sippy cups. There's more alcohol at a Little League game than at a Super Bowl party.

I don't drink, so I feel virtuous.

My mind races trying to find a way to get out of this pee test. "I'm going to take the dog for a walk, and maybe I'll pee when I get back."

I put our dog on his leash, grab a Tupperware container from the kitchen, and hide it under my sweatshirt.

It's dark outside, and I walk him around the cul-de-sac. Every minute or so he stops and lifts his leg, and when he does I quickly put the container under the stream and catch it. I think this will only take a few minutes, but each leg lift produces such a tiny amount that I have to walk him for over an hour to get enough.

Once we're back in the house, I hand the dog off to DJ, grab the cup from his hands, and flounce off to the bathroom. I lock the door

and then pour the dog's urine in the cup. Luckily it's still warm. I hide the Tupperware under the sink, open the door, and hand the cup to DJ.

He does the test while I stand by self-righteously.

The dog tests clean.

I say, "I told you so. How dare you not believe me? You should look in the mirror the next time you want to accuse someone." And the strange thing is, in that moment, I believe I am who I'm pretending to be.

It didn't cross my mind to say, "I have a problem and I need help." I have never said that sentence out loud to anyone.

I graciously accept DJ's apology.

~

Today, DJ and I are put in the same van after leaving the tombs. The driver is playing music and ignoring us as we whisper.

"I want to escape," he announces.

"What?"

"I'm not going to prison. We could drive to Costa Rica."

I don't want to go to prison either, but I can't imagine us on the run, and I'm not even sure if you can drive to Costa Rica. I've always been bad at geography.

There have been escapes before. There's a girl in G who walked away from Blaine Street. She was caught down at the local diner a quarter mile away and now she's not allowed to go back to Blaine Street. As far as I know, nobody has ever escaped from the main jail.

I glance at the driver and back at DJ and put my finger to my lips. "I'll think about it," I whisper.

It's hard not having an out date—an official sentence. I envy the girls in G who have hand-drawn calendars, and every night they get to make a big X through the day. It feels like progress. I'm in purgatory, and for me, there's no progress in purgatory.

DJ slips me a kite right before we get out of the van. I panic for a

moment because the guards pat you down when you return from the tombs. I quickly tuck it in my bra. Hopefully the guard won't be too handsy during my search. I'm furious that DJ has given me the kite directly. It's so much safer to write me via sandwich.

When I get back to my cell, after a mercifully light pat down, I tuck under the covers and open the note. When I do, a folded-up note within drops onto my sheet.

"Hey Homegirl, I love you and miss you so fucking much. Remember that thing I never tried, well I tried it and it was amazing! Here's a little early Xmas present. Who always takes care of you???? Open it privately and carefully!!!!"

I read the note over and over, trying to make it mean anything other than what I think it means. That thing he never tried is injecting heroin. I am shocked. *DJ is shooting up? In jail? Which means he could only be sharing a needle.* My heart races and my mouth waters. I am ravenous for whatever's inside this kite-within-a-kite. I am only about six weeks clean, but I am clean. The idea that DJ isn't makes me both angry and jealous.

Everybody is trying to get high in G. Some are trying to smoke banana peels leftover from breakfast. Others are ripping out pages from the Bible and rolling up coffee grinds to make a caffeine-laced religious blunt because somebody said they heard smoking coffee gets you high. When the med cart comes, one girl on methadone holds it in her mouth and then spits the warm syrupy medicine into three other mouths. One girl didn't give her albuterol inhaler back to the nurse and sprayed it on the sink until it dried into a faint powder that she could snort.

When somebody sneaks drugs in, she is rushed to the top tier where Daddy and Vivian and Kiki embrace her and shuttle her into a room while Nina keeps lookout.

I don't feel great clean, but I don't particularly feel bad either.

I'm not invited to the top-tier drug parties, and I'm okay with that. I want to be clean. Or I did. Now I have whatever DJ gave me, and I'm questioning why I shouldn't use in here. If there's anywhere that calls for some mental escape, it's here. I go into the bathroom and over to the corner where there are no cameras. My hands are shaking as I unwrap the mini kite. Inside is a tiny plastic baggie full of white powder. I assume it is meth. A part of me is sad it's not sticky brown heroin that I could pop in my cheek and suck on like a lozenge. I don't know if that's a thing, but I can imagine doing that. I flush both kites down the toilet and tuck the baggie in my bra.

I don't know what to do. I get into my bunk and close my eyes.

Back when DJ and I were keeping our drug habits secret from each other, I found three pea-sized baggies just like the one in my bra. I had searched his gym bag while he drove the kids to school and found them inside a sock. Only those baggies had tar heroin in them—goopy dark brown pebbles. I felt triumphant.

While he was driving carpool, I took down a box of dark brown sugar and a saucepan and boiled the sugar so it looked just like the heroin. Then I made three duplicate baggies and tucked them in his sock. I carried the real heroin in my pocket all day—constantly playing with the baggies like worry beads. Eventually I googled how to smoke heroin and locked myself in my bedroom with a straw and some tinfoil and a lighter. It didn't give me the magical rush of Vicodin on an empty stomach, but it made me feel warm. I had given up the pills for the millionth time and swore I would never take them again, so this felt like a good alternative. Easier. Gentler. It gave me a quiet boost of opiate energy, but I had to smoke a lot to feel it. Or maybe I just had to get better at inhaling. I wasn't sure if I was really high or just high because I should be but I kissed DJ when he got home from work and made a nice dinner. I don't know if he got high from the brown sugar, but he didn't mention it.

We played our parts. We played each other.

We kept our secrets.

I can trace that day to all the days in the year that followed. Telling DJ I knew he was doing heroin. Telling him I wanted to smoke it with him.

And then it was on.

We spent all our money.

I went out stealing, both to fund our habit and maintain our suburban charade. DJ bought the drugs, but I was the real criminal, stealing credit cards and going through other people's mail looking for money.

It was a year of misery and chaos and lying to everyone.

Those little baggies made me lose everyone I loved.

~

I get up from my bunk and walk to Vivian's room and knock on her open door.

"What's up?" She raises her eyebrows as I enter.

"I was in the van from court with my husband today."

She gives me a nod telling me to continue. I look over my shoulder to make sure there's no officer in G, and none of the girls are looking. She sees me glance out and gets off her bunk and shuts the door. I pull out the baggie and hold it out to her in my palm.

She smiles at me like we're best friends.

"Take it."

"What?"

"Take it, I don't want it."

She looks at me suspiciously. I shrug. "I'm trying to stay clean."

"I can respect that. What do you want for it?"

I start to say "nothing," but I've learned enough to know this is worse than asking for something. In G, altruism is always suspicious.

I don't have money on my books yet, although DJ said his mom

was going to put some on mine too. I haven't been able to order anything from the commissary.

"Do you have paper and an envelope and stamps?"

"I can hook that up. What else?"

I don't really want anything else—I just want to be able to write my boys and maybe write in general. But I can tell Vivian doesn't think this is an even trade yet.

"Give me two bear claws," I say.

She gives me a big smile and nods.

~

That night in my bunk, I again try to meditate. I take deep breaths. I try to focus on the breath moving through my body. I try to stop my thoughts by asking myself what my next thought will be. I try to be the self behind the self.

Metacognition is great and all, but not that easy when half the locked rooms are high on DJ's drugs and the party goes on all night long.

I pull the blanket over my head and cry—this is my meditation tonight.

~

The only thing that's happened in our court case since our arrest, besides continuances, is that the judge denies a request to reduce our bail. It's still $250,000, which seems excessive considering the only violent moment I've ever had in my life was throwing a head of iceberg lettuce at my high school boyfriend when I was sixteen.

Needless to say, no one has bailed me out. My mother-in-law could bail me out, but apparently she's too angry to consider it. She blames me for DJ's crimes.

It's almost Christmas, and I'm no closer to knowing my fate than I was on the day I arrived. I try to call Kaden on December 12, his

fourth birthday, but there's no answer at Bryan's house. Some days it feels like there is no outside world. It's just three meals a day and music videos. I feel listless and tense. I only have a year, or I lose Kaden forever. A judge will say I'm no longer his mother, and legally it will be true. It doesn't matter where I am. The clock ticks just the same. Unless I can have a certain number of supervised visits with him, stay clean, provide somewhere to live, get a job, go to therapy, take a parenting class—I will lose him. None of it is hard to do, but all of it is impossible to do from G.

I just want to know what's going to happen one way or another. The not knowing is the worst. Every day is like that moment when you lean back in a chair and you go just a little too far and have to jerk yourself upright. I'm not upright, and I haven't fallen; I'm suspended in that space of muted panic.

Things get tenser in G as Christmas approaches. Just like on the outside, holidays are triggering and make everyone even edgier. Arguments happen over the hot pot and someone double-dipping her colored pencil directly instead of putting the hot water in her mug. The cleanliness of the shower is another powder keg waiting to blow. The lack of new videos in the rotation have some cursing the country music channel in two languages.

Today tension is high because a woman named Elena was brought in last night and Daddy suspects her of ratting out a friend of a friend of Daddy's. There's something about a motel room, counterfeit money, and a setup.

Daddy is raging at Elena, trying to bait her, trying to get her to respond. Elena just ignores Daddy and watches the videos.

Daddy's rage is escalating. She's on the top level yelling down at Elena and getting zero response. I'm annoyed that the yelling is interrupting the music. Finally, Daddy comes barreling down the stairs, and I lift my head and watch as she slips on the bottom step and falls.

Everyone laughs, even her minions. Daddy does not like to be laughed at. I quickly jump up from my chair and stand between Daddy and the tables. Her face is red with embarrassment. Even under her buzz cut, her scalp has turned red.

I give her my hand and as I pull her up, I whisper, "Real power is quiet power."

She freezes, her head next to mine.

"If you lose control of yourself, you lose control of them," I add.

Daddy pulls me into the bathroom and doesn't say a word. Everyone stops laughing.

"Explain," she commands.

"If you rage at Elena, you give her power over you. Over your emotions. She becomes stronger than you." Daddy nods. "If you fight her, you'll get pulled out of here, and then you really won't have any control." I'm making shit up now. I have no idea what the guards do when there is a real fight.

I recall the time I dumped an entire box of cereal onto the middle of the kitchen floor to shock my kids into silence so I could take a business call and not have the client know I was at home with three little boys.

"You have to create cognitive dissonance—do the unexpected thing and she'll do something different." I'm not sure if this is what cognitive dissonance means, but the words impress Daddy.

"I get it," she says. "Dope."

She turns and walks out of the bathroom. I follow behind her, not sure what she's going to do. She walks over to Jolly Rancher, who's sitting next to Elena, and motions for her to get up. She sits down next to Elena and doesn't say a word, just stares at her.

When lunch comes, she doesn't eat. She just sits and stares at Elena. And when Elena moves to a different table, Daddy follows her.

All afternoon, she sits and stares and never speaks.

When the meal trays come for dinner, Daddy is still staring, and Elena is increasingly nervous and uncomfortable. When Daddy doesn't eat dinner, everybody in G goes silent.

Elena runs to the bathroom and pushes the panic button.

Two guards come in. "Roll me up," she says, pulling her things down from her bunk. "I need to go to another unit."

The guards know that a girl rolling herself up really means the other inmates are rolling her up. She's not wanted. They don't argue when someone wants to be rolled up, and they don't ask questions. It's how you keep peace in the unit, and the guards want zero problems and zero paperwork. They look around to see if anyone is obviously causing trouble for Elena, but nobody says a word. Daddy just watches the television, disinterested.

"Roll it up then," one of them says.

After Elena leaves, Daddy walks upstairs and starts moving people around. I see bunks being shifted from room to room. Spider, the girl with the neck tattoo, comes downstairs and moves into the room next to Vivian. That girl moves out onto the freeway. I'm not sure what is happening until Daddy walks up to me.

"Get your stuff."

"What?" I'm shocked. Is she rolling me up?

"You're moving in with Patricia." Patricia is an older gangster woman and super chill. She has a prime room right at the top of the stairs, but mostly keeps to herself. People show her respect because she's so old. I grab my few things and Daddy picks up my yoga mat mattress. I can't believe I'm getting a door that shuts. Some quiet. More privacy.

I settle my stuff onto my bed and turn to say hi to Patricia.

"What you want?" she asks with a big smile.

Before me on her bunk lies a huge array of snacks from the commissary—chips, candy bars, ramen noodles, bear claws, Jolly Ranchers. The mother lode.

I pick up a Snickers and peel back the wrapper. Nothing in my life has tasted as good as this candy bar.

~

Everything changes once I'm on the top tier. During long conversations, I get to know everyone well. I stand at the railing and look down on the freeway and discuss the latest gossip in G with Daddy. We keep the peace. My thirty-two felony charges give me street cred I don't deserve, considering I didn't even know the phrase "street cred" two months ago. But I go along with it.

I develop some swagger.

I tell the girls how I decoded the algorithm to credit cards—the pattern of odd and even numbers that are used by each bank—so I could create working credit card numbers without having to have an actual card. It's not that complicated, but they're deeply impressed. On paper, it looks like I'm the scariest person in the county. Since I don't know the street world of Santa Cruz, I don't know who to fear, defer to, or lord over—I treat everyone equally. Now that I'm on the top tier, I quickly come to understand each subgroup, each clique, each gang, and each outsider, and I speak all jail languages. I can be gangster. I can be a Bible thumper. I can be a wise elder. I can do makeup with Kiki and Nina and flirt with the trustees who deliver the meals. I can also talk to the guards in a way that implies I don't really belong here by using big words they've never heard of but have to pretend they know so they can save face with an inmate.

I also become the unofficial welcome wagon, making sure that everyone who comes into G has what they are allowed to have. If someone is missing their hygiene kit or a towel like I was, I bang on the window and demand the guard go get it. I am a friend to everyone but not too close with anyone. It's exactly as it was in high school. I become whoever I need to be to survive.

But mostly I'm a mom with nowhere to put my mother energy, so I listen. Empathize. Word gets around that I have a master's degree so girls who've dropped out of high school start coming to me for advice. Problems are brought to me. Legal issues. I'm given a nickname.

Mama Love.

And like any good mother, I lead with compassion. But all it takes is one stern look to bring the miscreants in line. Eventually Daddy brings me her court and legal papers and we talk over options and prison. The minute the unit sees Daddy deferring to me, a peaceful transition of power happens. It's subtle and unspoken but real. When someone has a problem with being disrespected by someone, wants to move off the freeway, wants to move upstairs, wants to make a commissary trade, wants to roll someone up, I'm consulted. Daddy is there, too, but my opinion is always the final word.

I write a one-page narrative poem about the girls in G being hooked on H and they make me read it out loud over and over. They have never been written about, their lives and struggles never put on paper. When they learn that a short story of mine has been published in a real book, I hear them telling their family about me on their phone calls.

I don't tell them that a short story in a small press anthology doesn't make you famous or that right now is the first time I've written anything in ten years.

But now that I'm on the top level I have endless paper, so I start to write. I start a young adult novel about angel guides who fall into forbidden love as the two teens they are guiding also fall in love. I mail the first eleven pages to Ty and ask him if he wants to write the book with me. He's an avid reader and at thirteen has already written his first novel. He writes in the way people do who are madly in love with language—a maximalist who will go on to major in linguistics and speak five languages. I tell myself that his love of reading isn't for

the same reason I loved to read as a kid. I tell myself he isn't trying to escape trauma, but it's hard to do that when I'm telling myself that in jail. I write letters to my boys and ask them to read parts to Kaden for me. It's hard to talk to them on the phone some days because it's awkward and they are teenagers who don't love to talk on the phone to begin with. When they put Kaden on, he just tells me he loves his brothers but wants to come home.

"Soon," I promise. "I love you so much," I say.

~

The "real power is quiet power" mantra spreads through the unit, and people stop fighting so much and instead try to "out-quiet" each other. Power doesn't have anything to prove, I remind them.

None of them know that I actually feel more lost and powerless than ever. My future is in limbo and there's no power in limbo.

chapter 9

NEW YEAR, NEW YOU

It's a year of firsts without my children. My first Thanksgiving without them. My first Christmas without them. I miss Kaden's fourth birthday on December 12, and Cody's sixteenth birthday on December 30.

I am now someone who misses her children's birthdays because she's in jail.

Shortly after Thanksgiving, Darcy sends me a Christmas card that shows her and my four boys. They are making a pyramid at the beach, and they are all in Santa hats. I think I know why she sends me this picture, and it is not to wish me season's greetings. I try to focus on the fact that they're all together, and safe. While Bryan was not the best husband, he is a great dad. Darcy couldn't have children, and while we were friendly as she got together with Bryan, things have been fraught this last year during my relapse. Darcy hired an expensive lawyer, and Bryan took me to court over custody. They wanted

more time with them and accused me of being on drugs. They were right, of course, but I still denied it. I wanted to pretend I was fine and work things out with Bryan without lawyers or courts the way we always had. I didn't think it was any of Darcy's business, and I was afraid that if I had gone to them and said, *"Hey, can you take the boys for thirty days so I can go to rehab and get my shit together?"* they would have used that against me in court. I was stuck.

In jail, I choose not to think about the fact that my boys had said they didn't like Darcy. By their account: She screamed at them all the time. The house was never clean enough for her taste. She often hid out in her room. She got mad at them for eating her special food. She was always yelling at and fighting with their dad. Maybe it was true or maybe it was just kids complaining.

Darcy and I had long pretended to get along for the boys, but I always felt like she resented me when I did well and celebrated when I did badly. Underneath the pretense was the simple fact that, no matter what, I was always going to be the mother and she was always going to be the stepmother. She could never change that or, perhaps, forgive me for that. After months of dragged-out mediation over custody, my arrest had settled it once and for all.

I knew Bryan would take care of Kaden and love him while I was in jail. I knew Kaden would be happy as long as he was around his big brothers.

Darcy was a necessary evil, but better than strangers. I sent her as much love and light as I could. I hoped her heart would be open to Kaden. I was grateful to her and wary of her at the same time.

Now she holds my baby in this picture, and it feels like she is staring straight into my soul.

Now she has all my children all the time. She has won.

~

I push thoughts of Darcy away and try to stay in the moment. Jail is a great place to learn to meditate, and it's going to be my New Year's resolution. I sit on my bunk breathing every day of December—first for five minutes, then ten, then thirty, until I can meditate for an hour without feeling like more than five minutes have passed. It's a way to beat crazy jail time at its own game. After an hour of meditation there's a feeling that's almost like getting high. Not quite, but close. I wish I knew how many hours of meditation would equal twenty Vicodin.

When people speak to me, I practice being present and sending them love. I do this with the guards, with the judge and prosecutor when my case is continued yet again on Christmas Eve, with Daddy and Nina and Kiki and Vivian. I send love to the scared women who come in for their first time. I also make sure to tell them how everything works in G. I give them the orientation I never got. All day long I send love out to the world. To my children. My neighbors in Aptos. To DJ and Bryan.

I even send love to Darcy, but then I think of her clutching Kaden and I take it back. I'm not the Dalai Lama, after all.

The other women tell me that I will definitely be going to prison and that I should start working out now so I can try out for fire camp. We go in the courtyard and do sit-ups and push-ups and walk in endless circles. No one can figure out how many times around the small courtyard is a mile. The guesses range from fifty to a thousand.

On Christmas morning I wake up and walk around the courtyard for hours. I meditate as I walk. I meditate all day long so I don't have to think about life outside G block.

~

The time between Christmas and New Year's is extra boring, so Daddy and I hatch a plan to break up the monotony. Leah, who is pregnant, will fake labor pains. She's only seven months, so Daddy has

determined that this will be too serious for normal medical and as a holiday gift to us, she will get paramedics into the unit for our viewing pleasure and just to break up the monotony.

She and Leah come into my cell as they are plotting the details.

"I need to know what labor feels like," says Leah. "You have a million children, coach me."

I have nothing better to do so I agree. "Do you get period cramps?"

"Yeah," says Leah.

"It's nothing like that," I say. "It's like this pressure that builds, kind of from the back, and then it wraps around and tightens." I think back to all my labors with Dylan, Cody, Ty, and Kaden. "It's like no other pain there is when it comes. A tightness and a squeezing and sometimes the pain is so bad it takes your breath away."

I know this is pretend, but I see in Leah's face the realization of what awaits her when she has her baby. She looks scared.

I am about to say it's okay because it's all worth it, and you have this beautiful baby, and you fall in love like you've never felt love before, but I stop myself. Her baby will be taken away from her in the hospital. She will give birth handcuffed to a bed. She will fall in love and have her heart broken at the same moment.

~

Everyone is excited to start the New Year with visions of paramedics. Daddy pushes the panic button and calls the guards.

"Leah is going into labor. She's in pain, come quick!" she yells. Leah has taken over an empty bunk on the freeway, so everyone can witness the performance.

Two guards rush in and hover over her.

"Oohhhh it hurts, it hurts . . ." she moans. They try to get her up, but she screams louder and says she can't move. Her performance is

high-school-theater level, but it convinces the guards. One talks into his shoulder radio and instructs someone to call 911.

It only takes about ten minutes for the paramedics to arrive. Firefighters also. There are four of them, and they are young and gorgeous. The guards lock everyone in the cells, but we watch through the windows as they stand around Leah. Within minutes two more paramedics come in with a gurney.

We watch in disbelief as Leah is wheeled out of G. Right before she's rolled out the door, she flips us all the bird.

The guards unlock the cells, and Daddy asks where they are taking her.

"Dominican Hospital," one of the guards says.

As soon as he leaves the room, there's a mad rush to the phones. Three girls call their drug dealers and tell them to get to Dominican Hospital emergency. Leah is on the outside and will be coming back in once they realize she's not in labor.

This wasn't the plan, and I feel my power in G slip a little. Did Daddy keep this part of the plan from me? It's no secret that I don't use the drugs DJ sends me. I don't know if this was the real plan all along and Daddy says no when I ask.

I'm not thrilled at the idea of more drugs in G, but I could never say that. It's so hard to stay clean in G and I'm almost at sixty days. I'm proud of myself, but when they are around, the cravings are stronger than my meditation. In recovery they always say, "If you don't want a haircut, then don't hang out at a barber shop."

There's no catchy platitude for when you're locked in the barber shop twenty-four hours a day.

Leah doesn't come back before lockdown, so I go to sleep not knowing if she was met by a cavalcade of drug dealers in the ER.

I am awoken by yelling. Patricia and I jump up. I slept in my

clothes, but she is in her bra and underwear only. There are about ten guards in G shouting, all the doors are open, and the lights are on.

"Everyone out on the floor, now!" they scream. Girls are running down the stairs. Patricia tries to grab her clothes, but the guard yells at her not to touch anything. There's yelling from Daddy's room, but I don't have a chance to turn back before we are all rushed out of G block. Shakedowns have happened before but there's usually some warning and people have time to hide their second mattress in the shower or tuck any contraband away in hidey-holes around the unit.

Not tonight.

The entire unit is marched through the jail until we get to the big holding room you pass through before you go to court. There's a giant wire cage in one corner of the room. It's square and looks like the temporary fencing that goes up around construction sites. We're all herded into the cage and stand there stunned as it's locked from the outside with a giant padlock.

I look around at some of the regulars to see if this is normal, and I can tell this is not normal for anyone. I don't see Leah; she must still be at the hospital. I think about all the calls made to drug dealers. I had heard girls talking about the trick we played on the guards over the phone. After a while it's easy to forget that the guards are always listening to everything.

It is freezing in the cage, and poor Patricia is half-naked and shivering. "Hey," I yell to one of the guards.

"Yeah?"

"Can you get her some clothes? She's freezing." I nod toward Patricia.

"Yeah, sure, no problem."

Thank God for small kindnesses.

I give her a big fake smile and say, "Thanks so much! Hey, do you happen to know what time it is?"

"Why? You have somewhere to be?" She laughs and walks away. I'm guessing it's 2 a.m., maybe three.

Girls are huddled together on the floor trying to fall back asleep. Daddy and Kiki and Vivian are whispering. I need to see what's up with them, but first I need to get Patricia dressed. The guard brings her some reds and a big beige coat.

"Whoa," I say, "I've never seen one of those before."

"Blaine Street coat," says Patricia. "So they don't get cold walking over to the kitchen."

It's a huge coat, with thick canvas material on the outside and soft flannel inside. It's warm. It's luxurious. It's amazing.

We're left in the cage for hours. Daddy is pissed because she has a lighter in her cell and doesn't want to get another demerit. The more demerits you get, the less credit you have to shave days or even weeks off your sentence.

We sit in there through what would normally be breakfast time, and it's almost light out when they bring us back right before the shift change at 7 a.m. The guards don't say a word as they march us back to G. None of us have any idea what they were looking for or what they may have found.

G is in shambles. The freeway mattresses are scattered all over the floor, and everything from the cells has been dumped haphazardly along the tier: books, letters, legal papers, blankets, clothes, toothbrushes. Family pictures painstakingly glued on the walls with toothpaste have been ripped down. Shelves engineered from empty maxi pad boxes have been crushed. Commissary items are scattered. It's like a Category 5 hurricane hit G. This wasn't an investigation—it was punishment.

We're all trying to sort whose belongings are whose when Leah comes back in with a big smile on her face.

I can't deal with all of this and the temptation of drugs at the same time. I assume that's what she's smiling about. I quickly get on the pay

phone to call my boys. If anything will strengthen my resolve it will be talking to them.

Because DJ always has money on his books I use his S-number whenever I need to make a call. The system will charge his account. I dial his S-number and the operator says it's not valid. I think I must have done it wrong so I try again. I keep trying. If there wasn't money, it would say not enough money and to call collect. I have never heard the not-a-valid-number message.

This is not possible. I run to my room and pick up one of his letters from the floor and look at the number on the envelope. I don't have the number wrong. I try to call again as panic sets in.

My mind starts to conjure all sorts of disaster scenarios. He's overdosed and in the morgue. He's been shanked and is in the morgue. He's been taken off to prison now even though we haven't even had a trial or been sentenced.

My hands are shaking. I don't know what to do. I have no money on my books to make a call. I call my mom collect. No answer.

I don't want to call my mother-in-law. I've tried to avoid her because I'm pretty sure she hates me and it's just too much to deal with. I pace nervously around G, not sure what to do after the mess is cleaned up. I keep trying to use his S-number. Maybe the jail found out I was using it for my calls and shut it down. Maybe that's what the not-valid number means. Maybe this is more punishment.

G block is excitedly listening to Leah's account of the ambulance ride and the real ice cream they gave her in the hospital. No drugs got through because they took her to the maternity ward rather than the ER.

"Braxton Hicks," she yells at me as I stand at the bank of phones. "You forgot to tell me about Braxton Hicks contractions."

I shrug. I'm just glad there are no drugs to tempt me.

I gather my courage and make a collect call to my mother-in-law.

I wait for it to connect, and I hear her accept the charges. There's a shuffling and cracking sound as if the phone has been dropped, and then I hear a man's voice: "Hello?"

"Hello?" DJ says again.

"Hello?" I whisper.

There is a long pause, and I feel as if G block just flipped sideways. I press my hand against the wall to steady myself.

"I got bailed out," he says.

"You mean your mom bailed you out . . ."

"Yeah." He's trying to keep the glee out of his voice, but I hear it.

He is sleeping in a soft bed and eating good food and taking hot showers. He's been getting high all the time while I fight to stay clean, and he is free. I want to scream. I want to cry. But I swallow it all and try not to choke as it goes down.

"Amazing," I say.

"Look, baby, I'm going to get you out of there, I promise. We'll be together soon."

"When did you get out?"

"A few days ago."

"Have you talked to Kaden?"

He doesn't answer right away, and then he's angry. "I'm not going to call that fucking house!"

"Have you not talked to him since we were arrested?" I am shocked. I never asked, but I assumed he was trying to call and talk to him as much as I was. "You didn't call him on his birthday?"

I can hear DJ inhale deeply, and I realize he's smoking. "Look, I have to go, we're about to go to lunch."

"Well, I don't want to keep you from lunching."

"It's not like that, I need to do what my mom says, you know how it is . . ."

"Okay. Can you at least put some money on my books so I can call

113

the boys?" I realize that he's been out for a few days and hasn't done this yet. I know what he's doing with any money he has.

"Of course, and I'm going to get you out. Who always takes care of you? I will sell everything we have."

I doubt we have anything left to sell, but I don't argue.

"Call me tonight," he says.

"Wait," I say before he hangs up. "You need to call CPS! You can do supervised visits. You can take the parenting class. You can start all the requirements. You need to right away or we'll lose Kaden!"

"Gotta go. I love you, homegirl."

I hang up and head back to my room. I imagine DJ free and me in prison for years. I vow never to call him again.

When I get back to my cell, Patricia has everything in order. She still has the coat, and it's laid across her bed like a comforter.

"Look what I found," she says, a huge smile on her face. She's holding a small radio.

"How the hell did you get that?"

"It was on the floor outside the cage. When we left, I scooped it up and hid it in my nice big jacket."

She adjusts the antenna, turns the dial, and gets a local pop station. And when Beyoncé's "Single Ladies" comes on, Patricia turns the volume all the way up and moves the radio to the doorway. Everyone stops cleaning up the mess and starts to sing.

I don't think about DJ anymore. I don't think about my boys. Just for tonight, G block is the only family I know. The only family I want to know.

I smile and shimmy until lights out.

~

That night Patricia is snoring, and I stare up at the darkness wide awake. I've never been able to lie to myself between 2 a.m. and 4 a.m.— those hours have always been when my conscience wakes me up with

the truth—since I first stole my aunt's jeans. I'm too exhausted to use any of my Tolle tricks, so I lie in the dark and let every worry and fear and regret and pain settle in.

I press play on my life and watch all my mistakes flicker past my mind's eye. I see my fake smiles and my posturing and my decades of pretending everything is okay when it isn't. I see all the lies I have told, all the untruths, all the omissions.

I see every bottle of Vicodin I have stolen. I see every credit card I have taken. I see everyone I have hurt—my boys, DJ, Bryan, Darcy, my mom, my neighbors, my friends. I see every ridiculous story I have told to hide my addiction.

I see all the moments, years really, where I could have easily asked for help but my ego, my denial, and my shame prevented me.

The thought that I was already in jail before I was in jail floats around in my mind, but it's both too ephemeral and too complicated for me to unpack.

I try to look at my life as if it's a story and trace the plot that has gotten me to this bleak place, but there are too many missing pieces. I want to blame some moment for my addiction, some trauma, some loss. But mostly I want to blame somebody. Someone has to be responsible for who I have become, so I put the people in a lineup and try to pick out the perpetrator.

My older sister was killed in a car accident.

My brother died of a heroin overdose.

My other brother had mental health issues and a gambling problem and often threatened suicide.

I never had a father.

I never had a mother who was present.

I never had a normal family.

My first husband cheated on me.

My second husband is an addict who just abandoned me in jail.

I don't know the language of grief or loss or emotions at all—it was never spoken in my home. I can't remember a single time in my life when someone asked me "How are you?" and I answered honestly.

I don't think I have ever known how I am, or who I am.

I have always felt like an actor playing the role of me. My whole life I had pretended to be a beautiful, happy, shiny person in the hopes that would somehow make me a beautiful, happy, shiny person. I fit in everywhere because people love beautiful, happy, shiny people. But the problem with me trying to fit in everywhere is that I have never actually felt like I belonged anywhere. Or with anyone.

I couldn't reach out for help before the police came knocking on my door because I was so desperately playing the suburban mom role I'd created. *This is how a real mom shows up to school board meetings. This is what a real mom makes for snacks. This is how a real mom should sacrifice herself for her children.*

I vowed to be the mom I never had, but she and I turned out to be just the same. Absent. Gone.

If my children need me tonight they can't call me.

I wonder if showing up as a fake version of yourself is just as bad as not showing up at all? I run this idea around in my mind, poking and prodding at it to see if it holds up. It doesn't. The truth is, I would have preferred any version of my mom to being alone. So I am actually worse than my mom.

I can study the people in my lineup and make them turn right and then left, but every time I try to point my finger at someone or something, I can't.

There is no one to blame but me.

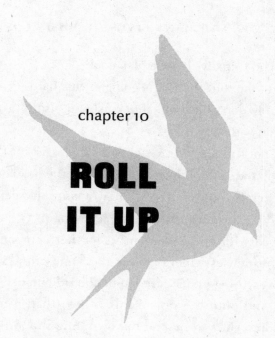

chapter 10

ROLL
IT UP

Our public defenders are trying to work out a plea deal. Elizabeth comes to see me, and she is not happy that DJ is out, but super happy that I am still in.

"You're safer in here," she says.

"Really? It doesn't seem all that safe."

"If you were to get out and commit a crime, do drugs and get caught, the plea deal doesn't happen. You will go to prison. I won't be able to do anything."

"Do you know how many drugs are in this jail? I haven't done any, and I could have. A lot."

She gives me a weak smile, but I want applause. I need some kind of validation. If I said that in a recovery meeting, I'd get a standing ovation. It's the one thing I miss about twelve-step programs. They applaud anything as long as you don't use. You can burn your house down in a fit of rage but as long as you don't pick up, you're a hero.

"Do you think we'll get a plea deal?"

"I'm trying, but the DA is going at this hard. Probation too. They really, really don't like you. Your husband also, but they seem overly focused on you."

"But not the actual DA, right? It's the assistant DA?"

"It's all the same. But it's the ADA and the head of Probation. They want prison. If you weren't a white woman, you'd get prison for sure."

I nod because it's true. Mimi, a Latina in G, just got sentenced to four years for embezzlement: using her company credit card for personal expenses—more or less the same crime that put me in G block. Everything in her case happened ridiculously fast. Arrest, sentencing, and onto the prison bus in less than a month. Mimi has two children she's raising on her own. She supports her parents and grandparents too. When she left, she said she'd see me in Chowchilla. She assured me that prison is much better than jail—easier. She had family members in prison, she said, so she knew what to expect. You get more visits, you get classes and workshops, you can work and stay busy.

"Does the DA look at all the cases?" I ask Elizabeth. "Like does he know about them?"

"Of course."

It's probably not helping my case that I once dated the current district attorney, and by dated I mean had a torrid affair with him while he was living with another woman. It was 1989, and I was in my last year of college and working as a manager at Player's Pizza—a sports bar and grill around the corner from the courthouse. He would come in after work, alone or with coworkers. He was tall and blond and while he introduced himself as Tom, I immediately renamed him Sven because he looked like a Nordic god. I flirted with him shamelessly, and he began to stay at Player's until closing time, waiting for me to get off work so we could spend time together. Sometimes he

would take me into the courthouse after hours and make love to me in all the offices, even once in what he called the gun room.

Gun rooms are sexy, and I don't even like guns.

He would spend hours at my small studio apartment, letting me read through his confidential case files and discussing strategy. He was a new assistant district attorney then, a decade older than me, and I was about to go off to graduate school. When I moved back to Santa Cruz after Dylan was born, we reconnected as friends, and I would sometimes visit him in his offices at the courthouse, where, knowing my writerly curiosity, he would tell me about cases he was working on and let me listen to 911 calls. He had never lost a trial, a fact he was very proud of. He was also bitter about his first marriage ending and shared how hard the divorce was and how upset he was about the claim she had made on his pension. When Tom ran for district attorney in 2002 on a family-values, law-and-order platform, I had to laugh. There were definitely no family values happening in the gun room, but that felt like a lifetime ago.

Our friendship petered out as life went on, and now was impossible given that he was technically prosecuting me. It couldn't help my case that his new wife was high up in the probation department. I didn't know if she was aware of my history with her husband, but when Elizabeth says that Probation is taking a hard line on my case, I have to consider it a possibility.

On one of our early court appearances, I saw him off to the side in a huddle with other attorneys, and I wondered if they were talking about me or one of the dozens of other cases before the court that day. I was too ashamed to meet his eye, and I imagine he wasn't eager to acknowledge me either.

"I'm going to keep at it," Elizabeth assures me. She puts a hand on her belly again. "How's your son?"

She used to be a CPS attorney before becoming a public defender.

"He's good. He just turned four. I talk to him when I can, but it's so hard . . . he doesn't understand why I'm not with him." I tear up.

"Hang in there," she says kindly.

~

When I get back the unit is in a tizzy. Rooms are getting switched, and when I ask Daddy what's going on, she says that they got word Princess was in booking.

"Who's Princess?"

Daddy looks at me like I'm crazy. At times like these my position in G feels tenuous. I don't know the players on the streets. I know there are girls everyone is afraid will come into G, and other girls they wish would come in. Apparently Princess is a big-time meth dealer—the original lady boss—competing in a man's world and making a killing.

Patricia and I are split up, and I move into a room with Kiki. It's the last room on the top tier. A corner room, so it's the biggest. Daddy is next door. Patricia moves to the bottom tier. I'm happy to move in with Kiki. She's smart and funny and tough and sweet. She's barely older than Dylan so I feel most like Mama Love around her.

I'm anxious that Princess's arrival will mean more drugs in G. It's almost rude of me not to do drugs that are offered, but I really don't want to. I'm working on my YA novel and mailing pages to Ty to type up. My mind seems full of creative ideas. I jot down notes for short story ideas. I long for a keyboard. In prison I would have access to a computer. It's the only upside of prison I can think of.

When Princess arrives, Vivian and Daddy rush her upstairs. She doesn't look like a drug dealer: She's tiny with long strawberry-blond hair, pale eyes, and freckles on her face and arms. I'm obligated to meet her, and when Daddy introduces me, she just flicks her eyes in my direction and ignores me. I leave their huddle in Daddy's room and lie down on my bunk. I don't want to see what she brought in.

That night Kiki gets permission from one of the guards—the one who brought in the McDonald's—to spend the night in Daddy's room. She asks for a sleepover, and he laughs and says okay. I can hear them through the wall all night long. It's a meth party for sure. And when the moaning starts, I recall Kiki telling me that when she does meth she just wants to watch porn and fuck.

My meditation is no match for the threesome next door, so I just stare into the darkness. I think about my boys asleep just a few miles away and wonder what they are dreaming about. I send them love and light and sweet dreams. I hum their favorite made-up lullaby: "Mommy loves you, yes she does, Mommy loves you just because . . ." Dylan, Cody, and Ty are too old for lullabies, but I sing it to them anyway. I imagine myself scratching Kaden's arm so he can fall asleep.

I hum all night long until the lights come on for breakfast.

Kiki doesn't eat breakfast. Neither does Daddy, Vivian, or Princess. They divide their meals among the other girls when the guards aren't looking. If a group of inmates stops eating, it's a sure sign there's meth in the unit.

The meth bender lasts for three days until the drugs run out. Nobody in the unit sleeps. It's a G-block rave, and the guards don't say a word. Everyone but me from the top tier is in a sleepover cell. Eleven girls crammed into two rooms. The guards even unlock the doors so the girls can go downstairs and get hot water from the hot pot for commissary cocoa. They must know there's meth, but there are no searches.

Kiki is back in my room, and she's exhausted. She looks like she's lost ten pounds in three days, but I don't comment. It's commissary night and because my mom had put twenty dollars on my books I receive a batch of chocolate and ramen and new sandals. It feels like Christmas, and the unit is busy comparing hauls and making trades like my kids do with Pokémon cards.

Suddenly, the intercom in our room crackles.

Kiki and I freeze.

"Love, roll it up!"

I look at Kiki and she looks at me. "What did he say?" I ask in disbelief.

"He told you to roll it up," she whispers.

I walk over and press the intercom button.

"Yeah." It's the same guard.

"What did you just say?"

"I said, 'roll it up.'"

"Why, what did I do?"

"You made bail; roll it up. You got five minutes."

Kiki and I look at each other in silence, and then she screams. She runs into the hallway and announces, "Mama Love's getting bailed out!"

Daddy and Vivian run out and congratulate me. I hand them my commissary food and give Kiki my new shoes. I grab all my legal papers and letters. It's not much, but I look around the cell frantically. I hand Eckhart Tolle to Kiki. "Read it," I say.

She laughs. "I hate to read!"

"Read it anyway," I say. "Trust me."

Kiki folds up my mattress, and Vivian grabs my blanket and sheet. We all head downstairs just as the guard comes in yelling my name. Daddy walks behind us. It's all happening so fast, and I call out my goodbyes.

Daddy grabs my arm. I think she's going to hug me, but she pulls me in close. "You know what to do when you come back."

I pull back and look at her blankly.

"You will know the date when you will be remanded. You will have time to prepare. Got it?"

I nod quickly. She's talking about drugs, but there's no time to

clarify what she's asking for specifically because the guard is walking out the door, and I'm running after him with everything in my arms.

I'm rushed through booking, where I turn in my reds and change into the clothes I was wearing when I was arrested. When I walk out of the jail, DJ is standing beside his mom's car waiting for me. He hugs me, and I hang on to him for a long time.

The night air is crisp, and there are stars in the sky.

"I told you I would get you out. Who takes care of you?"

"You do," I say. "You do." And in this moment, I believe it's true. I feel warm and safe in DJ's arms, and for a brief mindless moment I believe it will all be okay.

~

My mother-in-law is waiting in the car, and she barely speaks to me as we drive away. It's only when we start to drive over Highway 17 toward San Jose that I realize we aren't going to our home in Aptos.

"Where are we going?"

"We have to go sign some papers at the bail bond place, and then we're going to stay at the Saratoga house and my mom's going to the San Jose house," DJ explains. His mom owns two houses in Silicon Valley that she splits her time in. He's talking so quickly that I wouldn't be surprised if he's high.

"Not our house?" I ask.

"We can't go there, remember?" He looks back at me from the passenger seat. When I don't say anything he's suddenly angry. "When they set that fucking ridiculous bail, they also set fucking ridiculous conditions."

"What conditions?" I should know this, but I wasn't planning to be alive for long, so I hadn't paid attention in court. And I haven't wanted to read the legal papers because I didn't think there was anything in

them I could take issue with. After all, I was guilty of everything they'd charged me with.

"We aren't allowed in our fucking neighborhood, so we're not allowed back in our house. The house we own.

"I don't know how they can do that when we haven't been convicted," he rages on. "It's supposed to be innocent until proven guilty. We can't go to our home, they can search us at any time, no alcohol, no drugs . . ."

For the first time, I realize I'll never see our home again. I didn't appreciate it while I had it, and now that it's gone, I miss it desperately.

". . . no computers, no contact . . ."

I stare out the window as he rants. Even though I've been inside for only two and a half months, the world looks unreal to me. I think about what's happening in G right now and whether my boys know I'm out.

"Will we be able to see the kids?" I ask.

"Tomorrow we have to see our public defenders, then go to CPS and meet with the social worker. There's a lot to do tomorrow."

I haven't had an "a lot to do" day in a long time. I can't imagine myself in offices, talking to people, dealing with reality. One of the best things about being locked up was that the outside world was locked out. I scan myself for inner strength, but all I sense is a faint pulse. If I rolled down my window, I believe I could float out of the car like an errant balloon.

I feel untethered.

My mother-in-law drops us off in Saratoga and heads to her home seven miles away. "Thank you," I call after her as she drives off.

I walk around her house like I'm visiting the moon—it all feels so foreign and strange. It's a big, single-level ranch-style home with a giant pool out back surrounded by grapevines. We used to bring

Kaden here to swim; it was always sunny and bright—my favorite place to spend an afternoon. I open the fridge and gaze in awe at all the food. Eggs and butter and bread and fruit and vegetables. I open all the cabinets and find crackers and coffee and chips and almonds and pistachios. Four kinds of cereal. I sink into her leather couch and savor its softness. It has been so long since I've felt softness.

"I'm going to take a shower," I say. "Hot water . . ."

"Want company?" DJ gives me a little leer, and I smile.

"Let me do the first one alone."

I go into the bathroom and lock the door behind me. I reach out and open the medicine cabinet to see what's inside. There's nothing but deodorant and Band-Aids and eye drops. A bottle of Tylenol. Only after I close the cabinet do I realize what I've just done. What's still automatic for me.

I turn on the shower and there's a knock at the door.

"Yeah?"

"My mom grabbed some clothes from the house. I have no idea what she brought you. She just threw a bunch of stuff in a box. It's next to the bed."

"Okay, thanks."

I feel awkward with DJ. The few times we saw each other on the way to and from court felt furtive and dramatic and a little exciting. We were separated lovers. Husband and wife torn asunder. But now, here in this domestic setting, I feel just like I did before the arrest.

We were headed toward divorce. In the last year, while we were ripping and running, I had cheated on DJ with a man I met online who lived in Oregon. When I was loaded, I had gone to a website that married people visit when they want to cheat. I had seen the man only a few times, and they were thrilling. DJ had found out, but we never really dealt with it, and then we were arrested.

I look in the mirror before I get in the shower. I am still thin but

not as gaunt and gray as when I was arrested. My diet of bear claws and mystery meat has not given me the rosy glow of health. Everyone in jail is dehydrated—living on the equivalent of one glass of water a day. The water that comes out of the bathroom sink tastes like rust, and no one can stand drinking more than a few sips at a time. I bet there would be less fighting, less depression, less severe mental health issues in jail if there were clean water, fruits and vegetables, and food that wasn't so processed and rancid.

I turn around slowly on tiptoe, trying to see my whole body. I haven't had a real mirror in so long, just the murky fun-house mirrors in G. I have more muscle thanks to the fire camp workouts. But I also have the corpse-like pallor of someone who hasn't felt direct sunlight in months.

The shower is like going to church. I stand in the stream of hot water, awed by its majestic power, and wash away G block until the water runs cold. I want to cry, need to cry, but I feel so disembodied that the need isn't connecting to my tear ducts. In my mind I am sobbing and shaking because I'm so scared of whatever might happen next. But after stepping out of the shower I feel robotic.

In the bedroom, DJ has lit candles, and he holds out a soft robe for me. We make love, and it feels like nothing at all. I fake the pleasure to get it over with. Even with the full weight of him on top of me, I still feel alone and lost. After, I lay awake for hours among the soft pillows and blankets worrying about our attorney visits the next day, about what CPS will say. And I think of my boys asleep in their beds. I'm even farther from them now than I was in G. At least in G I could think about them possibly driving by the jail on their way to basketball games or their friends' houses. When I took a breath in the courtyard, I could imagine them breathing the same air nearby. Sometimes I would exhale and imagine my breath flying through the sky, across town, and under the crack of the door in the house where they slept.

I imagined that my breath washed over them, settling into their skin, their pores, burrowing deep until it joined the blood cells traveling through their bodies. I imagined that for a brief second they could feel my love as my breath pumped through their hearts.

~

In the morning, we take Carol's car to go to our appointments in Santa Cruz. As codefendants we have separate public defenders, mostly in case one of us wants to turn on the other at trial. DJ drops me off at my attorney's office and promises to pick me up when he's done. Elizabeth is grim and angry when I walk in.

"This is so dangerous," she tells me. "I'm working on a plea deal for you. I'd rather you were locked up and safe than out. We talked about this."

"I didn't know I was getting bailed out," I say. "It was a surprise."

"Well, that surprise could end up meaning prison time."

"I'm not going to do anything wrong," I say. "I promise. I'm over two months clean."

She ignores my words and my sobriety. "If you steal, if you do drugs, if you break any laws—you will go to prison. If you go to trial— you will go to prison. If you do what your husband does—you will go to prison. This plea deal is tenuous. People are really angry and they're going to be even angrier that you're out on bail."

"What people?"

"Your neighbors. Your ex-husband's wife. The DA is getting all kinds of calls from them. You really pissed people off. They are putting lots of pressure on him, and he's angry at you because they're angry at him."

"Wait, the DA or the assistant DA prosecuting us?"

"It's all the same, the ADA is the DA's office. The DA represents the people. The people are mad."

"I swear I won't do anything wrong." I don't know what else to say. She seems satisfied she's made her point and that I've heard her.

"We're working on a plea deal. You're looking at a year in jail, completion of drug court, and five years of probation plus restitution."

"How much is restitution?"

"Around nineteen thousand dollars."

"What? That's impossible."

"And you have to pay half up front in order to get the plea deal."

She shows me all the crimes I'm charged with. I read down the list—many of them I actually didn't do. I try to protest, point out that I never stole anything from a vehicle at Costco, and that I don't know these people listed here who say I stole from them.

"It doesn't matter, you can only argue each charge at trial. With a plea deal it's all or nothing. You'd have to plead guilty to thirty-two felonies. With a trial you could be in jail just waiting to go to trial for as long as the plea deal sentence. And if you're found guilty it will be a much longer sentence."

"So I either plead guilty to all of this—even the things I didn't do—or go to trial and most likely go to prison?"

"That's it," she says. "With drug court you can get your record expunged once you successfully complete it. That's a yearlong program after you get out."

It feels unfair that I must plead guilty to crimes I didn't commit, but I shove that feeling away. I don't have the luxury of fairness. I get it—every unsolved credit card crime, every property theft, needs to be solved, and someone needs to pay restitution. The DA gets to clear a bunch of crimes off his slate, the victims will get paid by me, and I avoid prison. I have no legal grounds to demand I pay only for what I've done. I also have no money and no idea how I'll pay. But I'll plead guilty to a hundred felonies if it means I can be with my boys sooner. If it means I can get Kaden back before the CPS clock runs out.

I feel nauseous. I push the list over to Elizabeth, but she hands it back to me. "This is your copy."

Elizabeth hands me the restitution list, and I see all the money various victims and nonvictims say I must pay them, based on pain and suffering and days of lost wages because they had to cancel a credit card. I am surprised to find any of these people on a restitution list. If a credit card company or bank wrote off the debt, shouldn't I pay back the company or the bank? If you report a card stolen, you don't have to pay the charge. I see on the list one of my neighbors claiming lost wages at $150 an hour. She works as an assistant in a medical office. That would be over a $300,000-a-year salary. There are a million different ways for people to steal, but not all stealing is considered a crime. Nobody was going to get prosecuted for stealing from me. I shake this thought away. Who am I to judge? I'm in no position to assess morality or integrity. I have no high ground to stand on.

"With the time you've already served, and time off for good behavior, we're talking six or seven more months in jail. You'll get moved to Blaine Street, and hopefully it won't be so bad."

I start doing the math in my head—trying to figure out if I will have time to complete everything CPS will require me to do. The one-year clock to get Kaden back started ticking almost three months ago. I obviously need to be out of jail. I need a job. A place to live. Drug testing. I need to take a parenting class. I need to go to counseling. I need to have supervised visits and prove to CPS that I can and will keep my son safe.

I'm not even sure I know how to keep myself safe, but for the first time in a long time, I feel hope. I don't care how much I have to pay or who I have to pay it to. A year from now I could be back with all my children. This could be behind me. I could be free.

"Do you really think I can do the plea deal? What about DJ?"

"He will have the same deal. Restitution will be joint and several,

meaning you are both equally obligated to pay it back. And you both have to accept the plea."

"I don't know how we would pay nine or ten thousand up front."

"You'll have to find a way."

"I guess I could put it on a credit card . . ."

"Not funny!" she snaps.

"And you have to go see Probation while you're out. They do an assessment and will make a recommendation to the court on sentencing. Call and make an appointment right away."

"Okay, but if there's a plea deal . . . ?"

"They still make a sentencing recommendation. Anything can happen. The judge could reject the plea deal. It doesn't happen often, but it can."

I say my goodbyes and stand out on the street waiting for DJ. It's all a lot to take in, and I'm not sure I understand all my obligations. DJ finally arrives about half an hour later.

"Where were you?"

"Maya was quick, so I went and met up with some homeboys who I was in with."

Maya is his attorney. "Did she tell you about the plea deal?"

"Yeah, it's all some fucking bullshit with the charges and that restitution."

"But we're going to take it, right?"

"I want to go to trial."

"We can't, we can't go to trial. Kaden. Think about Kaden!" I am instantly angry and slightly hysterical. "You have to agree, you have to take this. We both do. You don't want to go to prison. Are you crazy?"

"Relax, we're going to take it, it's okay. It's just some bullshit, though." In a way I envy DJ's anger. His lack of shame. "Did you see that charge from . . ."

"Stop!" I say. "I don't want to talk about any of it. I can't handle

it. Do you understand? That was so hard to get through, and I have nothing left in me today."

"Okay, but now we have to go to CPS."

"I know. Let's just go and get it over with."

~

The harried social worker seems surprised to see us even though we have an appointment. She shuffles through large stacks of files to find Kaden's.

"What about seeing Kaden?" I ask. "Can we see him?"

"I'll have to talk to the Parents Center—they are who we contract with to supervise the visits. They will coordinate with the foster parents and you. We just didn't know you would be out to do this."

I realize there are no visitation plans in place because she didn't think we'd ever be out. "I'll call you when I know more," she says.

DJ and I drive away, and all the hope I felt earlier is gone. I'm hungry and tired and overwhelmed.

"Let's just go home," I say. Part of me craves the simplicity and isolation of jail.

"I just have to make a quick stop," says DJ.

I lean the passenger seat way back and close my eyes. When I open them, I see DJ has pulled into a hospital parking lot. It's the hospital where I gave birth to Cody.

"Wait here," he says. "I'll be right back."

"What are you doing?"

"I just have to pick something up," he says, jumping out of the car. It's almost 5 p.m. and getting dark. I sit in the parking lot for over an hour. We don't have cell phones or I would call him. A security guard taps on the window to ask me what I'm doing, and I explain that I'm waiting for my husband.

"Is he a patient?" he asks.

"He's visiting someone," I say, the lie rolling off my tongue with ease. I suddenly feel guilty and afraid. It helps that I'm sitting in my mother-in-law's Mercedes. I am still skinny from my pre-jail diet of Vicodin and chocolate, but I'm dressed nicely for our appointments so I don't overly concern the guard. And I haven't done anything wrong.

DJ finally shows up, breathless and hurrying. He doesn't explain his absence, and I don't ask. My anxiety is building, and I recall my attorney's warnings.

When we get over the mountain and away from Santa Cruz, he passes the exit to Saratoga. I still don't say a word.

He pulls into an IHOP in a strip mall in San Jose and parks on the outskirts of the lot away from the other cars. He reaches under his seat and pulls out a velvet bag. In it there's a small metal tin, a lighter, a rubber band, and a clump of black tar heroin about the size of a silver dollar.

"I told you I met with some guys from jail while you were in your meeting," he says. "And then I grabbed this from the hospital." He reaches into his pocket and pulls out a long, skinny object sealed in paper and plastic. In the dome light I can read the words BIOPSY NEEDLE and STERILE.

"It's huge," he says, "but it's all I could find."

I have been driving in a car with drugs in it. I was in the getaway car while he stole from the hospital. I have already violated the terms of my bail agreement.

"You're going to love this," he says as he pushes up the sleeve of my sweater. I am mute as he melts the heroin into liquid and draws it into the needle. Yes, this is something I swore I would never do. But I don't have the strength to resist. He ties the band around my arm. I watch as if from a distance as he sticks the needle in my vein. It stings and tugs and burns, and then he pulls back a little on the plunger. I see my own blood folded into the brown liquid, and then before I can

even take a breath, he presses the plunger aggressively and empties the needle into my vein.

For a moment I feel nothing, and then warmth spreads through me. Excitement. Joy. Energy. Every good feeling flows through me. The shower wasn't church, this is church.

All the day's pain washes away. A part of me marvels at this new, more efficient way of getting high. No inhaling smoke through a straw for hours. No swallowing twenty pills. I've always loved efficiency.

I don't think about the fact that it's also a more efficient way of killing myself or that this is what killed my own brother.

My attorney's words of warning are forgotten. My brief, fragile sobriety is gone. As the heroin swallows me like a pill, I close my eyes and pretend this is good.

I pretend this is love.

THE
NEIGHBOR
FROM HELL

The heroin makes it easy to cope with what's to come, and I quickly learn how to shoot up all by myself. DJ's mom wants us to be where she can keep an eye on us, so we move into the spare bedroom in her San Jose house where she now lives full time. We lock the door and sit on the floor and start our day with the ritual of injecting heroin. Breaking off a chunk of the black rock and holding a lighter underneath a tiny, silver-dollar-size metal pot DJ has acquired from some DIY crafts store so that it liquefies. I have no idea how much heroin is enough, or how much is too much. DJ seems to be an expert, so he measures it out and draws it into the syringe. He has gone to a needle exchange place, so the giant biopsy needle has been replaced by dozens of tiny needles like the ones diabetics use.

"It's great," he says. "You bring back the used, and they give you new ones."

Once in a while I try to talk to him about the risk we are taking—

how we are violating the terms of bail and putting our plea bargain in jeopardy—but he shuts me down. He assures me that because we live outside the county we won't be surprise searched. The more times I shoot heroin, the less I worry. I am living in the moment. It's a bastardized version of the present I learned about in *The Power of Now*.

DJ and I soon realize that it's impossible to subsidize a heroin habit without getting a job or committing a crime. A job is out of the question since we're due to be sentenced in a month. Plus, getting high is once again our full-time work. So we have to brainstorm. One morning DJ disappears into the master bedroom closet. When he comes out, he is holding three suit jackets, all with the tags on them.

"You won't believe what's in there," he says. "Tons of new clothes. All from Nordstrom."

I don't understand what he's so excited about. The jackets are obviously his stepdad Freddy's, who is currently living in Iran.

"Nordstrom has the most amazing return policy," says DJ. I shrug like he's maybe lost his mind, but I want to be polite about it.

"The tags are still on. We can return these. For cash."

I see where he is going with this, but I also see a problem. "We don't have the receipts," I say. "We can't return something without a receipt."

"You can at Nordstrom," says DJ. "Let's go!"

When we get to the store I refuse to go inside. I don't even like returning things that I have legitimately bought, so I'm certainly not going to return something I didn't buy. They will see my guilt a mile away.

I sit in the car and watch all the shoppers passing by. Are any of them doing nefarious deeds—or am I the shadiest person in this lot? After half an hour, I start to get anxious. What if DJ has been arrested? The minute I think this, the drugs wear off. I am me again, and I am wondering what the fuck I'm doing here. I vow that if DJ comes out,

we will get clean. We will not do anything shady. We will focus on what's important—getting Kaden back. I start to pray.

When he finally emerges, he's not carrying the clothes and he's not in handcuffs. I exhale and try to read his face to see what emotion he is conveying.

He looks pissed.

I don't say a word as he gets behind the wheel. It's only when we are pulling out of the parking lot that he turns to me. "A little over three hundred," he says before I can even ask. He says this so proudly, like a stockbroker with a bullish pick that has paid off. "There was such a long line at returns; we need to go to a different Nordstrom next time. And they gave me a hassle without the receipts. Asking how I had paid for the suits so they could refund the correct payment method. I got it done, though."

And just like that I forget my parking-lot vow to get clean.

The next time DJ goes into the closet he comes out with a giant bag of receipts. "I think Freddy has every receipt for all those clothes."

"It looks like he has every receipt he's ever gotten."

We empty the bag onto the dining room table and start pulling out the Nordstrom ones, and then we try to match the receipt numbers to the clothes in the closet that still have tags on them. It's time-consuming, so I ask DJ why we are doing this if the return policy is so great. "Insurance," he says.

With our habit fully funded, we can focus on getting shit done. We meet with our separate probation officers for our reviews and find out they are recommending four years in prison. I'm glad the twenty-seven years is no longer on the table, but four years means we will lose Kaden. The plea deal must go through.

CPS wasn't prepared for us to be out on bail, and because we are temporarily living in a different county, they are stymied about how to handle this new development. I call the social worker every day to

see if I can have a supervised visit with Kaden, go to court-ordered therapy, take some positive-discipline classes, anything that will move me closer to meeting their requirements for reunifying with him by the one-year deadline. But nothing moves quickly in the system, and CPS is waiting to see if I'm sentenced to prison before they start me with services to reunify.

I haven't seen my older boys once since I've been out. Every time I try to arrange something with Bryan and Darcy, they are magically busy. I'm desperate to see my boys, see how they are, see if they are angry or sad. I talk to them on the phone, but I need to hold them. I need to look in their eyes and be sure they are doing as okay as they say. I need to look in their eyes and see if they still love me.

It's a tightrope to walk because while CPS has barred me from seeing Kaden without CPS arranging and controlling the visit, Dylan, Cody, and Ty aren't under the control of CPS. But they are under the control of Bryan and Darcy. I can't just show up at their house because that's also where Kaden lives. I don't feel like I'm in any place to demand my right to see them. I'm not even sure what my rights are while I'm out on bail. All I know is I don't want to make Bryan and Darcy angry.

DJ's ex is fine with him seeing Hailey and Logan while he's out, but I skip those visits. I don't have the energy to be a stepmom to them when I can't be a mom to my own. It's not kind, but it's true. Plus, I feel safer in San Jose than in Santa Cruz. I'm too afraid I will run into a neighbor or a friend from recovery or a parent I know from school or the deputies who arrested me. I feel exposed in Santa Cruz. Vulnerable. In San Jose, I'm anonymous.

Cody is on the high school varsity basketball team, and when I find out last minute that they have a game in San Jose near where we're staying I decide to go to the gym. I can't wait to see him, even from a distance. I want to cheer him on.

It's a workaround that doesn't require talking to and scheduling with Bryan and Darcy, and DJ agrees to go with me. When we arrive it's halftime, and the minute I step through the doors I look across the court and my breath catches. Kaden is dribbling a toddler-sized basketball. Our eyes lock, and he drops the ball and sprints over to me. I scoop him up and smother him with kisses and hugs. Bryan walks over.

"Hey," I say.

"Hey."

"I had no idea you would be here, he would be here. I don't know what the rules are with CPS when I run into him in a public place. I'm sorry, I had no idea. I'm not trying to do something . . ."

"I'm not worried about it," says Bryan.

"I can just leave," I say, but Kaden is already holding on to my leg.

"It's fine."

Kaden sits on my lap for the second half of the game, and I kiss his cheeks and the back of his head every few seconds. He is warm and soft, and I close my eyes and inhale his scent over and over. He looks small to me, as if he hasn't grown a bit since I was arrested. I bring him back to Bryan when the game ends.

"Thank you," I say.

Bryan just laughs—it's not a real laugh, just the way he laughs when things are awkward. I give Cody a big hug.

"Can I take the older boys to lunch in a couple of weeks?" I ask Bryan. "Please?"

He is quiet. DJ is on the other side of the gym. He doesn't want to talk to Bryan, and I'm annoyed that he can't be gracious toward my ex. Thankful, even. If it weren't for Bryan, Kaden would be with strangers.

"I guess so. Let me talk to Darcy."

"You're their dad. It's not really up to her," I say quietly.

I want him to grow a spine, but I get it. He just shrugs and picks

Kaden up. "Let's go, buddy." I blow kisses to Kaden over Bryan's shoulder all the way across the gym and until he's out the door. Cody lets me hug him again even though he's sixteen, and his teammates are watching, and I'm his mom who's out on bail. "I love you," I whisper in his ear. "And I'm so, so, sorry."

"It's okay, Mom," says Cody. "I love you too. Just get better, please."

We are halfway home and I'm in bliss, not because of any heroin, but because I got to hold Kaden, see Cody. When my cell phone rings, I answer it without looking at the number.

"What the fuck do you think you're doing? You are going back to jail!" I recognize Darcy's voice immediately. She's screaming. "You aren't allowed to see Kaden; you just violated the CPS order. I'm calling them in the morning."

I panic and try to explain that it was an accident and that I had no way of knowing he would be there. "Bryan said it was okay," I say. "I offered to leave when we came in, but he said it was okay."

She hangs up on me.

"Oh my God," I say to DJ. "What do we do?" I start to hyperventilate.

"It's fine," he says.

"It's not fine. It's not going to be fine." I'm so scared I can barely breathe. Following all CPS rules is a condition of bail. If we violate bail, the judge won't accept the plea.

"Call the social worker."

I call the social worker and leave her a long, rambling message about what happened. It gets cut off, so I call back and start all over again.

I am awake all night watching the clock. I call again at 8 a.m. and beg the social worker to call me. All morning I sit and stare at my phone. Finally, at 1 p.m. the social worker calls. She seems unconcerned. "It happens," she says. "It's okay." She doesn't tell me if Darcy called her or

what was said. "We're trying to arrange a supervised visit for you while you're out, but it's been . . . umm . . . difficult."

I think I know the name of the difficulty—the one screaming at me on the phone last night.

When we hang up, I lie on the bed, relieved. *This all has to stop*, I think. We need to stop using. I say it and I mean it, but the truth is, I can't stop. I won't stop. And I have no idea why.

My attorney was right, I was safer in G. I'm not ready to be out in the world. I'm not recovered, not even close. I'm worse than I ever was. I can't stop hurting myself even when I know it's hurting my boys.

I don't know how to cope with the normal everyday world of minor problems without drugs, so I certainly have no way to cope with life when my freedom is at risk. When my children are at risk.

I fall asleep to these thoughts and wake up an hour later in so much pain I can't breathe. My left arm is swollen from elbow to fingertips. It looks like a giant balloon animal. If balloon animals were covered in track marks. I have no idea what it is.

DJ is sitting on the floor preparing his medicine.

"DJ," I whisper.

"Yeah?" He looks up.

"Can you take me to the hospital?"

~

In the emergency room the triage nurse takes my vitals and looks at my arm, which is now twice as big as it was when I woke up. It's so swollen I can't bend my fingers. I have to hold the entire arm up with my right hand. I'm like the girl in *Willy Wonka* who blew up into a blueberry.

"Why did you do this to yourself?" she asks.

"I don't know," I say.

I wish I knew. I wish I could say I did this because this one thing happened to me this one time. It would be so much easier for

everyone. I wish I could trace it to being born prematurely, or early-childhood attachment issues, or being abandoned, starved, abused. I wish I could say it's because every time in my life I've wanted to say no to someone I never have. I wish I could say it's because of karma. A past life where I agreed to be an addict in this life. I would blame it on my brain chemistry if I could, or a mental health diagnosis if I had one. It would be so much easier if every addict knew why they were destroying themselves. When I'm on drugs, I feel happy, I feel like I belong in the world, I feel joy no matter what else is happening around me. Drugs give me what I'm looking for, what I need and crave.

The truth is simple: Getting high feels better than not getting high. And until that changes, no addict will change.

~

I am admitted to the hospital and immediately placed on IV antibiotics. The heroin has caused a massive infection in my arm, and most likely it's been building for weeks. I just hadn't noticed. The doctors are worried about sepsis. When my fever spikes dangerously high I make DJ promise nobody will know I'm here. "They can't," I say. "Not Bryan and Darcy. Not the boys. Nobody!"

The doctors are pumping morphine into my system for the pain in my arm, which prevents me from detoxing. A week after I've been admitted DJ comes to see me.

"My mom and I went to the Aptos house and packed everything up. I got permission from the judge."

"Did you see any neighbors?" I ask.

"No. And I wouldn't care if I did."

I don't understand DJ's anger. It's like he doesn't feel bad for what we did. I would be mortified if I saw anyone and I'm grateful I didn't have to pack up our home.

"They're foreclosing on the house," DJ tells me.

I close my eyes. A part of me thought maybe I would still have a home for my boys when this was all over. I just want to make them breakfast and dinner. I want to be annoyed that I have to pick up after them. I want to sit on the edge of their beds and hear about their friends and their schoolwork. But it's gone. All of it.

When I open my eyes, DJ is fiddling with my IV.

"What are you doing?"

"I brought you a present." He pulls out a needle with brown liquid in it. "Watch this." He quickly inserts the needle into my IV port, and the heroin flows through the tube and into my arm. A warm rush floods my system and I close my eyes.

I surrender.

This is who I am.

This is what I do.

~

There's an angry mob of about twenty people outside the courtroom doors. The mob is composed of my neighbors, and Darcy almost seems to be its leader, with Bryan by her side.

Who is watching Kaden if they're both here watching me?

DJ and I spent the night in a motel near the courtroom. We are to officially plead guilty to thirty-two felonies, and per the plea deal will each get one year in jail and a year in drug court. The judge still has to approve the plea and sentence, though. And after the court appearance, we'll go directly back to jail.

We were up all night using and preparing to go back inside. When we get to the courthouse our attorneys meet us outside the courtroom and escort us away from the mob.

"We have a problem," says my new attorney, Jonathan. He's Elizabeth's husband, and he's taken over my case while she's out with the baby.

"Someone told the DA who told the judge that you were bragging about your light sentence. Someone told all your neighbors the same thing."

I am shocked. I never bragged about anything, and I haven't talked to anyone about the plea deal.

"We're going in to speak to the judge now, but I need to know what you said and who you said it to."

"I . . . I've . . . never bragged or talked to anyone."

"You must have. Someone knows the details of the plea."

I suddenly recall the sushi lunch with my older boys. Bryan had agreed, and we had gone to one of their favorite restaurants. I had told them it was good news, that with good behavior, in six months I would be out of jail and we could get back to our lives. I wasn't bragging, I was reassuring my children their mom would be okay. I told them I could get my record expunged. I was trying to cheer them up. They must have told someone, who told someone, and like a twisted game of telephone, someone went to the prosecutor and the neighbors with a distorted version.

"Someone told the neighbors and the DA you were laughing at them all."

I don't want to think it was Darcy in a last-ditch attempt to put me in prison. I'd much rather believe it was an angry neighbor; and given the sentiment of many of my neighbors it could well have been. Still, nothing gets the ex-wife out of the picture more completely than a long prison sentence. The extreme public humiliation is just a bonus. I shake the thoughts away, because ultimately it doesn't matter who it was. It's happened.

It's happening.

I risk a glance at the crowd. Darcy is staring at me, her hair perfectly coiffed, her makeup done just so, and her thin lips sneering. She is the Queen of Hearts yelling "Off with her head!" Her vitriol

feels palpable. Maybe I am reading her wrong, maybe I am projecting, but it all feels surreal and I just want to be anywhere but here.

Jonathan clears his throat. "The ADA and I are going to talk to the judge in his chambers. Sit here until the bailiff calls everyone in. I'll see you in the courtroom."

We sit on a bench and wait for the bailiff to call us in. I can't look at my neighbors—people I used to think of as friends. People whose houses my boys still play at.

I care about these people. I care about their children.

Their anger is hard to face. In the entire crowd of my neighbors, I stole from only two of them. It was wrong. I violated them, I know this. I am the perpetrator and they are the victims. They trusted me and I betrayed their trust.

I want to run up to each one and say I'm sorry. I want to hug them and tell them it wasn't personal, that it wasn't the real me, but I can only sit here with my head down.

I think about the dollar amount I stole from my neighbors—it amounts to a little over five hundred dollars for one family and I used another neighbor's social security number to get an Amazon credit card so I could buy a Kindle and a few parenting books. All together it's less than a thousand dollars that I have stolen from this mob of neighbors.

We had to pay back nine thousand to get the plea deal.

I know that what I stole amounts to more than just dollars—I know that I betrayed all of their trust, their sense of safety in their own homes, and because I have hurt some, I have hurt all. I betrayed this community of cul-de-sac parents not only because I was their friend but also because addicts and criminals aren't supposed to host playdates and work on fundraisers and they aren't supposed to look like me. Addicts aren't supposed to look like them.

Criminals are never supposed to live next door.

~

When we go into court, I see someone with a camera off to the side. Every time he aims it at me, I turn away. I try to hold my hands over my face as much as possible and thwart his shot. I can't cover my face while the judge addresses me, but otherwise I think I've avoided him getting a clear view. DJ sits next to me, and in the middle of the sentencing he falls asleep because he's high. I poke him in the ribs to wake him.

One person speaks on our behalf, the director of a local rehab program who knows us and the judge. She stands up and says this is a health problem, a drug problem, not a criminal problem. The jail is overcrowded with people whose crimes are a symptom of their addiction. We are good people, she implores the judge, and the judge acknowledges that many people from the recovery world, people I helped in my six years of sobriety, have written to him on my behalf.

DJ and I don't speak. Jonathan expresses my remorse for me. DJ's lawyer doesn't say a word. When the judge approves the plea, I glance over at Darcy. She is frowning. Everyone against me is sitting together with Bryan and Darcy on the opposite side of the courtroom. She and my ex don't even live in Aptos, so I don't know how they have become so close with our former neighbors. It's like a sad wedding where no one is sitting on my side during the ceremony, and the other side is all waiting for their moment to object.

Our time out on bail has almost killed me, and I'm relieved that it's over. Two weeks in the hospital has left me weak. Two months of injecting heroin has been two months too many. I just want to get to Blaine Street. CPS has agreed to bring Kaden once a week to see me there. He can sit in my lap, and I can kiss his chubby cheeks. My boys can visit me on the weekends if Bryan brings them. They couldn't

come to the main jail where visitors are separated by plexiglass and have to speak through telephones. In Blaine Street we can visit in person, we can talk.

I am wearing a long skirt and a light blue sweater. When I hold my arms out to the bailiff to handcuff me, I see that blood has seeped through the arms of my sweater. He sees it too.

What he doesn't see is the tobacco, Vicodin, heroin, and two needles packed into an overstuffed condom and hidden inside me. It was uncomfortable sitting in the courtroom with a vagina full of contraband, and it's even harder to walk behind the bailiff. I can feel the package slipping.

The van takes us to the main jail, and DJ and I sit in the reception area. We have to get new mugshots taken for our ID cards. A man in his early twenties is sitting in one of the plastic seats behind us.

"What are you two doing here?"

"Going to jail," I say.

"Together? That's so cute."

I turn to see if he's serious, and he is. It's not cute, and I'm exhausted and just want to get to my bunk and lie down. I know I'm going to detox all over again in G, but hopefully it won't be worse than the first time, which was bad but not so bad that a few hot water bottles didn't make me feel better. I know the girls in G will take care of me. Especially when they find out what I'm bringing them.

I can't go to Blaine Street until the classification officer sends me. Hopefully it will happen within the week. Now that I'm sentenced, I can count down the days until I'm out. Now that I'm sentenced, I can make a plan with CPS for reunification. Now that I'm sentenced, I can separate from DJ. I know I'm about to be locked up again for three times as long as before, but in many ways it feels like freedom. I don't have to worry about anything on the outside besides my boys.

DJ leaves first, and then a female guard I don't recognize takes me into the big room where we spent the night in the cage. I know there is a lawsuit pending about strip searches in the jail, it's been all over the local news, so I've been pretty confident I won't have one. But now that I'm here and about to change into my reds, it hits me how stupid it is to be carrying drugs in. If I get caught it's another charge, and I definitely won't get to Blaine Street.

The guard has me walk through a metal detector, which is new. When I do it goes off: a loud shriek and a flashing red light. I hold out my hands, and then I show her I have no pockets. She pats me down and has me walk through again.

Everything lights up and I begin to sweat.

Fuck.

I walk through for a third time and when it goes off I grasp at anything to explain it to her other than the needles in my vagina. "I'm wearing an underwire bra," I say. "Look." I lean forward so she can look down the V of my sweater.

She is quiet for a moment and then shrugs and says okay. She takes off my handcuffs so I can change, and I surreptitiously shove the package back up inside me while putting on the jail-issued granny panties. She gives me my bedding, and this time I know to ask for my hygiene and a cup.

When I step into G, there is a moment of silence before everyone starts yelling, "Mama Love! Mama Love!" Kiki and Vivian and Nina run up to hug me. Daddy is on the top tier next to a woman I don't recognize who is giving me the once-over and looking skeptical. Kiki pulls me up the stairs and into the room at the top I used to share with Patricia.

"This is our room," she says.

Daddy and Vivian pile in after her while Nina stands watch outside

the door. I am happy to see them all, but I just want to sleep. A long day in court has taken its toll, and I can feel myself starting to detox. I'm not ready for that. I'm hoping to use what I brought in to medically detox myself—taper my dose a little bit each day.

I pull out the condom and empty the contents on Kiki's bed. While they look at the gifts I've brought, I flush the condom down the toilet. The guards go through our trash.

"I brought two needles," I say. "One is mine. You guys can share the other one or not, but I don't share mine."

I break off some heroin and give each of them a piece. "We'll share the tobacco," I say. "The pills are mine to help with detox."

Nina opens the door, startling us. "Don't forget about me," she says, quickly scanning Kiki's bed and our hands to see what we have.

"Never," I say, and I break off a piece of my heroin for her.

When everyone leaves, Kiki and I quickly catch up. "Did you get the deluxe chocolate package I sent to you from commissary?" I ask.

"Was that you? I had no idea. It was massive. Thanks so much!"

"Of course," I say. I couldn't use my real name when I ordered the commissary, because I had used a fake credit card number to purchase the pack. Kiki had helped me, and I wanted to help her. Plus, she loved chocolate. "How are things in here?" I ask.

She settles in to give me all the gossip from the two months I've been gone. "Things aren't the same in here since you left," she says. "There have been some bad fights. There's this one chick locked in solitary in Nina's old room below us. She's a fighter, but they don't have room anywhere else for her. Did you see all the sleds?"

"What are sleds?"

"The plastic things all over the freeway that look like snow sleds?"

I hadn't noticed anything when I walked in. "The jail is at, like, double capacity. They are going to put sleds in all our rooms too. It's

such bullshit. They aren't allowed to have so many people in here, but nobody cares."

I look around the room and try to imagine another body living in here—it seems impossible. "I'm getting to Blaine Street as fast as I can," I say. "They're going to let Kaden visit me there. I got a year sentence but with what I've already done and good time I can be out in September."

Kiki squeals and jumps up to hug me. "We need to make you a calendar," she says. "I have paper and pencils. What's your out date?"

We rummage through my court paperwork until we find my out date. "After dinner we'll get a little buzz on and then make your calendar. This is the best day ever."

I smile. "I just need to take a little nap though, okay?"

"Okay Mama Love, whatever you need!"

Kiki bounces out of the room, and I know the giddiness she is feeling. It's the high before the high. Her dopamine is firing just thinking about the little piece of dope hidden in her bra. I get under the covers and curl up on my side. I push the images of the day in court—Darcy, my neighbors, the reporter—out of my head, and I sleep like I have just run a marathon.

When I wake up the next morning, I see that Kiki has made me a calendar and taped it on the wall beside my bed. Yesterday is crossed off. It feels like progress. Like hope.

When breakfast comes, there's a guard I haven't seen before. He's about my age with short brown hair with a little gray at the temples and a big smile. He's someone I would talk to if I ran into him at a bookstore or a bar—he's tall and cute and I've always been a sucker for gray temples. He hands me my tray and I give him a big smile. "Good morning," I say. "Thank you."

"Wait," he says as I start to turn away. "I have something else for you."

When I turn back around, he's holding today's paper. "You're famous. Or infamous. Should I call you 'The Neighbor from Hell'?"

"What?"

"You can have this one." He hands me the *Santa Cruz Sentinel* and on the front page, in full color, is my face looking up plaintively. The reporter got the shot. My picture takes up the full half above the fold, the article is below.

I see the headline and my stomach drops.

APTOS "NEIGHBORS FROM HELL" SENTENCED IN MASSIVE ID THEFT CASE.

The guard laughs and picks up the next tray. I bring the paper over to the table and sit my tray on it so I don't have to look at my picture. I think about my boys going to school today and seeing this. I think about everyone who has ever known me seeing this. I used to coach Little League, I was on the school board, I was a real estate agent way back when I first left Bryan—everyone I ever did business with is seeing this. I think about the parents of all my boys' friends, their teachers, their coaches—all reading this headline.

Massive ID Theft Case.

Daddy sits next to me with her tray. "Why did he give you a paper?" she asks.

"Because I'm on the front page."

"No way. Give it to me."

"No," I say, but Daddy has already pulled it out from under my tray, and she's hollering, "Mama Love is in the papers!"

"Stop, please . . ."

Daddy starts reading the article out loud. I don't want to know what it says. Everyone gathers around as she reads it. G block thinks this is funny, but I can't listen. I put my hands over my ears and run up the stairs to my room. I can't breathe. My ears are ringing. This isn't

funny, it's a disaster. It's my disaster. I will never be able to show my face again in Santa Cruz. When I get out of here, I will have to move.

Daddy and Kiki come into the room with the paper. "Hey, sorry," says Daddy.

"It's okay," I say. "I get it."

"It's a great picture," says Kiki. "Your skin looks so good."

They're trying to be kind, and kindness is precious in jail. I offer them a weak smile.

"You want your tray? Nina is guarding it."

"No, I'm not hungry."

Daddy has the paper in her hand. "Here," she says.

"I don't want it. Can you rip it up and throw it away?"

Daddy nods.

"At least we can have coffee and a cigarette. Should we post up on the steps outside?" Kiki seems antsy and I know it's because of the stuff I brought. I throw her the tobacco and papers. "You go ahead."

After she leaves, I look at Daddy. "So how bad is it . . . the article?"

"It's not great."

"That's what I figured."

~ /

I stay high for the next few days and try not to think about the article. When my heroin is finally gone, I go to bed early but wake up a few hours later, shortly after lights out. I am feverish and sick. It feels too quick, but there's no mistaking this for what it is—I'm detoxing, and it's coming in hot.

I run to the metal toilet and vomit. "Sorry," I say to Kiki when she wakes up. "Sor . . ." I can't get any more words out, and the vomiting goes on for hours—long after there is nothing left to get out. I hang on to the toilet's cold rim and shiver and shake while Kiki softly snores. In the early morning everything comes out the other end, and I beg

Kiki to give me privacy. It's only 4 a.m., but I can't be so sick sitting on a toilet with someone in the same small room.

"The doors are still locked, where can I go?" Kiki asks grumpily.

"I know . . ." I cry. "I'm sorry."

When the locks pop at breakfast, Kiki runs out of the room. I have never felt so ill. Liquid is pouring out of my nose and eyes. I have never detoxed like this. I know there is Vicodin under my pillow but it won't help me now. I can't even swallow water. Kiki checks on me at lunch. I am lying with my cheek against the cold cement at the base of the toilet. I can't get up, but I tell her I'm fine. One minute I am freezing cold and the next I am burning hot. This is death, I think, this is the death I deserve.

At dinner, Kiki comes back in. I try to tell her again that I am fine, but my mouth can't form words. I vaguely hear her yelling and I think she is pushing the button, but I am watching from far away, and she is just a tiny, blurry speck on a vast horizon in this small cell. I don't register the two guards pulling me off the floor and half carrying me down the stairs and out of G.

~

I come to in the medical unit, and the nurse is pissed. The classification guard is standing over the bed as well. "You must have brought something in with you to be so sick now," he says. I think of the drugs under my pillow, and I hope Kiki hid them. They will search the room. I am so, so stupid. I risked my whole family yet again for what—to belong in G? To be a big deal there?

"I just have a slow metabolism," I whisper.

He shakes his head in disgust.

"You need fluids," says the nurse. She hands me some Pedialyte. "And there's an abscess in your arm. It's infected. You're going to get antibiotics three times a day until it clears."

I have nothing to say in my defense so I sleep.

When I get back to G days later, the worst of my detox is over. Kiki is waiting in our room and seems nervous when she sees me.

"I've never seen anyone so pale before," she says. "I thought you were dead."

"I was," I say.

"I kept pushing the button and screaming until they came. It fucking took forever, the motherfuckers."

"Thanks," I say. I look over at my pillow. "Did you hide the stuff?"

Kiki looks down and away. "Yeah."

"What's wrong?"

"Well, I didn't think you were coming back . . ."

I realize she must have taken the rest of what I brought in and used it or traded it. In the normal world of jail this would be cause for someone to get rolled up and probably a beatdown.

"I don't care," I say. "I'm done."

Kiki is relieved and instantly solicitous. "Let me make you some hot water bottles. Oh, and mail came last night for you. It's under the blanket."

I pull out a large manila envelope and get under the blanket. I don't recognize the name or PO box for the return address. It says Mary Hill. I don't know a Mary Hill. I open it up and there's a giant stack of printed pages—at least fifty. The first few pages are a photocopy of the newspaper headline and article. Somebody made sure to reduce the size so it fit on a normal page of paper. After the article and in the dozens of pages after is a printout of what must be the online comments to the article. I start reading them and don't stop for an hour.

Someone writes "her poor boys," and then I see a comment from what must be Darcy writing back: "the boys are fine." Others talk about how they used to see me at NA meetings—so much for twelve-step

anonymity. I can figure out who a few of the commenters are by their usernames. Others are strangers, though. Hundreds of them. Saying I should be in prison, calling me a sociopath, saying I am the worst kind of person in the world. People who are outraged that I am not going to prison. And then there are the more ominous ones.

There are ways to make sure people like that go back once they get out.
They will get theirs on the street.

I read the comments over and over. And each negative word burrows through my skin and latches onto my bones. The hatred, the vitriol, the threats become a chorus in my head. It sings to me a song of my own badness, and the melody settles in and plays on repeat. Everything I have been before this moment—daughter, sister, student, teacher, wife, neighbor, volunteer, employee, boss, coach, friend, mother, human—is gone. The community has spoken. Everything I have been is now erased. There are so many names for me in these comments. I am a criminal, a thief, an addict, a felon, a plague on society, a sociopath, a liar.

The Neighbor from Hell.

chapter 12

PUSH
AND PULL

I can't go to Blaine Street until the abscess clears, and each pass-
ing day makes me more anxious. Daddy leaves for prison, and two
of the girls that people had feared coming in from the streets have
arrived—Christina and Denise. We shuffle the rooms, and Kiki and I
move back to the big corner room. There are almost more sleds than
bunks on the freeway and almost every locked-door cell has a sled in
it too. Christina moves into our room and takes an instant dislike to
me because I don't fawn over her. I have no idea who she is from the
streets, but Kiki defers to her. Because Christina doesn't like me, Kiki
starts treating me differently when she's around. It hurts.

Every day for a week, a new fight breaks out because someone
looked at someone wrong. The overcrowding has made everyone
grumpy, and girls press the buzzer to go on time-outs every hour. The
guards are stressed. Tensions and tempers rise. Mama Love's way of
doing time in G is no longer the way. There is bloodshed, there is di-
vision among races. The whites and the Latinas who affiliate with the

157

southern, or Sureño, gangs fight with the Blacks and the Latinas who identify with the Norteño, or northern, gangs. There is also rivalry between the Westside and Eastside Gs of Santa Cruz, which, despite the confusing geography, also line up with the Sureños and Norteños in ways I can't decipher. Christina has brought in meth. She and Kiki do it and are up all night having sex and I am forced to listen. The next day Kiki takes me aside.

"You need to do some meth."

"What? No . . . why?"

"Christina doesn't trust you—she thinks if you don't do some, you're a snitch."

"That's ridiculous," I say. But there is no logic in G and certainly not with Christina. Her man is a big-time drug dealer, and all the girls are afraid of him. His power gives Christina power. I don't know him, and unless she's driving carpool someday, I doubt I will ever see her after G. I can't have any trouble if I want to get to Blaine Street. Kiki is stuck in G for her entire two-year sentence this time because she has too many marks against her for smoking and fighting. She's also banned because one time when she was in Blaine and working kitchen duty she walked up to the edge of the river that runs along the parking lot and they called it an escape attempt. But she just wanted to see some real water on her way to work.

"She's talking about fighting you."

I laugh at the idea of fighting Christina, of fighting anyone. I don't know how to throw a punch.

Kiki is quiet. "I don't think you get that this is serious." She whispers, as if Christina is in the room with us. "You want to get to your son, you need to do a line and hang with her. Or she can make it so you don't get to Blaine. Even if you don't start it, if you are in a fight, you can't go. She'll make sure the guards know you two fought. She's done it before. And you can't tell her I told you this. And if you tell

her the reason you are not doing it is because of your son, she will make sure you don't get to Blaine. She has two kids in the system. No parental rights. They were adopted."

Kiki seems legitimately scared, and now I'm scared too. When Christina comes in, I avoid looking at her and just stay in my bed and turn to the wall.

"Love," she snarls, making my last name into something sarcastic.

"What?" I turn around and see that she's standing over my bed.

"Are you going to party with us or what?"

Kiki is nodding over her shoulder. "I don't do meth," I say. "It makes me too annoyed at everyone. I'm not into speedy drugs." I say this like I'm telling someone I don't drink boxed wine. I even sound snooty to myself.

"Do it or move to the freeway," she says. I look to Kiki, but she's not meeting my eye. "And if you move to the freeway we are going to meet in the downstairs bathroom. Or you can be chill and roll with us. I only have a little left, you should be grateful I want to share with you."

I am not grateful.

"You don't need to waste it on me," I say.

"It's not a waste, it's insurance. I don't know you or who you reppin'."

"I'm reppin' Aptos," I say, and I make an "A" with my hands. She doesn't think it's funny.

Kiki is getting agitated. I can't get in a fight. It's a no-win situation. "Maybe just a little," I say.

Kiki stands watch while Christina shakes out a small line of meth on the edge of the sink. She hands me a rolled-up page of a book as a makeshift straw. I get up slowly and walk over to the sink. I look Christina in the eye, so she thinks I'm unbothered. I lean over and snort the meth as gently as I can. It burns my sinuses, and my eyes water, and I can feel it hit my system instantly. I really do hate speedy

drugs, and not sleeping is my least favorite thing to do in G. Now I will be up all night with nothing but regret and racing thoughts to keep me company.

I hate the meth immediately. I am anxious and self-conscious and paranoid. After lights out, Christina tells a pointless hour-long story about when she was four and thought her toys were real, and I want to jab a spork in my eye. I feel stupid for being afraid of her, for pretending like I did it because it would be rude not to. Like refusing a glass of wine at a book club, or not eating the cookies at a PTA meeting. I realize I could have just rolled myself up. What do I care where I wait to go to Blaine?

I lay in the dark listening to my cellmates' meth-fueled sex in the bunk above me and wishing for sleep. When they're done, Christina starts talking.

"Hey, Love . . ."

"What?"

"You ever been to Blaine Street?"

"No." She knows I haven't—she knows this is my first stint in County.

"Well, I hope they don't come tomorrow for you to go over."

"Why?"

"They drug test everyone there first thing, and if you test dirty, they send you back to the main jail and you don't ever get a chance to go there again." She and Kiki start laughing.

I've been set up. Kiki was an accomplice, and her betrayal hurts. After they fall asleep, I get up and go to the sink. I put my mouth under the faucet and drink and drink as much of the rusty rancid water as I can. I don't know how long a little bit of meth stays in your system. When I can't drink any more without vomiting, I lie down.

In the morning I pack up my stuff and move down to the freeway. I don't speak to Kiki again. Vivian tells me I can come to her room,

but I don't want to. I am done with the upper tier. I just want out of G, desperately.

An hour before lunch a guard comes in and asks who wants to go to church service. I throw on my red shirt and grab my ID card. Anything to get out of here.

In the service I tune out on the Bible readings and get lost in my head. I know I can't have a life and use drugs. I know I will have to find something other than drugs to fix whatever is broken in me, but I don't know how to do that.

I realize I haven't thought about DJ since we were sentenced a couple of weeks ago. I am relieved to be away from him. I will need to fix that, too, one way or another.

I'm so disappointed in myself for doing the meth. I gave in to Kiki and Christina's stupid plan. I put my head down on the table and cry silently. I know that the only thing I need to change is everything.

The chaplain, a woman about ten years older than me, tells us that anything we ask for sincerely in prayer, if it's for the greater good, will come to us. She tells us to pray right now before we leave. I pray for my desire to use drugs to go away. Forever. I cry silently into my arms, and when everyone gets up to leave I am the last one. The chaplain stops me at the door.

"Did you pray for something?"

I nod.

"Something big?"

I look at her, and my tears start flowing again. She opens her arms and I go into them. She hugs me, and I hug her back. She's not allowed to, but she does. This hug means everything.

Back in G, I go straight to my bunk on the freeway and turn to the wall.

I continue my prayer. I don't know how I feel about God, so I pray to the universe. I pray to find my path, my purpose, my goodness, my

soul. I pray for the strength and power and bravery I've given lip service to. I pray that whatever I need, I can find inside myself, because that's all I have. I pray to the better version of me. I pray to the soul behind the ego, the brokenness, the fear. I pray to whom Eckhart Tolle calls the observer. The me that is watching me.

I pray to Eckhart Tolle himself.

I throw in Oprah because I know those two hang out a lot together.

I spend the next three hours praying and visualizing a new life.

I imagine writing about my experience.

I imagine standing onstage talking about my mistakes.

I imagine a home of sunlight and happy faces.

I imagine my boys all sitting around the dinner table. I try not to think that Dylan will graduate high school in a few months and I won't be there. That he will go off to college maybe before I even get out. I try not to think about the fact that our home is gone, my car has been repossessed, I don't even have my driver's license because I wasn't out to pay an old ticket in November. I have lost my business. I have no job to support me or my boys or this imaginary place where we sit at a dinner table with sunlight streaming through the windows. I have destroyed everything. I have no idea what I will do when I walk out of jail in September, or where I will go, or if anyone will help me. Who would possibly hire the neighbor from hell?

All these thoughts swirl in my head until I refocus and go back to prayer.

The only solution is to never use drugs again.

Today is March 18, 2009.

My new birthday.

~

I'm told to roll it up for Blaine Street a few days and many gallons of water later. I am nervous while I take the urine test, but I pass. I tell myself that this is the last drug test I'll ever have to worry about since I'll never use again.

Blaine Street has its own kitchen and serves meals that are cooked in-house. Other luxuries include a sparse backyard with a dirt track around it, a badminton net, a small gym with an exercise bike and a treadmill. There is no freeway like in G, only four sets of dorm-style rooms on two levels. Each quad, as they're called, is framed around a central dayroom with couches and chairs and its own television. There is a communal bathroom for each quad with actual stalls for privacy and porcelain sinks with mirrors and two genuine bathtubs. The bunk beds have real mattresses and even a pillow. There is a desk and a radio and a lamp. In Blaine we are given large T-shirt nightgowns to sleep in, and we get to change out our other clothes twice a week rather than twice a month. Blaine is the Ritz-Carlton compared to G.

Volunteers come in after dinner each night and teach us to crochet or tell us about reentry services. There is a class on relapse prevention taught by a woman named Tracy who I instantly love. She's direct and no-nonsense, and we hit it off immediately. There are even volunteers who will come in and do your hair. There's a chaplain and religious services. A computer class if you need computer training. Music. Board games.

And work. Lots of work. Each day you must clean your room before 7 a.m. Beds have to be made military style. Floors are mopped daily. Bathrooms cleaned. All are subject to inspection at 7 a.m. Once a week, on Sundays, it's double scrub—in-depth cleaning, closets organized, every surface, knob, and wall scrubbed to perfection.

Once the daily chores are done, the girls at Blaine Street go to the main jail to clean and cook for the entire facility—without them the

jail would cease to function. I'm assigned to clean the public lobby of the main jail and the sheriff's offices. I start work at 6 a.m. Only one deputy comes into the main office that early, and we chat it up every day. She calls her mom every morning, and after a couple of weeks she hands me the phone so I can say hello. Her mom always asks if I'm doing okay and staying out of trouble, and I assure her that I am. And I've let everyone know at Blaine Street I am not getting involved with anything shady. I know there are probably drugs waiting to be couriered under the tampon bags in the public stalls that I clean, but I don't look. If anyone asks me to check, I tell them to fuck off.

During my mornings emptying trash bags and cleaning bathrooms, I think about how much Blaine Street relies on women's unpaid labor. If Blaine were empty, the jail would be in trouble. No meals. No cleaning. It's a system completely disincentivized to rehabilitate people. Their business model doesn't function without a high recidivism rate. If all the women in County were successful, exhibited good behavior, and became productive members of society, it would break the county budget. The sheriff's department couldn't afford hiring actual workers, so local taxes would get raised. People could barely afford the cost of living in Santa Cruz as it was, and proposing higher taxes rarely went well for local politicians regardless of the reason.

Recidivism was the only financially viable path forward. The only way for the government to win is for the inmates to lose. It's as simple as that.

~

There's an actual library at Blaine Street, and I read every volume. My new favorite is *The Book of Awakening* by Mark Nepo. It's organized in daily dated essays, and I read it like a horoscope—looking for whatever wisdom I need to get through this particular day. It's uncannily

accurate. One of his observations resonates especially strongly with me: *Pain pushes you until vision pulls you.*

After lights out, I lay in my bunk bed and try to trace my life back to the moment when I stopped letting a vision for my future pull me and started letting pain push. Because I did have a clear vision at one point. And it didn't have anything to do with marriage or money or motherhood.

From the time I first escaped into books, all I wanted was to be a writer. I was going to write novels that moved people, that helped them understand the world and themselves better. I wanted to make people feel, whether it was laughing or crying. And if the vision also had me rich and famous and fabulous, I was okay with that.

Writing was always the only way for me to make sense of my childhood, my family, my fears, my emotions, my vast and confusing interior world. I was always a better version of me on the page. I was always at my most honest on the page. I could transcend every limitation I believed I had when I wrote. In high school I may have lived in a small apartment while my friends had big lawns but writing transcended class. Writing transcended loneliness. Writing transcended self-doubt and fear and heartbreak.

I never needed a drink or a drug to write.

When I took that first pill after Dylan was born, I stopped writing. I told myself it was having children, and financial troubles, and a difficult marriage that made writing impossible. I told myself there wasn't enough time in the day to write. But all the excuses were lies.

Opiates made writing impossible.

The drugs I took to avoid pain kept me from the one thing that helped me cope with pain. Writing was my survival strategy and a bridge to other people. It gave me a sense of self-worth. It gave me joy. But mostly it was how I let feelings flow through me. Once I stopped

writing, every bit of pain stayed in my body where it settled and weighed me down so much that the only way I could move through life at all was to take a pill as needed for pain. Then two. Then ten. Then twenty. Then sixty. And every time I tried to stop, tried to choose a life without something to dull the pain, I couldn't stop for very long. I couldn't stop long enough to realize what I really needed.

I needed the writing.

~

I start writing again. I write stories on the computer and print them out because we aren't allowed to save documents. I write an essay about anger. There's a woman in Blaine with the last name Doll who suffered horrible childhood abuse and I write a story about the million ways to break a doll. I read the story to Tracy, after relapse prevention class one night, and she sits in silence when I finish.

"Can you please read that to me again?" she asks softly.

I read her the story again. And then I read her my essay about anger.

"They're so great," she says. "I'm blown away. Can I take them to make copies?"

Every day that I write, I feel vision pulling me. It's not a clear vision, but there's a tug. Writing not only passes the time, it makes me feel like I am me again. The old me. The real me.

The me before the mess.

Tracy brings back many copies of my anger essay, and it gets passed around Blaine Street. When Jacinda, a thirty-year-old who looks like she's twelve, comes to me and asks if I can write her letter to the court asking if she can be moved from Blaine to a long-term residential treatment program, I'm not sure if I know enough to argue on her behalf for treatment.

We sit on a bench in Blaine's backyard, and I ask her why she

wants to go to an eighteen-month treatment program rather than just do her six months at Blaine.

"Because I don't want to come back here," she says. "I don't want to go to treatment, but I need to go to treatment. Look, it's eighteen months of structure and regular meals and therapy and support, but I'll be safe there. You feel me?"

Drawing on Eckhart Tolle's advice, I stay as present as I can while Jacinda speaks. She tells me about her ex who always finds her, and her mom who died two years ago, and her sister who has been raising Jacinda's son for so long that he thinks she's his mother. I have to put my own desperation to get out of jail aside—I would never trade six months for eighteen months—and really listen to Jacinda. I try to see the world through her eyes, understand her backstory. It's not pretty— one horrible foster home after another, running away from abuse, get- ting raped and kidnapped while high, getting locked up for the first time because she was crashing at a drug house that got raided.

"Okay," I say, after she's shared her stories for over an hour. "I'll write your letter."

"What do you want?" asks Jacinda.

I always forget about the quid pro quo of jail friendship. I'm trying to cut my carbs, so I'm done trading things for bear claws. I fall silent as I ponder what else I could possibly want in this place.

"I'll make your bed every morning," she says. "Please . . ."

I suck at making my bed. I can never get the corners as smooth and tight as the guards demand.

I nod and smile in agreement.

"And," she adds, "if I get released because of your letter, I'll make sure someone else makes your bed until you get out."

It's a great incentive, but when I sit down to write the letter to the judge, I'm not thinking about my messy bed. I'm imagining that I am Jacinda and all she's been through. I'm thinking about how many

times I've been in and out of jail and how badly I want the structure of the residential program. I write a long letter imploring the judge to send me to treatment, to give me a fighting chance to never come back to jail. As Jacinda I end the letter with this: "I never had anyone care enough about me to tell me when to go to bed, to make sure I was eating healthy, to ask me how my day was. I want to follow the rules. In Santa Cruz Residential, they may not be my family but it will still be the closest thing I've ever had to a real home. Please let me go home. It's all I've ever wanted."

Jacinda and I mail the letter, and for the next two weeks she makes my bed every morning before inspection. When the classification officer comes over from the main jail and asks for Jacinda, I go down to the lobby with her. He seems rushed and gives me a slightly annoyed look as I listen in on their conversation. He hands Jacinda a stack of paperwork.

"You get transferred tomorrow to treatment," he says. "Pack it up tonight. They are coming for you at six a.m."

Jacinda bursts into tears.

"Okay then," he says and walks away quickly.

Jacinda and I look at each other, stunned. She throws her arms around me.

"I'm so happy for you," I say. "You deserve this, you deserve a real chance."

"Thank you," she says. "I don't know how you did it, but what you wrote . . . it was just everything I've ever felt and didn't know how to say."

I hug her back tightly. There's a feeling I don't recognize that immediately overwhelms me and my eyes well up. I'm so happy for Jacinda but it's something else. I'm proud of myself.

And for the first time in a very long time, I feel good.

~

I don't see Jacinda the morning she leaves, but at 7 a.m. a quiet girl named Eve taps on my door and then walks in and makes my bed in silence. I try to ask Eve about herself, about what Jacinda traded her for, but she just smiles at me and shrugs. Whatever it is, she's not saying. She comes every single morning before seven. When she's not making my bed, Eve crochets all day, only breaking for meals. Her room is lined with hundreds of baby-sized caps and booties. The crochet volunteers collect them every month but where they take them is a mystery. I imagine a hospital or maybe the treatment center for pregnant women.

After Jacinda, I have a steady job ghostwriting legal letters, love letters, birthday letters, anniversary poems, arguments in family disputes. I even write eulogies for two women who get passes to leave Blaine for funerals. I break up with a few gangsters, and I tell one poor schmuck I need a divorce because I've fallen in love with a woman and now have a jail wife.

I prepare for each assignment the same way I did with Jacinda—by listening. Sometimes I worry I could get in trouble for pretending to be other people, especially since that's what put me in jail in the first place. But I'm helping rather than hustling now, so I don't worry too much about the fallout. I love pretending to be someone who isn't me. All my years writing fiction help me to be a different character. When I talk to my clients at Blaine I listen for their particular quirks of language and phrasing, the way they tell a story. There are only a few judges in criminal court in Santa Cruz so I'm extra careful to vary the voice in each letter and match the voice to their individual backgrounds, education, and culture.

The more letters I write, the easier it becomes to become another person. To think like they think. Reason like they reason. Occasionally I write how someone feels and they freak out because they didn't tell me that they grew up never trusting other women, or that because

they were abandoned by their father they always chose bad men just like him, but it's true for them.

It's kind of spooky, and the girls whisper that I must be psychic.

I don't discourage their suspicion because it's fun, it passes the time, and saves me from having to make my own bed. When I occasionally make a prediction about something entirely predictable that comes true, I gaze intently into people's eyes as I deny that I'm psychic.

And I don't explain that the reason I can write so accurately about their fears, their shame, their desperation to be loved, to be better mothers than they had, or their struggles to stay clean, is because in all these ways we are exactly the same.

I don't yet realize that what I am doing is honing my empathy— the superpower of all great ghostwriters.

chapter 13

MOTHER'S DAY

I get moved to kitchen duty at Blaine Street, and I get permission to grow a garden in the backyard. Each morning and night I work the soil, plant the seeds, tend to the vegetables that I will eventually cook and serve to my fellow inmates.

I have never been a gardener, someone who loved to get her hands in the soil. But it's different gardening in jail. Planting seeds feels hopeful and even the slow pace of vegetables growing feels exciting because there is something new being tended to and born.

Soon after I plant the garden, Amy, Kaden's CPS social worker, begins making plans to bring him for his first visit. I have called her every day since I got to Blaine. I am determined to do what I can from inside to get my boy back. Every week I ask her what I can do to move my case along. Rather than seeing her as a bureaucrat who wants to take Kaden away from me, I choose to treat her as my ally in getting him back. I choose to believe that the goal of everyone in CPS court is to return Kaden to me rather than take him away permanently. I try to

manifest this into being, and I tell myself that the judge, the attorneys, the social workers are all working with me toward this goal.

"What more can we do?" I ask them.

"What more can I do?" I ask myself.

This question becomes my mantra and consumes every waking hour.

I slowly become an advocate for myself and for the other women going through similar CPS cases. One of the requirements to reunify within the allotted year is a positive-discipline parenting class. After I'm released, there will be no way I can complete this class within the one-year time frame. I lobby hard on behalf of all of us at Blaine and get an amazing woman, a former mayor of Santa Cruz, to come to Blaine Street and teach the class.

Amy agrees to bring Kaden to a court-supervised visit once a week, but only if all the other girls in Blaine Street agree to stay in their rooms during the visit. It's the only way CPS will allow the visits to count toward our reunification.

All the girls agree to stay locked in their rooms. I don't know if it's because of the letters I have written for them, or because so many of them have already lost children to the system, and they empathize with me. These women—mothers, sisters, friends—are rooting for Kaden.

He is brought in for his first visit. We read books and play badminton. He sits on my lap, and I cuddle him and promise him I will be home soon, that we will be together.

I walk him along the side yard so the girls can see his joy, which their sacrifice has made possible. He smiles and waves to them all and blows them sweet four-year-old kisses. I think it gives them hope.

Because my new job in Blaine Street is running the kitchen, I can make him a snack like it's our own kitchen. I make him hard-boiled eggs, which he loves to peel. I squirrel away boxes of Froot Loops so I can pour him a bowl of sweet cereal when he asks for it every week. I

still worry that he hasn't grown an inch since my arrest, so I feed him as much as I can. We work in the garden and talk about how each plant grows bigger just like him. I will him to grow. Each week he tries to leave something with me, a piece of clothing, a toy, his shoes. "I want to live here with you," he begs. "Please, Mommy."

"I love you, Boo Boo," I tell him. "I wish you could live here, but it's not allowed, plus your brothers would miss you."

He clings to my neck when it's time to go, and I murmur "soon" as I rain kisses across his face until he laughs. I do my best not to show him my breaking heart. After he leaves, I grieve the loss all over again. When he cries to stay with me, I tell him Darcy and Bryan love him and are taking care of him for me. I want him to be happy wherever he is—and I do not say a negative word about Darcy, although he repeats cruel things she has said about me. I will never make him feel like his loyalty is divided or feel guilty for his happy moments away from me. I know I am his mom, and there is no ticking clock, or law, or judge, or social worker who can change that.

DJ hasn't yet made it to Rountree—the medium-security facility for men on the other side of the county. He has had no jailhouse epiphany like mine. If anything, jail is making him worse; he's affiliating with gang members and doing drugs, and the jail stops allowing letters between us because he's doodling gang symbols in them. When I ask the social worker what happens if both parents aren't doing what they're supposed to, she tells me the judge has the power to view each parent's requirements separately and give custody back to one parent and not the other.

"Of course," she adds, "if you are living with the other parent and he is using drugs or hasn't fulfilled his requirements, it would appear like you are not putting the well-being of the child first. Sometimes safety means there is only one parent in the picture."

I nod.

Pain pushes and vision pulls.
I'm done with pain.

~

Officer Lonnie is the main deputy who works the day shift at Blaine Street. I am amazed that everyone calls her by her first name until I realize Lonnie is actually her last name. She is there from 7 a.m. to 7 p.m. most days. Lonnie is about my age, with big brown eyes that can stare at you for an uncomfortable amount of time without blinking. She likes to think she doesn't miss anything that happens at Blaine, but she does. She wears her dark hair pulled back in a severe bun. The guards don't ever give out personal information, but from what I can gather, she is second generation from somewhere in Southeast Asia. When I get up at 5 a.m. to start cooking for the thirty residents of Blaine she offers me coffee. Real coffee. Guard coffee.

She finds the fact that I've never tried pho more offensive than my felonies. She tells me how her various relatives make pho, what they each put in it, the five main spices, and how the pho at the diner nearby compares. She also shares the latest Hollywood gossip with me in hopes I will share the latest Blaine Street gossip with her.

One day I ask Lonnie if I can make banana bread as a treat for the women of Blaine. I hand her a list of ingredients I will need. As a working mom, I never had time to bake and garden like I do at Blaine. I always thought of baking and gardening as luxuries of the idle or un-ambitious, but I was wrong. There is something about growing things and feeding people that makes my soul feel good again. I wish I had gardened and baked more when I had a home of my own.

"What do you have to offer?" asks Lonnie.

It's not as creepy a question as it sounds. Lonnie is trying to move up in the corrections department, and the more contraband she can

confiscate from inmates the better it is for her career. Confiscating involves a lot of work for her and a lot of stress for the residents of Blaine, so Lonnie and I have worked out a system: I collect contraband for her so that nobody gets in trouble and in exchange she brings in treats. It's a win-win, no-fuss-no-muss system for everyone.

"What do you want?" I counter.

"Two lighters," she says. Lighters are a coup in the guard confiscation world, since they are needed to smoke cigarettes or drugs, and they can also start fires.

I come back with an offer of one lighter, and the deal is done. There are lots of lighters at Blaine, so it's easy to get a volunteer to give one up for the possibility of banana bread. When I ask for two DVDs and cake mix and frosting, we have a harder negotiation. She wants three lighters and a pack of cigarettes. We settle on two lighters and five cigarettes in exchange for a full movie night experience for Blaine Street where we can stay up until midnight.

We are drinking our morning coffee when I finally get up the nerve to ask her about going to the Gemma Program—an eight-week reentry program where about ten Blaine Street residents get to leave in street clothes two days a week and take classes at a local church in relapse prevention, nutritious cooking, music, yoga, résumé writing, and life skills like how to balance a checkbook.

"I'd like to do it," I say.

"You don't really need it," says Lonnie.

"Please!" I beg.

"It's not up to me. You have to meet with Cassandra, she's the program director. She's coming to do interviews tomorrow for the new session. I just refer people to her that I think can be trusted and who will benefit from it, but it's her decision."

"Will you refer me?"

She says nothing, just smirks at me between sips of her coffee.

"What?" I ask. "You don't think I can be trusted?" I ask this lightly, but my voice shakes a little. It hurts. I want people to trust me again.

Lonnie sets her coffee down and laughs. "I already referred you."

Lonnie doesn't show much emotion, nor is she moved by others' emotions. But she does have compassion, and I'm grateful to her.

Cassandra pulls me out to the lobby to interview me. She's a large Black woman who exudes joy from her purple-glitter eye shadow to her flower nose ring to her colorful flowing scarves.

I'm afraid she's seen the newspaper headline and read the online comments. I read them constantly, trying to figure out the identity of each username. I know which comment is from Darcy. I know which are from people in recovery. I know which name is an old boss. But the bulk of the comments seem to be from strangers—people who read the article and have a lot to say about who I am and what I've done. It's almost like reading your horoscope every day and trying to see yourself in the description—if your horoscope threatened you and called you a sociopath. Reading them is like poking at a wound that's trying to heal. They are the opposite of positive affirmations, but I can't seem to stop.

Cassandra and I chat for twenty minutes as she tells me about the program, the classes. She asks me why I want to attend and I don't bullshit her. "I really want to leave here twice a week," I say. "I'm not going to lie about that. But I also love school, learning, and home-work. I want something to focus on besides cooking and cleaning and waiting for visits from my boys."

"I think you'll make a great addition to the Gemma Program," Cassandra tells me. She has the kindest smile I have ever seen, and she beams it at me as if I am worthy of such kindness.

"But . . ." I stammer, "I just want you to know . . ."

She looks at me expectantly, still smiling.

I don't know how to say what I want to say. I feel inarticulate and like I need to make sure she knows what she's getting into so that she doesn't regret offering me a place. "There was this headline," I begin. "I have thirty-two felonies, and I just want to make sure you know . . . that I'm really, I mean everyone thinks I'm really . . ."

I finally blurt it out.

"I'm a bad person!"

Cassandra tilts her head and stares me straight in the eye. The kindness and warmth don't leave her face. What I say doesn't seem to shock her, but she doesn't speak for a good thirty seconds.

"My son was in the paper once. I'll tell you about it someday, but meanwhile I'll be here at seven a.m. on Tuesday to pick you up," she finally says.

I nod and thank her. As I stand up, she hugs me. Lonnie, watching from the guard station, doesn't stop her. Lara the mom gets hugged and cuddled by Kaden every week. But Lara, the neighbor from hell, has never been hugged like this. I fold into her and rest my head on her broad shoulder. Her perfume is sweet. I want to stay here forever. She murmurs "It's going to be okay . . ." over and over, and we stay like that for a few minutes.

In Cassandra's arms, I feel like I am good.

~

The Gemma classes are taught by local volunteers, and the church gives access to the meeting room and the kitchen for free. A few weeks into the session I find out some girls have been stealing money from the collection box at the church. I put a stop to it right away, making them return what they stole and confess to Cassandra.

When they protest, I remind them that I control the Blaine Street kitchen, which also means I control the cheese. In relapse prevention someone said that there's a chemical in cheese that's identical to one

in heroin. I don't know if that's true, but I do know that in Blaine who-ever controls the cheese controls the women.

Halfway through the program, Alice, a volunteer, gives us homework where we have to list all the pros and cons of restorative justice versus punitive justice. Back at Blaine, we all gather in the computer room and talk about what it would be like to sit in a circle with the people we have harmed and hear their experience of our crimes. Some girls say they'd prefer a judge to facing their victims, and I think about sitting with my neighbors and trying to explain why I stole their checkbook and wrote a check at the grocery store. Or why I used their social security number to get credit to buy a Kindle. I don't know if I could explain it in a way that wouldn't sound like I wasn't taking responsibility. *"I was out of my mind"* doesn't cut it. *"I just wanted to read parenting e-books"* makes me sound inane. I didn't want to hurt them. But my life for the last year was like driving at night in heavy fog; I could only focus on a foot in front of me. I had no peripheral vision for anyone or anything else.

I definitely couldn't see my neighbors.

I can't imagine one person who was in the courtroom when I was sentenced choosing forgiveness over punishment. I don't think I could make that choice if someone hurt my family, violated my sense of safety and security. Restorative justice was great in theory but we Gemma girls couldn't imagine forgiving ourselves, much less asking others to forgive us.

I am the fastest typist in Blaine, so I help all the girls type up their homework and print it for class.

At the next class, Alice and I are sitting across from each other, at two ends of a large conference table. The rest of the girls are on either side.

"Did anyone have any problems with typing it up?" she asks. "It's okay if you had to handwrite it."

"I helped everyone type it on the computer," I say brightly. The

weeks are flying by now, and I'm in great spirits. Tracy, the relapse prevention teacher, had challenged me to stop reading the newspaper comments about me so I have, and it's lifted my mood considerably.

I smile at Alice, but she doesn't smile back. She says sharply, "I'm not comfortable with you being on any kind of computer at all."

My stomach flips, and I study Alice more closely to see if I know her from anywhere outside Gemma, Little League or Montessori maybe, but she just glares at me with open disdain.

Nobody says anything. One of the rules of Gemma is that you never talk about anyone's crimes. The volunteers are there to help and support us because they believe in reentry and rehabilitation. Like our homework assignment, Gemma itself is based on restorative justice, not punitive.

I can't respond, and my cheeks burn. I keep my eyes on the table for the rest of the class. When the day is over, and we are putting chairs away in the supply closet, I step inside and start to cry. I feel defeated. Ashamed. I silently berate myself for my optimism. If a Gemma volunteer has such vitriol toward me, then I have no chance out in the world.

Cassandra pushes her way into the closet. She's livid.

"She had no right to say that to you," she says angrily. "I'm going to talk to her."

"I can't come back," I say. "What's the point? I'm done." I have no anger in me like Cassandra does, but then anger has always come out as sadness for me.

"You will be back. You'll be back on Thursday, and you'll be back every week after until you graduate. I promise you, nothing like that will happen again."

I shrug and tell Cassandra I'll think about it.

When I walk into Blaine, Lonnie takes one look at me and says, "Who died?"

I tell her what happened.

"So your feelings got hurt," she says. "Do you like Gemma?"

"Yeah . . . but . . ."

"Then get over it. Show up and hold your head up."

"But . . ."

"Or no more getting out of double-scrub by having your minions do your job."

This makes me laugh. Lonnie always knows more than I give her credit for. "How about some ice cream for the girls? Ice cream always cheers me up. I like vanilla."

"Figures you like vanilla. No deal. You don't get rewarded for pouting, so suck it up, Love. And finish what you started."

Lonnie's right. I want to finish Gemma, so I will. Later that night Lonnie calls me to her window and hands me the office phone. It's Cassandra.

"I spoke to her. Apparently she's friends with your next-door neighbor."

"Oh, great . . ."

"It won't happen again," says Cassandra. "Not on my watch. And you don't have to do her class anymore. And she won't be coming back next session."

"Thanks," I say. "I guess I'll see you Thursday."

"You bet your ass you will."

~

On Mother's Day, Bryan brings Dylan, Cody, and Ty to visit. It's always awkward to see Bryan, and even more awkward when he keeps telling me how good I look.

"I mean, you look so healthy," he adds.

It's true. I exercise every day, I meditate, I go to bed early, I have lots of friends. But mostly I feel hopeful. At first it felt like I would be

in jail forever, but now I see an advertisement for a movie coming out in October and I think, *I will be out of jail when that movie premieres.*

The boys and I sit in Blaine's backyard and talk. I tell them stories about the other girls, silly fights people get in, how we trade lighters for cake mix, and I give them the beanies I have crocheted for them.

"I got into Cal Poly," says Dylan. I scream and hug him. My first-born is headed for college.

"I'm so proud of you," I say. "When does school start?"

"The end of September."

I will be out, I think. *I will be out of jail to see him off to college.*

Cody talks about basketball and his new girlfriend. Ty talks about his friends in junior high and the academic awards he's winning even though he skips classes whenever he can. "I believe in cutting out the middleman," he says.

I look at him, puzzled.

"The teacher." He laughs. "I don't need the teacher to learn or to do well on the tests."

The old me would have freaked out on him, told him he can't skip school and that teachers are important. The new me just listens and understands.

Because it's Mother's Day there's no time limit on the visits, and the boys and Bryan stay all day. We play badminton and check out the garden, but mostly we just sit and talk and laugh.

"I've been writing," I say. "I've missed it so much. I don't know why I stopped writing."

"Don't stop, Mom," they say. "You should do what you love."

Sitting in the shade under a tree outside the jail with my boys should feel weird and painful and awkward. But there's so much love between us under that tree that I realize I didn't need all those trappings to prove I was a loving mom. I didn't need a big house and a big car and private school and fancy vacations. None of that mattered or matters.

I realize in this moment that I am a better mom in jail than I have ever been outside jail. Our conversations feel more real, more raw, more honest. We're not fitting into any preconceived roles—we can't. I used to think the most important thing was that my boys get into Stanford, or some big Ivy League college like Harvard, but now I realize it's not that important.

Dylan is happy to be going to Cal Poly, so I'm happy. If he'd told me he decided not to go to college, I would have still been happy. Bryan and I aren't fighting, and every time one of the boys says something funny our eyes meet in shared understanding: We did this. As flawed and fucked-up as we were, we created these beautiful humans. The Love boys have always had each other, but now, thanks to my arrest, they have their mom back. I'm not keeping secrets. I'm not pretending. I'm just here in my green and purple loving on them.

I never thought I would be overwhelmed with gratitude spending Mother's Day in jail, but I am.

Thank you. I am alive.

Thank you. I am their mother.

Thank you, thank you, thank you.

~

A few weeks later, we have a Gemma graduation at a hotel near the courthouse. We are given graduation gowns. We are each expected to give a speech. Friends and family, judges and attorneys and city officials, and even some guards attend the ceremony. I invite my sons, but only Dylan and Cody can make it. For many of the girls, this will be the only graduation they'll ever have.

I have graduated high school and college and graduate school, but I feel most proud of this commencement. It feels like a celebration. When we come out to begin the ceremony, we all dance out one by one to "Superwoman" by Alicia Keys.

It should have been embarrassing for all of us, in our maroon caps and gowns, swaying and dancing and celebrating because we graduated from a basic life skills program. The audience of judges and guards is slightly uncomfortable, and my boys are mortified, but our dancing is an act of rebellion. Who are we to celebrate? Who are we to laugh and smile? Who are we to wear our caps and gowns proudly and share our speeches with confidence? Who are we to identify as Superwomen?

We are women full of possibility and hope.

In my speech, I talk about the experience of time in jail. I talk about how I used to treat time as a limitless resource, and not the precious and rare commodity it actually is. I try to convey how often the past is present when you have only your own mind for company, and how the future is unknown. I talk about the obstacles we all will face when we are released. I talk about pain pushing and vision pulling. I talk about missing Dylan's high school graduation the week earlier but how he is here to see me graduate, and I ask the audience to cheer for him. And then I promise my boys, the guards, the judge on my case who is watching, that I will never miss another graduation of any of my children.

My old boyfriend, the district attorney, is at the graduation. Cassandra is flabbergasted because he has never attended one of these ceremonies before. I see him watching me dance, staring at me intently while I give my speech. He gets up to leave when the reception is about to begin, and I track his movements to the door.

He turns around at the doorway and our eyes meet.

He smiles.

I smile.

In this small moment we are friends again. We are on the same side.

~

It's a long summer without Gemma to break up the monotony, but I work in the garden, and Lonnie lets me do landscaping in the evenings in front of Blaine Street. I am always working during shift change at 7 p.m., so the main jail guards all see me out front with no locked doors between me and the outside world. Some have started to wave to me every evening, others just frown and look concerned. I love these evenings of freedom—pruning rosebushes, pulling weeds. Plants never judge you. Some nights, I almost think I can hear the summer sounds of people laughing at the nearby beach. I think of all the times I took my boys there—riding the baby rides on the boardwalk until they were big enough to go on the Giant Dipper roller coaster. Kaden would still be on the baby rides, and I imagine us eating cotton candy and playing carnival games together.

On nights when the summer fog rolls in, it makes me moody and nostalgic for everything I have lost. I don't want to cook dinner for thirty women; I want to cook dinner for my family. I don't want to mop jail floors; I want to mop a floor in my own house. I don't want to prune the jail's rosebushes; I want to plant my own garden in my own backyard. Each night I go to sleep thinking I am one day closer to all these things.

And each morning I wake up not knowing how the hell I'm going to make any of that happen.

At the end of June Michael Jackson dies. Lonnie and I discuss his demise over coffee. It's got to be opiates, I tell her. I'm pretty sure he was an opiate addict. Lonnie disagrees, and we fall into a heated debate. In July, reports emerge about his history of abusing pain medication. Even though she runs a jail filled with women who suffer from substance abuse disorders, Lonnie still doesn't understand how someone who has everything can throw it all away. Such behavior doesn't fit her no-nonsense, deal-with-it mentality, so I try to explain how the drugs just take over. How they make nothing else matter.

"But you know what you're doing," she says. "You still know right from wrong."

"Of course," I say.

"Then if you know you are doing the wrong things," she says, giving me a pointed look, "then you should know enough to stop."

"It just doesn't work that way," I say.

"Well then you ask for help . . ."

I think about all the times I could have asked for help and didn't. In my mind, there was no way I could ever be away from my children for the thirty days it took to go to rehab. It feels ironic now that I've been away from them for nine months.

"There's so much stigma and shame," I say. "For me, it would have meant admitting that I didn't have my shit together. I was afraid of being judged. Seems like a small price to pay now. I was super invested in pretending like everything was fine, and I was the perfect mom. Perfect moms don't go to rehab."

"So how'd that work out for you?" Lonnie asks. "And you still knew right from wrong when you were out there committing all those felonies."

I think about it for a minute. "It wasn't that I forgot right from wrong," I say. "Drugs don't do that, at least not for me. But they did make me forget who I was, if that makes sense. I didn't forget the law, I forgot myself."

"What does that mean?"

"It means I forgot that I'm someone who would give you everything I have before I'd ever steal from you. It means I forgot that I'm someone who's happy and fun and likes people. I forgot that I'm creative and loving and careful and thoughtful and generous."

"You didn't seem to forget that you're full of yourself." Lonnie laughs.

"But I did," I say. "I completely forgot to be full of myself. But mostly I forgot I'm someone who wants to live."

Lonnie clears her throat.

"Are you going to cry?" I ask.

Lonnie scoffs. "You wish."

~

In August, the jail announces plans for an early-release program to help with overcrowding. They are going to release some inmates ahead of their official out date, but you have to come back to the jail every day from eight to four and work. There's lots of excitement about this program, but it only reminds me yet again how much the county depends on women's unpaid labor.

Soon after this plan is floated, Lonnie calls me over the loudspeaker on a Friday before shift change.

"What's up?" I say.

"I was just looking up your husband's record on the computer. He was caught with street clothes under his mattress."

"What?"

DJ and I haven't been able to write each other in months, and since we're done with court dates, I never see him. Or think about him. I declared my love for him in my letters, but I didn't really feel anything for him anymore. I didn't hate him; I didn't love him. And I didn't know what to do about it.

Lonnie reads through the reports on DJ. "Wow, he's had a lot of trouble in jail. I shouldn't be sharing this with you, but I want you to know—you guys seem like you're on different trajectories."

I don't know what to say to this, so I just shrug. I don't know if this is Lonnie my friend advising me about my future, or Lonnie my jailer scouting for information.

"You should get rid of this guy, that's all I'm saying."

"Well, it's not like we're dating right now." I laugh, but Lonnie is stone-faced.

"You qualify for early release with the new program. You are out on Monday morning."

I am surprised. I thought I had another three weeks. I have no idea where I'm going to live or how I'm going to get to the jail to work each day. The jail doesn't care about these challenges, and for now neither do I. With freedom so close, it's hard to think about how hard homelessness will be.

"I'm not working this weekend, so this is goodbye," she says.

Lonnie and I look at each other. I can't tell her that I'll miss her because that's just awkward given our circumstances. But I appreciate her, and I will miss her friendship.

"I don't want to see you again," she says.

"I promise I will never be back here. I will never go to jail again. No offense."

"Do you know how many times I've been told that, and then two months later I see the person right back here again?"

"A million times?"

"Probably more. I think you might have a chance—but you need to get rid of the guy. Everyone here thinks so. And if you come back, I will not let you have your own room. I will bunk you up with the most obnoxious person in here."

"Deal," I reply. "But what do you mean by 'everyone' thinks so?"

Lonnie laughs. "You don't think the guards talk as much about you guys as you do about us?"

When shift change happens, I am outside tending to the roses. Lonnie drives past and yells out her window, "Try some pho!"

I give her a little wave and go back to deadheading the rosebushes so that the tender new buds have room to grow.

~

I don't tell anyone I'm leaving on Monday. The few days before some- one's out date are always precarious. Sometimes girls sabotage them- selves and get into trouble that requires them to stay, and other times another inmate sabotages them. Like any place where thirty women are living on top of each other, each dealing with their own trauma, their own sobriety, their own regret—it can be all kumbaya and girl power until it isn't.

I have nightmares all weekend before my release—where I'm run- ning because I'm being chased, or I'm trying to save my children and I can't. I know that I'm walking out of Blaine a different person than I was when I walked in—but I don't know exactly who I am now. I have been so many different versions of myself that I don't know which is real. All of them? None of them?

On Sunday night, right before lights out, I tell everyone I am leav- ing in the morning, and we have a spontaneous dance party in our quad. Janelle and Mandi help me fold the blanket I have made in crochet class over the last few months. I want to give it to Dylan to take to Cal Poly when he leaves in September. I've missed almost his whole senior year of high school. His football games and SATs and prom and graduation. I have missed my oldest son's most important year of school, and the guilt is all-consuming. In my fantasy life I imagine being back in a home with all my boys, but I realize that be- cause Dylan is going off to college he will probably never live with me again. This realization that some things are just lost to me forever is like jumping into icy waters. It takes my breath away.

I shake off the cold reality and focus on my last night with my Blaine Street family.

The blanket that I have been blindly crocheting during my months at Blaine has grown to be at least twenty feet long and ten feet wide, and the folding party devolves into dark hilarity.

"At least you'll have something to keep you warm when you're homeless."

"You could cut it up and have an entire crocheted wardrobe."

"You can hide under it when Probation comes knocking."

At one point, all thirty of us try to fit under the blanket like it's a fort. It's all fun and games until Janelle pees her pants from laughing so hard. I go to bed that night smiling, hopeful, sure that the hard part is out of the way. I have done my time.

On August 17, 2009, I walk out of Blaine Street forever.

~

When I leave Blaine, I must go immediately to the probation department to let them know my address and get the terms of my release. I have no address, only a prepaid room in a seedy motel called the Hitching Post not far from the jail, where I will spend the next few weeks. An uncle I haven't seen or heard from in years has offered to pay for this, my mom tells me. I am grateful, but also hurt that no relative of mine ever wrote or visited me in jail.

I know that part of my sentence is attending drug court once I'm released, but I don't know when or how this starts. Drug court is usually an alternative to jail that involves night classes twice a week, random drug testing, immediate incarceration for a weekend if there's a failed drug test, and the promise of a clean record upon completion of the program. Drug testing is also part of probation, and part of the CPS reunification requirements. Every day I must call three different numbers and see if any of them requires me to get a drug test. I will have three hours to get the test from the time I am alerted. Meeting all the CPS requirements is a condition of my criminal case plea deal; meeting my drug court requirements is a condition of the CPS case; and doing whatever Probation wants trumps all. The various parts

of the system are precariously stacked like a Jenga tower. Make one wrong move and it all comes toppling down.

I will walk out of Blaine with no car, no phone, no friends, and no idea how to navigate the confusing and conflicting requirements of three different parts of the same system.

It feels like a setup because failure at anything means I'm back in jail on a probation violation.

The early-release program also means I report to the jail every morning at eight to do yardwork and landscaping.

When I leave Blaine, my mom is waiting outside and takes me to breakfast. She has made the hour-and-a-half drive from her home in San Francisco, and I hope that she will stay longer, but after breakfast she drops me off at the probation department and leaves.

I give the woman at the front desk my name, and she looks at me blankly.

"I just got out of jail," I say. "They told me to come here and report in or get oriented or something. I have to do it within seventy-two hours, but I'm here today."

The woman has me wait in the lobby for over two hours and then finally the probation officer on duty comes out.

"You're here too soon," he says. "We don't have any paperwork from the jail yet. Come back in a few days."

"But I'm on the new work-release program and I have to be at the jail working from eight to four starting tomorrow. You guys aren't open before eight or after four."

"What's your name again?"

I tell him and then he has me follow him back to his desk. He gets on his computer.

"You just got out?"

"A few hours ago," I say.

"Yeah, we've already had a call about a probation violation. You

need to appear in criminal court, Department Three, at eight tomorrow morning. And drug court is at three on Fridays."

"What did I do? What probation violation?" I am shocked.

"I'm not your probation officer, you'll get assigned one once we get your paperwork. But you need to be in court tomorrow morning."

"I have to be working at the jail at eight," I say. "I just got out. I haven't done anything wrong."

He just shrugs.

"How," I ask him, "am I supposed to be in both places at once? What do I do? And drug court is at three but I'm supposed to do work release until four."

"Not our problem," he says. "But if you don't show up in court that's another probation violation."

I walk outside and sit on the front steps of the building. My body starts to shake, and I'm hyperventilating. The busy street in front of me narrows in my vision like I'm looking at it through a telescope. I watch the people passing by in their cars—running errands, going to work, getting lunch, driving their kids to and from activities. I bury my face in my hands and cry. I imagine throwing myself into the street, not to die, just to get injured, so a hospital will take me in, and nurses will take care of me.

I think about all the girls in the main jail who were released one day and then booked back in the next day for stealing, or fighting, or trespassing, or public drunkenness. One mother and daughter who were in G and then Blaine at the same time used to joke that it was the best home they ever had together. Only they weren't joking. I always questioned how they could be so stupid to land back in jail so soon, and now I know.

Alone on the outside makes together on the inside feel safer.

I sit there for an hour, and then I wipe my eyes and make a plan. First, back to the jail to tell them I have to be in court in the morning,

then I will walk to my public defender's office. I don't know if she's done with her maternity leave or even still my attorney now that I'm out, but she's the only one who might take my side and tell me what I should do.

DJ won't be released for a few weeks at least, and I know that if I can survive until then, my mother-in-law will help us find somewhere to live. Maybe lend us a car.

I just have to take the first step. And then another. And then another.

My attorney isn't in, but the receptionist tells me that Elizabeth will meet me at court in the morning and to get there fifteen minutes early so we can talk.

"Do you know what it's about?" I ask. "Do you know who called?"

"I have no idea, sorry."

That night I triple-lock myself into my room at the Hitching Post. Every surface is both greasy and dusty. *No double-scrub here*, I think. I only have the forty dollars that my mom put on my books so the jail would give me some cash when I was released, and I don't know how long that has to last. I don't have clothes for court. I don't know what I could already be in trouble for. How can I violate probation before I'm even signed up for it?

I consciously try to stay awake because I don't want to have nightmares in this strange place. Twenty-four hours ago, I was laughing and hopeful. Now I feel like prey.

chapter 14

ALL BUSES LEAD TO THE SAME PLACE

E lizabeth meets me at 8 a.m. in front of the courthouse. She is noticeably not pregnant, but we don't have time to chat about newborns, sleep schedules, breastfeeding, or any of the other experiences I would normally discuss with a new mother.

"Someone called Probation a half hour after you were released," she says, "and said you violated CPS terms."

"What did I do?" I ask in panic. "I was at the jail, went to breakfast, then Probation, then back to the jail, then went to your office."

"The caller said you were seen driving by Kaden's daycare. The caller knew that following CPS requirements is a part of your probation."

"I don't even have a car." Obviously, the person didn't know that. "I haven't even talked to anyone. I don't have a phone or a car or a way

to reach my boys to tell them I'm out. I wouldn't do that." I'm begging her, but I'm not sure what I'm begging her for. To believe me? To fight for me? My voice sounds high-pitched and shaky in my own ears. If I didn't know me better, I would think I was lying. "Who would make up something like that? Why would someone do that?"

Elizabeth pats my shoulder. "Look, anyone can make up anything and tell it to Probation. It happens all the time. People want revenge, or they just want to cause trouble for people when they get out of jail. They file false CPS reports. They file false probation violation reports. They make accusations."

My mind jumps through all the possibilities. I don't want to think Darcy would stoop so low, but while I'll never know, she's my most likely candidate. I want to scream. I want to cry.

I don't want to go back to jail.

"I would be on camera outside the jail," I say frantically. "Do they have cameras at Probation? I can prove I didn't go anywhere else but the main jail, breakfast, Probation, back to the main jail, and then to your office. I was in the lobby at the jail. I talked to the deputy on duty at the window. I can prove it! There will be a receipt from breakfast!" I'm angry, but my anger comes out as tears.

"It's okay," she says. "I'm going to go talk to the judge. I know you didn't drive by daycare. Sit in the courtroom and wait for me to call you up."

I follow her inside and sit near the door. A part of me wants to run. I'm going to be one of those girls who go back to jail the next day. The judge walks in, and I meet his eye. It's Judge Marigonda, the same judge who sentenced me.

Elizabeth, the assistant district attorney, and the probation officer all approach the bench. I can't hear what they are saying, but at times they all glance in my direction. I eye the bailiff nervously. I've done

nothing wrong, but I feel guilty and stare with mounting dread at the handcuffs on his belt.

After about fifteen minutes, the ADA and probation officer go back to their table, and Elizabeth waves me up.

"Ms. Love," the judge acknowledges me.

My mouth is too dry to speak so I just nod.

"Ms. Love, we understand you have been released early for good behavior and as part of the work-release program."

"Yes, Your Honor." My voice is small and weak.

"Ms. Love, we have decided to modify your sentence."

I look over at my attorney desperately and take a big inhale to speak, but she shakes her head at me and smiles at the judge.

"We are going to take you out of drug court and send you to Family Preservation Court. You have probation requirements and requirements from the CPS court and will also have requirements from Family Pres-ervation Court. I want to see you in my courtroom the morning after every appearance you have in Family Preservation Court. Commissioner Siegel oversees that court, so I will be getting updates from him directly on your progress. If you mess up, you will be remanded. Is that clear?"

I nod.

"I need a verbal answer, Ms. Love."

"Yes, Your Honor."

"I saw you walking to Probation yesterday as I was driving to the courthouse," the judge adds.

I nod again.

"I saw with my own eyes that you didn't have a car, nor were you driving by a daycare at the same time I was driving by you. You have a big uphill battle in front of you, Ms. Love, but I trust you are up to the task. I was also happy to see you at the Gemma graduation. We're going to be seeing a lot of each other now."

I swallow nervously.

"Thank you, Your Honor," my attorney says.

I mumble "Thank you" and turn toward the door.

"Wait for me outside," Elizabeth whispers.

In the hallway I blink at the bright lights, not sure what has just transpired.

When Elizabeth emerges from the courtroom, she pulls me to a quiet area in the hall where her husband, Jonathan, joins us. I haven't seen him since my sentencing. "They know the call was a fake," says Jonathan. "So you don't have to worry."

"But what about the next call?" I ask. "Can anyone just call Probation and lie about me?" My freedom, so newly won, feels fragile. What a fool I was to believe that I only had to do the right thing and it would all be okay.

Elizabeth and Jonathan have no answer for me.

"What is Family Preservation Court?" I ask. "And why did I get moved there?"

"Look, your husband is going to be out in a few weeks," says Elizabeth. "The court and Probation want to separate you from him. He will be in drug court, and you will go to Family Preservation Court, which includes outpatient treatment at night, testing, and court appearances on your progress, with the CPS attorneys and social workers in attendance. It's a good thing. It's a reward. It will help you get your son back sooner."

"But what about getting my record cleared and getting off probation when I finish and all the other benefits of drug court?" I ask. "Will I lose those?"

"No, you're not being punished. They want you to succeed. And they think you'll have a better chance of succeeding if you're in a different program from your husband. Although I've never heard of a criminal court wanting you to appear every time you have Family

Preservation Court. Marigonda really wants to be able to lock you up if you relapse, like they do in drug court."

"Will you be there in criminal court with me?" I don't understand how probation works or if public defenders are still your defenders after you get out of jail.

"One of us will be there. We represent you."

"But how do you get paid?"

"We are private attorneys, but we contract with the county public defenders' office. You and your husband couldn't have attorneys from the same place. It's a conflict."

I nod. I don't know why I didn't know this ten months ago, but it makes sense.

"You can't relapse," says Elizabeth. "Drug court only locks you up for the weekend. I have no idea what this judge will do. He could put you away for much longer as a probation violation. You don't have the wiggle room of drug court."

I'm not worried about relapsing—I know my rock bottom has been bad enough. I won't mess up. I take a deep breath.

"Does DJ know I am out?"

"He's not our problem," says Elizabeth.

"I know, but . . ."

"He shouldn't be yours either." Elizabeth says this softly, and Jonathan nods.

"Well, does the jail know I'm here or am I in trouble with them already?"

"You can leave work release if you have court, or if Probation calls you in, or if you have to drug test. Just tell them in the lobby the day before or if you get called in to test, just let them know who's requiring it that day so they can confirm. You can explain why you're late today, and if they're worried about it, they will confirm with Probation."

It seems complicated and inefficient, but I nod.

"We have to go. Call the office if you have any questions."

"Thanks," I say. I don't add that I don't have a cell phone because I am tired of my own voice bringing up problems.

~

I am more fucked than I thought.

On Thursday I go to Family Preservation Court as a requirement of probation. There, I learn that one requirement of Family Preservation Court is attending Sobriety Works—an outpatient three-night-a-week-for-three-hours program at the other end of the county. Every Monday, Tuesday, and Thursday night for a year I will go to group treatment, be drug tested by yet another entity, attend outside twelve-step meetings, and meet with a private counselor.

CPS also requires me to meet with a different private therapist.

Probation doesn't care about therapy, but they do require me to get a job and go to a different set of meetings.

I have no idea how I'll manage all my new responsibilities: going to three different courtrooms, pee testing for multiple agencies at different sites, seeing two therapists, going to twelve-step meetings, working at the jail, and supervised visits with Kaden. I write lists of each agency's requirements, cross-reference them against each other, and tape them to the wall of my motel room like a murder board.

Every Thursday morning I go to Family Preservation Court, where the judge and the CPS social workers and Sobriety Works treatment counselors will discuss how I did that week, check that I've been going to recovery meetings, and log it all into the system that will feed into CPS court and criminal court. On Friday mornings I go to criminal court and stand in front of Judge Marigonda, so he can read the report from the Family Preservation Court judge and tell me whether I have

fucked up and am going back to jail. Both judges then send reports to the CPS court judge.

So many judges, so little time.

~

I've never been great at peeing on demand, so all this random drug testing requires me to hydrate excessively each day. It's a pain, but on the plus side, my skin looks fabulous.

It's stressful not having a car and never knowing when you are going to be required to trek across the county to a drug test. It's a full-time job meeting all the requirements—complicated by the fact that one of the requirements is getting a full-time job.

The first time I have to take the bus across town for Sobriety Works, I give myself two hours to travel the eight or so miles. I haven't been to Aptos since I was arrested, and I live in fear of running into one of my former neighbors. I know they would never take the bus, but still I'm afraid someone will recognize me. In my mind, everyone who looks at me for more than half a second knows that I am the neighbor from hell.

There's a fine line between shame and narcissism.

At the bus stop, I try to make sense of the schedule, the bus numbers, and the routes, but it might as well be hieroglyphics. It's raining, and I jump on the first bus heading south. After more than an hour, it pulls into a large mall halfway to Aptos. Everyone gets off but me.

"Last stop," says the bus driver.

"But I'm trying to get to Aptos. The seventy-one is supposed to go to Aptos." I say this with more conviction than I feel, because I'm not even sure I'm on the 71.

"This isn't the bus to Aptos."

"When is the next bus to Aptos?"

"Look at the schedule, but probably not for another thirty minutes. Maybe more."

"Can't you take me to Aptos?"

"I'm not a taxi, this is a public bus." He shakes his head.

"But I didn't know I had to get off here . . ." I don't know why I am telling him this. He has nothing to do with the obstacle course I have to run every day.

"All buses go to the same place," he says.

I don't know what to say to this. For some reason, it strikes me as profound. Like a black-and-white photo, or anything said in a British accent. But it also drains me of hope.

This moment breaks me. The darkness outside, the fact that I will be late to my first night at Sobriety Works, and all the horrible consequences I imagine has me ugly crying in the back of a bus. I don't have a car, a job, a friend, a partner, an ally. I don't have anyone to help me get where I need to go in this new life of mine. Even when I get Kaden back, I won't have a home to fit the rest of my boys. All I've focused on is getting out and getting Kaden back. That is how I've triaged my life. But always in the back of my mind this painful truth has lurked. Never again can I wake them up in the morning for school, nag them to do their homework, curl up on a couch and watch a movie with them. I can't pick them up from school, drive them to their basketball games, or sit in their room at night and talk about their day.

I have lost my three older boys in those ways forever. And I miss them so much I can't breathe. I miss being their mom. I hate myself for what I have done to them. Kaden may be young enough to forget, but my older boys never will.

I am their torment, the source of their shame. I will be their college essay topic and the star of their therapy sessions for years to come.

And now I am lost on a bus at an empty mall on a Monday night,

grieving for the life I took for granted, grieving for my children, grieving for all the mundane moments that now feel like lost treasure.

The driver interrupts my tearful reverie. "This is the end of the line. You have to get off."

His face in the rearview mirror looks worried and maybe slightly afraid.

He looks over his shoulder at me.

"Seriously, you need to get off."

I wipe my eyes as I walk toward the front of the bus.

"I'm sorry," he mumbles as I pass him.

"No, I'm sorry," I say, and I rush down the stairs into the rainy night.

~

The only good thing about working outside the main jail all day is that it's exhausting. I doze off early at the Hitching Post and sleep dreamlessly. I'm also happy that there are cameras outside the jail. I make sure to walk directly in front of them every two hours and go inside to ask the officer on duty a random question about the weed whacker or the pruning shears or whether there are more gloves handy.

I need to make sure nobody can say I am somewhere I'm not. The fear of someone calling Probation again has turned me chatty. Every night before I go to sleep, I write down who I talked to and at what times and what I did all day. The days turn into weeks, and I discover that I love blowing autumn leaves with the leaf blower. It's the only thing that makes me feel powerful.

I have the leaf blower backpack on during my last day of work release when I feel a hand on my shoulder. I turn around and it's DJ. His head is completely shaved.

I drop the backpack and give him a big hug.

"What are you doing?"

"They let me out a few days early," he says.

"Are you . . . okay?" I ask. I scrutinize him for signs of drug use, but he looks clear-eyed and healthy.

"All good," he says.

"How did you get here?"

He tilts his head toward the parking lot where his mom sits in her Mercedes. "What time are you done?"

"Four p.m. It's my last day."

"I know. I think that's why they held me until now. I should have been out on work release too."

"I think they are trying to separate us. Did you know I got moved to Family Preservation Court instead of drug court?"

"Yeah, Maya told me. It's some more bullshit."

"I think it's good. It's going to help us get Kaden back."

He wraps his arms around me tightly. "Nobody is going to separate us again. They can do what they want. It's me and you."

I murmur agreement and rest my head on his shoulder. It feels good to not be alone, but I close my eyes so I can pretend I feel more than that for the husband I have not seen in such a long time.

"We'll be back to get you at four p.m. My mom is going to help us find a place."

"Are you serious?"

"Yep. I told you I'd take care of things."

I look over at Carol in the car and give her a big smile and a wave. Finding a place is the first step to getting Kaden back, and I'm so grateful she's willing to help. My mind flashes on all the girls in G who won't have help finding a place so they can get their babies back. There's Section 8 housing, but the waitlist is three years long. I applied for it from G, but with a wait that long almost everyone's CPS clocks would run out before they get bumped up the list. Then you have to find a landlord willing to take a voucher, and those landlords are rare.

"We only need a one-bedroom," I say, "so Kaden can have his own

room, and we can sleep on a futon in the living room. Maybe even a studio, and we could divide it. He needs his own room in some way." My mind is racing. *What does CPS require? What does Kaden need to feel like he's home?* I know that he needs me, but I am not enough for CPS.

"We're going to look for places while you finish up. Try to find something we can look at in person today. My mom's booked us a hotel until we find a place."

"I have a few more days at the Hitching Post . . ."

"There is no way I'm staying at the Hitching Post. We'll grab all your stuff from there too."

"Okay . . ."

It feels disconcerting to have someone else making decisions for me suddenly. It's another big change, and any change right now gives me vertigo.

"And what the hell did you do to your hair?" asks DJ.

I could ask him the same question, but instead I touch my head self-consciously. Last week, I bought a four-dollar box of brown hair dye and darkened my hair in my Hitching Post bathroom. "I don't want people recognizing me," I say. "I feel like I'm getting stared at a lot on the bus. I want to be anonymous."

"Fuck those people," says DJ.

I'm afraid of *those people*. Maybe people don't see the "neighbor from hell" when they stare at me, or maybe they do. All I see when I look in the mirror is that headline staring back at me. I don't want to be who I am, and the brown hair helps. I look in the mirror and I don't recognize the scared, anxious, brown-haired girl looking back at me.

I was worried about how Kaden might react to my new hair color, but he hadn't even noticed. When we're together, we're just looking in each other's eyes and playing and talking and laughing. I could be bald and he wouldn't care. I'm just his mom and he's just my KK, my "Cakes," and we don't care about anything but being together. Dylan,

Cody, and Ty came to see me at the motel, and they were happy but cautious, especially Dylan. "Trust is something you have to earn, Mom," he said, and he's right. All I can do is show up each day and do the next right thing.

I don't care if DJ hates my hair. Plus, if someone calls Probation with a fake report, they'll give the wrong description of me.

My brown hair is my biggest safety net right now.

~

Carol helps us rent a four-hundred-square-foot apartment, and we move in a week later. She lends us a car too. The rent is a thousand dollars a month. Our mortgage used to be more than five times that, but now I have no idea how we will pay. Carol will help us for a few months, but we both need jobs. I have no idea how to find a job that will hire a felon, much less allow me to leave on any given day for one to three hours depending on whether Probation, Family Preservation Court, or CPS demands a drug test. Since it's all County-related, you would think one of the agencies could do the random drug testing and share the results with the others, but it doesn't work that way.

After two months of supervised visits and drug tests and drug court for DJ and Family Preservation Court for me, our social worker comes to inspect our apartment. It's only one bedroom, but I deck that out with books and art supplies and a bunk bed with a slide that I know Kaden will love. Some of it is stuff from our old house, others are things I find at Goodwill and the dollar store and garage sales.

You can pretty much see the whole apartment once you step in the door, but I show our CPS worker the entire place like I am giving a grand tour. It's not much. It's not fancy. But it has a bedroom for Kaden, I explain. It's safe. It's a home. I show her how the futon turns into a bed and say that's where we will sleep while Kaden has the bedroom. I doubt he will sleep on his own, but I don't tell her that.

After the tour, she says she will allow unsupervised visits, then over-nights. If all goes well, we can be reunified before his fifth birthday in December.

This feels like the first victory I've had in a year.

"It's a cute place," she says. "I'll see you in Family Preservation Court next week." I thank her profusely.

DJ is standing behind me during this exchange, and as soon as she leaves he goes into the bathroom.

I can see Kaden living here. I can see reading him books as he falls asleep. Two more months and I'll be able to breathe again. Sleep again. I open the bathroom door to tell my husband how excited I am, how for the first time I see a glimmer of a path forward, how I feel hope again.

He startles when I burst in. It takes me a while to register what I'm seeing. A mirror, white lines of powder on the mirror, a rolled-up dollar bill.

I have no words.

"I failed my drug test," he says. "Drug court is remanding me for the weekend."

"What do you mean they're remanding you?" I ask. I know what *remanding* means; it means the bailiffs are going to take him back to jail and lock him up. What I don't understand is how this could be happening. How he could say he's taking care of us and then do this.

"I tested dirty, so I have to go back to jail from tonight until Monday morning." He says this slowly, as if I'm an idiot, and shrugs like it's no big deal.

"What did you test dirty for?"

"Heroin."

I point at the white lines on the mirror. "What is that?"

He looks surprised at the question.

"It's no big deal."

It's a big fucking deal to me. I feel stupid for not knowing. For somehow thinking we were on the same page. That we were a team. That he had finally changed.

If I stay with DJ, I will end up back in jail, and I will lose Kaden. I can't go back, and I won't lose him.

"Get out," I say quietly. "Take all your stuff. Take the car your mom gave us. Get out."

"It's no big deal," he insists. "I'm snorting my antidepressants. I just did heroin once last week with my homeboy from jail. That's why I tested dirty. This is just my antidepressant."

"You have ten minutes to get all your stuff."

He swears and punches the bathroom door.

"Eight minutes."

He piles his things into the car. I know his mom won't pay the rent now that I've kicked him out. I know that without a car it will be hard to get to all the courthouses and drug tests and therapy sessions, but I will find a way.

He pulls a towel from the closet and stacks it on his suitcase. His face is red except for the dusting of white powder around his nostrils.

"You hypocrite. You're just looking for a way out of this marriage. You're making a huge mistake, you heartless bitch!" he shouts.

I don't have anything to say to that, but I'm not heartless. I'm Mama Love, so I open the linen closet, pull out a washcloth, and place it on top of his towel.

He slams the front door as he leaves, and I rush to lock it.

In jail it's not okay to snitch, but I'm not in jail anymore.

My hands shake as I dial our CPS worker, but my voice is strong as I tell her everything.

chapter 15

JOINT
AND
SEVERAL

I get word that Kaden will be allowed to move in with me right before his fifth birthday. Darcy brings over all his clothing vacuum-sealed in clear plastic bags. Right now she controls access to my older boys, so I smile at her and pretend I have forgotten all the ways I believe she tried to thwart this reunification.

"I'm not sure what I will do for his birthday, but you're welcome to come," I say.

She smiles a big fake smile and looks around my minuscule apartment. "You might want to do something at my house. Well, in the yard. I don't want you in my house."

I fake smile back at her while Kaden grips my hand tightly.

When she leaves he and I just look at each other.

"Do you want to cuddle?" I ask. "Read a book?"

He just holds his arms out to me. I pick him up and he clings to me and nestles his head in my neck. I carry him to the couch, and he

stays wrapped around me as I sit. I kiss his head and face and soak in the warmth of him. We've had two overnight visits, but he knows today that he doesn't have to go back. As long as I don't do drugs, we can stay together forever.

And then I remember all the probation requirements that can send me back to jail even if I do nothing wrong. A missed phone call. A missed test. A missed check-in at court. Anyone calling at any time to make something up about me.

But today he is with me, and I try to remain in the power of now.

I rock him and murmur sweet words into the top of his head.

We sit like this until he falls asleep in my arms. The memory of him sobbing and CPS pulling him away from my handcuffed arms flickers across my mind like it always does when I have a quiet moment, but I will it away. I vow silently to do everything I can to make this last year up to him.

My arms go numb holding him while he sleeps, but I will not disturb him by moving.

When he wakes up, we walk the two feet into our miniature kitchen, where I get him grapes and make him a sandwich. We sit at the tiny Formica table I found at a garage sale "Free" pile, and I ask him what he wants to do for his birthday.

He shrugs shyly.

"Hold on," I say. "I got you something!"

I run to his room and grab a balloon I bought at the dollar store. Kaden loves balloons, and he loves to play a game he calls pack attack, where you hit the balloon back and forth to keep it from touching the ground.

"We can play pack attack," I say, handing him the balloon.

He carefully cradles it in his hands.

"Thank you," he says solemnly.

He sets the balloon on the table, walks over to me, and wraps his arms around my waist. I hug him back, not knowing why he is so serious.

"Of course," I say brightly.

He looks up at me, all blond hair and blue eyes and chubby cheeks. "Thank you, Mommy. I love my birthday present."

I see what the last year has done to him. A single balloon is the most he can imagine from me.

"It's just a balloon," I assure him. "Not your birthday present."

"It's okay," he says, but I hear the doubt in his voice.

"I was thinking we could get some Star Wars Legos," I say, "and then we can build a spaceship!"

"Really?"

"Yes, really!" I give him big, loud smooches. He laughs at the smooches and then turns and grabs the balloon.

"Pack attack!" he yells.

I dive to keep it from hitting the ground and yell "Pack attack" as I send it soaring into the living room. He laughs and runs after it, and we spend the next hour chasing it around our tiny apartment.

Later that night when he's asleep, I swallow my pride and call Darcy. I ask her if I can set up a bouncy house in her yard for Kaden's birthday. I then ask her if I can speak to my older boys, and they agree to help me set up a treasure hunt on the beach for Kaden as well.

For Dylan's fifth birthday I had a huge party with Big Bird from *Sesame Street* and pony rides for all the kids. For Cody's fifth birthday we went to Disneyland. For Ty's fifth birthday we had a giant pool party and costumed Barney the Purple Dinosaur.

I stay awake almost all night, constantly checking on Kaden while he sleeps and wondering how I'm going to pay for a bouncy house and a birthday party and Legos. I know presents shouldn't matter to me,

but they do. Five is a big birthday and I missed his birthday last year. And Christmas. And everything for all my boys. I've been so focused on the acute crisis of not losing Kaden that I haven't begun to tackle the chronic problem of creating a home for all my boys. I need a big house. I need space for them. I'm embarrassed at the idea they will be embarrassed by where I live right now. I spent so much of my child-hood embarrassed by my family, and now I think my own boys must be embarrassed to have me as their mom. I'm certainly embarrassed to be me.

A part of me simply wants to give up. Call it. Game over. I will never be the mom they deserve. And another part of me knows I'm just feeling raw and hypersensitive and sober and alone. I want to give up, but I won't.

One birthday party at a time.

~

Every time I close my eyes over the next few weeks, I see Kaden's face turned up to mine in gratitude for a dollar-store balloon.

Within weeks his good behavior, his excessive politeness, ends. He is eating well, which is a relief, but now he offers up tantrums and random bursts of anger. I theorize that subconsciously he's trying to push me away just to see if I go. He tests me every chance he gets, and through it all I try to remain steady and nonreactive. I tell the CPS-ordered therapist that his rage is a relief.

"Why?" she asks.

"Because the good behavior meant that he thought his bad be-havior had caused our separation. That I left him on purpose because of something he did. I'd much rather he blame me than blame him-self."

She nods but, like a therapist, doesn't indicate whether I'm right or wrong.

"He thought I got him a dollar-store balloon for his birthday," I say.

"That sounds like a fine birthday present."

"No, it was the look on his face. He was so sad and serious and he was . . . he was caretaking me in that moment. I grew up thinking I was responsible for everybody else in my family—that their well-being depended on me. I can't have him think that, I just can't!"

I didn't mean to say all that. She works for the court and I need to focus only on Kaden's well-being.

"Trauma is tricky," she observes.

"Well, what should I do?"

She tilts her head in the way only basset hounds and therapists do.

"What do you think you should do?"

If I were president I would sign an executive order never allowing therapists or anyone to answer a question with a question. Especially not this question. If people knew what to do, would therapy even be a profession?

She must see the look of disgust on my face because she basset-hounds her head to the other side, turns over a sheet of paper on her clipboard, and clears her throat. "You might want to consider working to process your own trauma."

"What trauma?"

"Well, to start there is the trauma of your arrest, being in jail, Kaden being in the system."

"That's not trauma," I say. "I caused all that. All those things are *my fault*, not *my trauma*."

"Trauma is complex . . ."

"Will Kaden be okay?" I interrupt her.

"Like I said, he's a perfectly normal child. Five-year-olds have tantrums and meltdowns all the time. This is normal behavior. Don't read into it too much." She flips through his folder. "He does well in preschool, he's sweet, he's communicative, he laughs a lot, he plays, he

has friends, he's eating, he's sleeping, he's a happy and well-adjusted little boy, and he obviously loves you."

It's hard for me to believe it could be true. I desperately want it to be true.

The therapist clears her throat and sets the folder down.

"But tell me, how are *you* sleeping? When is the last time *you* laughed and played with anyone besides Kaden? Do *you* have friends?"

"What do you think?" I ask, tilting my head pointedly to the side.

~

I am nervous for our next CPS court hearing. Kaden is living with me full time, and as hard as it has been to meet all my requirements alone, it's even harder to do it with a five-year-old in tow. I was a single mom of three boys for almost ten years before I married DJ so I am no stranger to the challenges, but without a job, money, a car, or a friend it is like I am running an obstacle course designed by a sadist while carrying a five-year-old on my back. I can't put him down. I don't want to put him down. But we are clinging so tightly to each other that it's hard for either of us to get enough air to run this marathon.

A friend of my mom's has an old car she doesn't want. It barely runs, but it's mine if I can get up to San Francisco and drive it back home. I have to go to traffic court to get my license reinstated because I couldn't fix an expired registration fix-it ticket while I was in jail so my license was suspended. It's another fine I must add to the growing list of court fees that amount to service charges for being on proba-tion, for being monitored by the courts, for paperwork that's been filed. I can't opt out of these. These charges are yet another way the system makes it seemingly impossible to get past my past.

But my next visit to CPS court makes me think I can put my past behind me. Judge Guy has long brown hair, big brown eyes, and a warm smile. Our massive files are stacked before her, and she peers

out at us over the top of them. She quickly observes and interprets the fact that, for the first time in this courtroom, DJ and I are not sitting together.

"Both parents are responsible for meeting the reunification requirements individually," she reminds us.

"But do we both have to?" I quickly whisper to my new CPS attorney whose name I don't even know. "What if DJ doesn't do anything? What if he relapses? What if he's in jail?"

Judge Guy seems to know what I am whispering because before my attorney can even respond she says, "I'd like to remind all parties that this court also has the power to determine custody matters, both legal and physical. That can be done here and not in family divorce court. That can be settled prior to divorce court proceedings."

I let this sink in. If I meet all the requirements, I can get permanent custody of Kaden regardless of what DJ does or doesn't do.

Judge Guy asks me how Kaden is doing now that he's living with me. I report on his progress, and she tells me I'm doing a great job. She doesn't address DJ. I latch on to her validation like a life raft.

When the hearing is over, my attorney tells me that if I do all the work, DJ's actions will have no effect on Kaden's custody situation. "He can do drugs, go to jail, whatever he wants. If you have sole custody, it will be up to you to protect Kaden, to show you will do that even if it means keeping him from his father. If you don't, they can take him again."

It is one more weight I must carry. Kaden and his dad love each other, but I may have to keep them apart to keep Kaden.

~

Somehow, DJ graduates drug court early. I'm still on probation with two months left at Sobriety Works, but he's done with probation, with random drug tests, and the obligation to pay back our debts. The

probation department has even given him a thousand dollars, presumably to help him get back on his feet. Never mind that his mother is bankrolling him.

When he gloats about this bonus over the phone, I shoot back, "Why would they do that? What about our restitution? You're not supposed to get off probation until all restitution is paid."

"I don't know why, it's part of drug court. I didn't ask questions; I took the money. But our restitution is now your restitution."

"The restitution is joint and several," I say. "We're responsible together and equally."

"I'm off probation, which means I don't have to pay anything. The 'several' means you. You are responsible now."

The unfairness of this has me shaking. I'm so angry, but my anger always comes out in tears and a wobbly voice. "You aren't going to help?" I ask. "You're going to make me pay it all back myself?"

"My mom paid part of it so we could get our plea, that was my share."

"She paid that for both of us, for Kaden."

"Nope."

Paying off thousands of dollars all by myself is impossible. I will be on probation forever.

"Can you even look at yourself in the mirror right now?" I try to say this with righteous force, but it comes out weak and unsteady. Not the effect I was going for.

"Half that money is bullshit money for things we didn't do. I'm not paying anything."

"So I'm going to take care of Kaden, do everything for CPS, pay back the money, while you do . . . what?" I walk out the back door of our apartment so Kaden can't hear me. The minute I am outside, my voice matches the anger I feel. I am yelling. "Shoot heroin with your ridiculous homeboys? You grew up in fucking Los Gatos! You're going

to dress like you're a gangster now and go in and out of jail like it's what, cool? What gang do you represent again . . . the mortgage broker gang? The mommy-pays-your-rent crew?"

I sound ridiculous even to myself, but it's easier to get mad than to feel betrayed, abandoned, lost, alone.

After I slam the phone down, I take Kaden for a walk. We walk away from the beach toward Santa Cruz. It's only when we are a block away from the Gemma offices that I realize where I've been going. Gemma. Cassandra. Graduation. The last place I felt welcomed and celebrated. There's a new executive director named Cynthia who I don't know very well but who invites me into her office. She offers Kaden some toys, and he plays in a sitting area next to her office while I vent and spew to her about all my struggles.

"But you're doing it," she points out. "You are showing up every day and doing it."

"I'm so tired," I moan, and tears start to come. I quickly wipe them away.

"Of course you're tired." She looks through the open door at Kaden and then back at me. "But you're winning. You've already won. Look how much you've done in such a short time."

I nod and try to muster some sense of accomplishment, of pride, but I'm still wading in the unfairness of DJ's situation versus mine.

"I'm pretty sure you haven't made it this far by feeling sorry for yourself."

I laugh at this tough-love comment. Cynthia has multicolored hair and is short and small and beautiful. She also seems like a straight-shooter, which I appreciate.

"Definitely not," I say.

"Well then, it's probably not time to start. Besides, there's a lot of women who have it a lot worse." She glances over at Kaden, who stands in the open doorway, and gives him a big smile.

"I have cookies," she says. "Let's have some cookies."

So we have a picnic on her floor, and Kaden tells her about his bunk bed and how he wants to make curtains around them.

"I'm excellent at making curtains," she says. "Why don't we go to the fabric store?"

Kaden jumps up and down with excitement and looks at me to ask if it's okay.

"Let's go to the fabric store, then," I shout.

Cookies, curtains, and a new friend. Such simple gifts really, but they're just what I needed to get through another day.

~

I graduate Sobriety Works and Family Preservation Court, and a few months later Judge Guy gives me permanent custody of Kaden. As amazing as it feels, it also feels anticlimactic. Every waking moment was devoted to getting him back—it was all survival and struggle and fight. And now the war is suddenly over, and I don't know how to settle into a normal life.

I don't even know what a normal life is supposed to look like.

Maybe I never did.

~

When I ask my new probation officer about getting off probation and getting my record expunged, he tells me that's only for people in drug court, not Family Preservation Court.

"But I was moved out of drug court as a reward. I was promised the same benefits in Family Preservation Court."

"There's nothing in the case notes about that. There's no order from the judge about that."

"But my codefendant . . ."

"He was in drug court."

Yet again, I'm facing brutal and inexplicable inequity, and yet again, I can do nothing about it. I will be on probation for the next five years. At any time, I can be called in to drug test. Any member of law enforcement can search my home and person and car and computer at any time. I can't leave the county without permission. I have to pay off court fees and fines, which have compounding interest monthly, and I have to pay all remaining restitution.

Normal is still a long way off. And I was a fool to think the war had really ended.

chapter 16

FUCKING GOOGLE

In the real world, one graduate degree does not trump one felony, much less thirty-two.

Because one of my felonies is for drug possession, I can't get any cash welfare benefits. The welfare system automatically assumes anyone with a prior drug conviction will spend their money on dope rather than rent, utilities, gas, and food. It doesn't matter that all my drug tests are clean, or that I'm a graduate of Sobriety Works. The conviction is on my record and that's the only context that matters. If I had gone to drug court this wouldn't be an issue—my record would have been expunged. The only way around this is to go back to court, appeal this particular conviction, and get it reduced to a misdemeanor.

Another giant hurdle that my short legs can't clear. Plus, I don't have childcare and the idea of bringing Kaden to criminal court is untenable. I couldn't leave him sitting in the back of the courtroom while I stand in front of the judge. And what if something went wrong and they tried to take me back to jail? I can catastrophize at an Olympic

level, and I imagine him sitting alone in the back of the courtroom while I am dragged away in handcuffs.

Every job I apply for asks me to check a box if I have a criminal record and then explain the charges. There's not enough space on the application to list all my convictions. And, like welfare, there's no room for context in these applications, and certainly no place to explain that as long as I'm not on drugs I am a valuable and productive member of society worthy of employment. Online I check the box even though I know it means I'll be automatically screened out.

I could choose not to check the box, but, unfortunately, my recovery program is built on a foundation of rigorous honesty.

Rigorous honesty seems great in principle, but it doesn't translate well to a job search. Or the dating scene, where I'm not having much luck either. It's hard enough for any soon-to-be-twice-divorced mom of four to hook up, but add the *Sentinel* headline and my criminal history, and my dating profile should just show a picture of a red flag. I'm lonely but resigned to the fact my future will not contain romance. I also know that picking great life partners is not part of my skill set.

Sometimes, I sit on the back porch after Kaden is asleep and imagine someone loving me again. But the idea is as distant and unreachable as the stars I stare at. I feed my melancholy by listening to sad Irish love ballads by David Gray and sad American love ballads by John Mayer.

A part of me just loves to wallow.

Kaden starts kindergarten, and I am on high alert at back-to-school night and parent-teacher meetings, searching for signs that anyone recognizes me or knows about my past. He makes friends easily, but when other parents want to organize playdates I am at a loss. I'm embarrassed by my tiny apartment, and I don't want to face the prospect of taking Kaden to their homes and making the small talk

that would either reveal my felonious, addictive past or break my code of rigorous honesty.

I enroll Kaden in a subsidized after-school program for working parents so he gets to socialize, and I get to be just one of many harried parents trying to afford childcare who have no time or energy to make new friends or linger over coffee. We wave to each other at pickup, but it's from a safe distance.

Cynthia from Gemma calls and says she has a temporary job for me, and I lunge at the opportunity. She wants me to case-manage other formerly incarcerated women with minor children and help them find jobs in the community under a state grant for the Community Action Board. CAB is the nonprofit agency that the Gemma Program runs under. It's barely enough money to pay the rent, but it pays the rent.

My job is to convince employers to hire the formerly incarcerated, match women with the employers, and then case-manage the women so they don't fuck it up. Basically I have to Mama Love them into compliance—make sure they go to meetings, get out of toxic relationships that might interfere with their employment, help them find the right clothes, and coach them on how to act in different professional settings. I listen to their problems and work with them to find solutions. I do the same with employers. In theory, it seems like a no-brainer for business owners because half the employee's pay comes from the grant money, but most of my job with the employers is convincing them that a formerly incarcerated woman makes the best employee.

And it's easy, because they do.

Someone who's been behind bars already knows that crime doesn't pay. They've lost everything and appreciate the simple joy of having a job. They've dealt with prison politics, so office politics present no challenge. They understand power structures. Each is on probation

or parole, so they follow all the rules. They're used to getting up early and working hard for no pay, so they appreciate minimum wage. But most important, every one of them has something to prove. That they are valuable, worthy, and so much more than a criminal record.

I know this about them because I am them.

I met extremely smart women in jail—CEO-level smart. Former drug dealers who were sales and marketing geniuses, others who were hustlers and designers and innovators. I'd like to see Elon Musk design Ikea-level modular furniture out of Tampax boxes and toothpaste. I challenge any beauty influencer to create a full glam makeover out of hot water and a box of colored pencils. Or any Michelin-starred chef to make a delicious meal out of Cheetos, ramen, leftover hard-boiled eggs, hot water, and mystery meat.

I'm not great at advocating for myself, but I'm really good at advocating for others, and I make some great matches in the business community. I help the women I manage form a co-op with other women in the program to help with childcare. I reach out to other nonprofits to help with résumés, business clothing, and transportation vouchers. Arden loves books, so I find her a job at a local bookstore. Hannah tells me about her childhood love of horses—the thing that gave her meaning before meth took over—and I find work for her at an equine therapy program. After her wage subsidy runs out, they keep her on and promote her.

The women work harder than is asked, always taking pride in their jobs and exceeding expectations. By all measures, the grant is a success, but, for reasons I cannot guess, the state doesn't renew it.

During my work for CAB, I see that my struggles are hardly mine alone. The barriers to becoming productive members of society are huge for just about anybody who's been incarcerated. As a condition of probation or parole you have to have a job; to get a job you have to check that box that says you have a criminal record, which excludes

you from getting a job. In order to show up to work every day you need somewhere to live; to find somewhere to live, you must have a job. The system is cobbled together out of catch-22s. I learn that if you've been incarcerated, you're ten times more likely to be homeless, and if you're homeless, you're eleven times more likely to become incarcerated.

It's a crazy loop-the-loop that's somehow overlooked in all the conversations about how to reduce recidivism. The system is illogical in its design, broken in its execution, and guaranteed to fail those it allegedly serves.

~

When the grant ends, my job ends. I'm back where I started, which is nowhere.

Until Cynthia comes to my rescue again. She calls me shortly after the grant runs out and tells me Cassandra is leaving her position as program director of Gemma.

"I want you to apply for the job," she says.

"Are you crazy?"

"No, you're perfect for it. You know the program, you know the needs of the women in jail, you've been advocating for incarcerated women, and you have experience developing curriculum from teaching in graduate school."

When she puts it that way, I consider it. "What do I need to do?"

"First, you formally apply. And then there will be a series of interviews with me, with CAB, with the sheriff's office and the probation department. All of them contribute to funding the Gemma Program. I love working with you, you're amazing, and this is perfect."

The pay is twenty-two dollars an hour, which feels like a fortune. I know I will have to find childcare two mornings a week so Kaden can be brought to school while I pick up the women from Blaine Street in

the Gemma van and take them to the church. It's an obstacle, but I'll figure that out after I get the job.

My résumé is impressive if you ignore the felonies, and I've finally found a job that ignores them. I make it through three rounds of interviews. My final interview is with the deputy whose office I used to clean—whose mother I used to talk to. She's in charge of the jail now, and she is a tough interrogator, but I can tell by the smile and hug she gives me at the end that I nailed it.

Before Cynthia calls to officially offer me the job, I've already made lists of potential volunteers and classes that will help the women deal with life after incarceration. I know these women and what they need, because I know what I didn't know and what I needed.

I imagine this being my new career—advocate, changemaker, champion of the underdogs. I think back to the sunny winter day when I sat in Elizabeth's office newly out on bail and heard about the plea deal. Then I still believed, like the twelve million other people who were arrested that year and the two million who were behind bars, that paying for your crimes meant doing your time and following Probation's orders, and then your debt was paid.

I had no idea how wrong I was, and I wanted to do my part to change that.

I've told everyone about my new job—my mom, the boys, my probation officer. Cynthia calls me on a Monday to tell me my business cards have arrived, and I can start in a week. On Friday morning, I'm just about to go to a twelve-step meeting when Cynthia calls again.

"Hello, boss lady," I answer.

"Hi," she says. "Where are you?"

"I'm just about to go into a meeting."

"I have bad news," she says. "I'm so sorry."

My stomach flips. "What is it?"

I sit down under a tree.

"You can't have the job."

"What? Why?"

"It came from Probation. They said there is no way someone on probation is going to be allowed to take women out of Blaine and supervise them."

"But Probation was part of the interview process," I say. "This doesn't make sense. Probation was aware of this every step of the way."

Cynthia is quiet for a while. "It's coming from higher up. There's nothing I can do."

Tom, my old boyfriend, is still the district attorney. His wife is still high up in Probation. I ask if it was her.

"I don't know who it was. All I know is we can't hire you for the job."

"You can," I beg. "You're the head of the program. How can they tell you who to hire?"

"They can't," Cynthia says. "But they said Probation would pull their funding if we hired you. Without that money, there's no Gemma Program."

"I understand," I say.

"I feel so bad," says Cynthia. "I'm so, so sorry. And I'm furious, it's so unfair, it's . . ."

I know this isn't her fault, but I can't hear any more about the unfairness of the system I'm in from people who aren't. "I have to get to my meeting," I say, interrupting her. "I have to go."

"Okay, but . . ."

I hang up and walk back to my car.

I don't have the energy to go to a meeting and hear some old guy in recovery say that "some days you are the bug, and some days you are

the windshield," or hear platitudes like "your worst day sober is still better than your best day using."

It's just not true.

Because sometimes your worst day sober *is* your worst day ever and getting high seems like a really great day.

But what do I know . . . today I am just a bug.

~

I find an online job at a company called Content Divas where I write blog posts on different topics. There was no background check, just a writing assignment. I have to produce 1,600 words a day. First, it's ten different posts about savings accounts, then travel in Hawaii. The pay is only enough for gas and rice, but it's something while I look for a full-time gig. The writing is fun, and I like having a deadline each day and the creative challenge of finding yet another metaphor to highlight the benefits of an online savings account. I imagine walking trails on Diamond Head in Waikiki and write as if I am there, smelling the plumeria and gardenia and being transformed in such a profound way that readers are driven to book their tickets through Content Divas' client.

I'm all too aware of the irony that both a savings account and travel to Hawaii are far out of reach for me. The reality is that I am out of a job, out of money, and out of options. The car I got from my mom's friend now leaks oil faster than I can afford to replace it, and it can't accelerate uphill. Today I have an appointment at the county welfare office to appeal the rejection of my application for cash benefits because of my criminal record.

I've avoided Craigslist when looking for a job because I don't want to get scammed or murdered, but I realize it's the only chance of reaching employers without being disqualified by the criminal background

question. I decide that if I'm asked, I will reveal my background, but if not I won't volunteer the information. It's a don't ask, don't tell policy that I feel still jibes with my rigorous honesty policy.

I find an ad that's ten days old, which is a lifetime in Craigslist years, but I call anyway. The woman who answers tells me they are about to make a decision, so I should send an email immediately. It's an extensive ad for a part-time job as an assistant at a literary agency, but it seems like a fun writing exercise and a way to practice answering honestly without ratting myself out.

I think about how great it would be to work with books—my first addiction.

Along with my résumé, I'm supposed to write a paragraph about how I exemplify each required quality: organized, integrity, problem-solving, communicator, investigative, computer savvy, flexible, good with money, committed, and educated.

I quickly google the company and Doug Abrams to make sure he's not a serial killer, while at the same time doubting that someone who works with Archbishop Desmond Tutu is actually advertising on Craigslist.

I say a quick prayer and pull up a blank screen to write a letter to go with my résumé. I write about how good I am under pressure, at meeting deadlines, at multitasking. How there is no task too small or too unimportant for me to do, and that I'm willing to work hard. I share my education and my writing experience.

The integrity topic stumps me for a while, but I define *integrity* as keeping my word and showing up to do what I've committed to doing. I don't want to lie about my criminal background, but nowhere in the application does it ask me about my past. I read it over and am happy with my responses. I allude to mistakes I've made without saying what they are.

Don't ask. Don't tell.

That has to be good enough for now, so I send the email. Hours later, when I read it all over, I realize that I've misspelled my own email address on my résumé. So much for that job.

~

Five days later I have an appointment to apply for food stamps. Kaden is with me, and I spend hours trying to entertain him in a dismal lobby crammed with hard plastic chairs and miserable people.

We build Legos together while I rehearse in my head exactly how I will plead my case. How can they look at his cute face and then tell me that he doesn't deserve food because his mom once had a drug conviction? Punish me but don't punish my son.

My phone rings. I startle and drop the Legos. I quickly silence it and look around the waiting room apologetically. I may be a criminal, but I'm not rude, so I answer with a whisper.

"Hello?"

The woman on the other end tells me she is Michelle, Doug Abrams's assistant, and he would like to meet with me for the job at Idea Architects, the literary agency. Can I be there in an hour?

If I walk out of here now, I'm not sure when or if I will get another appointment to appeal my case. And even if I could interview in an hour, I would need to find childcare, change my clothes, print out my résumé, and get gas. If the office is up a hill, I'm not even sure my car could make it.

I can't go.

I hold the phone and watch Kaden walk over to the window and stare out. He needs a mom who is brave, who will feed him and protect him and love him.

I don't feel brave, but . . .

"Hello?" says the woman on the phone. "Are you still there?"

"Thank you," I say, with a loud exhale as I hurriedly pack up Kaden's toys. "I will be there in an hour, of course. I'm looking forward to meeting you and Mr. Abrams."

~

Idea Architects is a room attached to Doug Abrams's house. And it's up a steep hill. But I get there on time.

During the interview we discuss my résumé—my experience teaching English composition and creative writing at UC Irvine, the small literary press I worked for while I was in college—and nothing more. On my résumé I only listed "relevant work history" so Doug doesn't ask me about anything I don't want to share. I don't list the pet cemetery business so I don't have to talk about losing it because of our drug use and jail. At the end of the interview he also doesn't ask, "By any chance, do you have an extensive criminal background?" and I don't volunteer the information.

What he does say is, "I'd like to try you out on some tasks first, that way we can both see if we're a good fit."

"I love tasks," I say eagerly.

"And I'd like to have you edit something for me, and read a manuscript and tell me what you think. I'll pay you of course for these assignments."

I agree to all of it and spend the next two weeks researching minivans and HEPA filters for him as part of my task list, and when he asks me to edit a biography of Desmond Tutu on a Saturday, I quickly learn how to use track changes in Word and return twelve chapters to him by Sunday.

I read another manuscript he sent me—a memoir of a doctor who was diagnosed with esophageal cancer and had some crazy woo-woo experiences but was living in gratitude and joy even in the face of death.

I love this guy. I love his story. He makes me want to be someone who lives in gratitude and joy. The manuscript is a mess, though.

Kaden and I are driving home from a twelve-step meeting when my phone rings. It's Doug.

"What did you think of the manuscript?" he asks. It's after 9 p.m.

"I liked it, but it was pretty hard to follow the story," I say, not wanting to offend him. "It jumps around too much to track. As a reader I was lost."

"How would you fix it?"

I pull over so I can take my phone off speaker. Kaden is falling asleep in his car seat, and Doug is a loud talker.

"Well," I stall. I do have an idea, but I don't want to sound ridiculous. I am one hundred percent sure I have a solution to the structural problem, but I have trouble saying it out loud. Sometimes, one hundred percent isn't enough.

I'm not an editor. It's been a decade or more since I've been a writer.

I look at Kaden in the rearview mirror, and I think one hundred percent will have to do. I take a deep breath.

"I would frame the whole book within the day of his diagnosis," I say. "But before he tells his family, and then the next chapter goes back to when he met his wife." I lay out the rest of the chronology quickly.

"Hold on," says Doug. "I'm going to patch you in with the author so you can tell him your ideas."

"Wait, what?" I ask, but Doug has already put me on hold.

I haven't talked to any authors since my MFA days, and they were my professors. I've certainly never talked to an author with an agent before, and my heart starts hammering. I jump out of the car and stand in front of it so I can see Kaden through the window. I need to sound serious and professional for my surprise conference call. My previous conference call was an illegal three-way hookup in jail where

I had a girl patch in Dylan's cell phone so I could wish him a happy eighteenth birthday.

Impostor syndrome kicks into overdrive as I stammer out my approach to the author, but he loves it. He says it's brilliant. Doug tells him I will be working closely with him on the chapters and the proposal, and collaboratively writing it with him. I don't know what collaborative writing means.

After we all hang up, Doug calls me right back.

"That was great," he says.

"So does this mean I have the job?"

"You have the job. Congratulations!"

I thank him and do a little dance in front of the car, and Kaden starts laughing from his car seat.

I get back in the driver's seat and buckle up. "We did it, baby guy! We got the job!"

He smiles at me, half-asleep.

That night as I carry him asleep into our little apartment, it feels like a home. I tuck him into bed in his clothes and kiss his forehead gently. I sit out on the back porch and look up at the stars and thank the universe. The job is only part-time, but it's a real job. I can work while Kaden is in school. I can help create books that matter, and I feel like I might matter again. For the first time in a very long time peace settles upon me.

~

On my first day at the office, Michelle, who has worked with Doug for five years, greets me. She tells me the Wi-Fi, hands me the keys to Doug's house and a green pouch with a type of address book in it, and says here are all the passwords to everything and all the bank account and credit card numbers for the business and Doug's personal accounts.

And then she leaves.

For a minute I think I must be getting punked, and I stare after her as she drives away. I look around anxiously as if Probation is going to pop out at me. I am alone in Doug's house with all his credit card numbers.

No algorithm needed.

I shake my head at such naive trust at the same time as I vow never to break it.

Apart from the editing and writing, I'm going to be paying all the bills for the business and for Doug personally, scheduling meetings, coordinating with the bookkeeper, and doing the day-to-day business of running the agency.

I don't know exactly what this entails because my predecessor only gave me a thirty-minute orientation before she peaced out for good.

I open my computer and set up a company email address for myself. Michelle had told me that Doug wanted to send out a newsletter with the MyEmma program so that's what I should work on first. I have no idea what MyEmma is, but I find it online and then I look for the password in the address book and log in as Doug. I quickly learn the program and create a newsletter campaign.

The hours in the Craigslist ad said five to twenty a week, but because I want to do more than is expected I bring work home with me every night and don't tell Doug I'm working unpaid hours after Kaden goes to sleep. We quickly settle into a rhythm in the office and the five to twenty hours becomes twenty-five paid hours right away. At twenty dollars an hour this feels like a fortune. I work on the doctor's book proposal—a document that's an abbreviated overview of the book that Doug will use to sell the book before it's written—on the weekends on my own.

I don't have a desk, so I sit in a big comfy chair across from Doug

and work with my computer on my lap. I listen to Doug's calls with authors, with editors, with friends. He's smart and generous and curious about everything. He's enthusiastic and brilliant and full of book ideas. He has three children and a doctor wife, and they are all kind and loving. I sit in my chair watching out the window as his beautiful family passes by in the ebb and flow of their lives, and it makes me both happy and sad. Doug's son is the same age as Ty, and I love the sound of him and his friends coming and going. I love their laughter, their thumping, their mess, and their energy.

Doug and I bounce ideas off each other easily, and he asks my opinion about everything—covers, potential authors, book topic ideas, edits we are each making. It's like we have been working together for years. We are still in the awkward getting-to-know-you stage, and while at first I was a little suspicious of his kindness, I quickly see that he is just a really good guy. When he tells me I am brilliant, I drive home that afternoon in my leaky, sputtering car feeling brilliant. He doesn't know that on the day he says this it is my two-year sobriety birthday, but it still feels auspicious. My mind is clear. My energy for the job isn't chemically induced.

Five days later I'm still relishing my natural high and working away in my chair while Doug is on the phone with an author. I suddenly feel the air change, like when a hurricane or a tornado is about to hit, and the world goes silent, and the atmosphere gets thick and muggy and electric. I take a quick breath and slowly look up from my computer and meet Doug's eyes. In them, I see shock and horror.

He ends his call suddenly, his face pale.

He stammers as he says, "Gary was just telling me that employers now google all their employees, so I googled you."

For a second I can't breathe.

"I didn't check your references," he says slowly.

I don't know what to say or do. I want to run. I want to cry. I want to defend myself, but I can't.

"It says you were convicted of identity theft. That you are the neighbor from . . ." He doesn't finish the headline because even in his shock, he is kind.

My face feels hot, and the room spins. "I have two years clean," I say. "I made mistakes . . . I hurt people . . . but that's not who I am when I'm clean."

I want to tell him that because he trusted me so instantly and blindly, I would never betray that trust. I want to tell him that I'm trying to get my children and my self-esteem back, and this work is my opportunity to do that, and I would never do anything to jeopardize it. I want to tell him that I don't even drive a mile over the speed limit because I will never break another law as long as I live. I will never do anything that will hurt my children again. I want to say all of this, but my throat is dry, and I don't want to start crying.

"Why don't you leave now," Doug says. "I need to think about this and call your references and talk to my family."

I walk across the room and pick up the zippered bank pouch. I hand it to him along with the keys to the office.

"Come back tomorrow at eleven, and we'll talk," he adds.

"Okay," I say. "I'm sorry, Doug. I'm really sorry."

"We'll talk tomorrow."

I am embarrassed and mortified and ashamed and lost.

Fucking Google.

~

I call Cynthia as soon as I get home and tell her what's happened.

"He's already called me," she says. "I told him that you managed a million-dollar grant and had access to all our information, and I would trust you without reservation."

"Thank you," I say. "How did he seem?"

"Kind of stressed, to be honest, and a little mad at himself for not checking references before he hired you."

"Would you have told him I went to jail?"

"Not unless he asked," she says.

"I can't go back there," I say. "I can't drive back to that house and face him and lose my dream job all over again."

"You can, and you will," says Cynthia. "You have so much to offer, remember that. I think he's a good guy. I think he's going to do the right thing."

At about 4 a.m. I get up and sit on the porch until the sky gets light. The idea of seeing Doug again fills me with dread, but the idea of hiding from him gives me a worse feeling—regret. If he fires me, then he fires me. For a brief shining moment I was brilliant, and I can be brilliant again.

~

He is at his desk when I walk in and sit in my chair. Before he can say anything, I take a deep breath and start talking. "I'm sorry I put you in this position, Doug," I say, "I really am, but I want to say that I'm just as brilliant today as you thought I was before you read that article. And it's important to me that you know I didn't lie to you. If you had asked me, I would have told you. But let's face it, if I had told you before you asked, I would never have gotten this job. But I am sorry you had to find out the way you did." My voice quivers, but I speak firmly.

"I appreciate you saying that." Doug's voice is somber. "I did call all your references. I talked to my family. And I spent all morning really thinking about what it means to walk your talk."

I nod.

"Look, I can't work with Archbishop Tutu and not put into practice

235

his ideas around forgiveness, redemption, and Ubuntu. So what I want to say is I believe in you."

"You do?"

"Yes, and I want you to work here. Work with me. Idea Architects needs you."

Tears flow freely down my face. Doug hands me a tissue.

"But maybe we hire someone else to handle the finances, and you handle the writing and editing?"

"Fair enough," I say. It stings a little, but I understand.

We hire a woman to handle the bills, but I end up overseeing it all anyway. Eventually Doug hands me back the green pouch, the woman leaves, and we don't talk any more about it.

~

Five months into my job at Idea Architects, we find fraud on one of the credit card accounts—a $700 purchase for a gift basket that nobody ordered. We close the account, and the bank reverses the charge, and Doug seems not to be overly bothered by it since no money is lost.

I can't let the incident go, though. I google the name of the business on the credit card statement and call the number. I talk a store worker into telling me where they shipped the wine basket after he says he cannot legally give me the name. I Google-search all over Ohio until I find all the names that match that address. Unfortunately, it's an apartment building so there are lots of names connected to the address. I call the store worker back and try again to get the name on the order. He still won't give it to me.

"How about I just say some names to you, and you tell me if any of them sound familiar to you. That's not telling me anything. Please," I say, "my job depends on it."

It's not quite true, but it feels true to me.

I start reading down a list of names and he clears his throat after one man's name. "Does that name sound familiar to you?" I ask.

"It definitely sounds like a name I have seen before," he says.

"I would tell you I love you, but that would be weird, so thank you!"

I reverse address search until I find the phone number, a landline that matches the name and address. Easy-peasy.

I haven't thought this all the way through, and as the phone rings in Ohio I realize I don't know what I'm going to say. A man answers after about five rings.

"Hi," I say. "Did you order a gift basket in April?"

The man hangs up.

I call back and I'm surprised when he answers again. "Look," I say, "don't hang up. I'm not the police."

"What, then?"

"I just need to know how you got the credit card number you used for the gift basket." He's silent for a long time and then, for some crazy reason, decides to answer me.

"A guy I don't know gave it to me, said it might be a working number."

"Did this guy live in California?"

"I don't know him."

I know he's lying. I also know that sometimes people who work in restaurants will take a quick photo of your credit card when they're processing your bill and then send the number to friends in another state. This makes the crime untraceable to the restaurant worker, and because people usually eat in the same zip code they live in, the fraudster has everything they need to use or sell a working credit card.

"Look," I say, "the police are onto the scam. And because it's across state lines the FBI are involved too." I'm just making stuff up now, and I have no idea what scam I'm even talking about. "You will not get

another credit card number from any guys you know or don't know, okay? You aren't going to jail this time, but you could next time. And trust me, you don't want to go to jail."

He hangs up.

The next day I tell Doug I tracked down the name and number of the person who used his credit card for the wine basket.

"We should tell the credit card company," he says.

I call the company, but they just tell me to call the police.

I don't call the police, though. I hope I scared the guy straight with my crazy phone call. I don't want to be blamed for the fraud, but I also don't want this guy arrested. He'll end up paying for that gift basket for who knows how many years, and I don't wish that on anyone.

I tackled this gift-basket case like I was the love child of the CIA and the NSA, and I go to sleep feeling better. Not because I cracked the case, but because I am now using my powers for good.

THE
FOUR-MINUTE
MILE

Work becomes my new addiction.

I have taken over the finances and the personal assisting, and, after we rewrite the book proposal and sample chapters, the doctor's memoir sells for far more than anyone had imagined. I become the agency's official in-house collaborative writer.

~

When Doug tells me about another writing project he has for me, I reply, "You are crazy."

"No," he says, "I'm not. You are the perfect person to help write this book."

He's talking about *The Book of Forgiving* by Archbishop Desmond Tutu. I don't know the first thing about forgiveness. I know about forgetting, but nobody is publishing *The Book of Forgetting*.

I am on probation. I am going through a divorce. I am hated by

my community. I am the last person to help write a book about forgiveness. DJ is on a path of self-destruction and missed Kaden's last birthday—just didn't show up for his party. I have no forgiveness in me right now. I want revenge, but revenge is reserved for people who aren't on probation.

Plus, I have never cowritten a whole book before. The doctor had done a lot of his own writing, and I wrote bits here and there and reworded some of his prose. An entire book feels like too big an endeavor. In my MFA program I only had the patience for writing short stories, and those were *short* short stories. I have no idea where to begin.

"Let's make an outline of Arch's philosophy of forgiveness," Doug says. "A blueprint that you can write from."

He might as well be asking me to speak Mandarin. I'm a fiction writer by training, and I've never done outlines or blueprints. Some do, of course, but I've never been able to comprehend how you can know the structure of something before you begin writing. I go along with the program, and we loosely sketch out each chapter, questions we need to ask Archbishop Tutu and his daughter Mpho about what forgiveness is and is not. Doug has worked with him before, and they've been talking about this book since before I came to work here, so he has a clear idea what each chapter will be about. My job will be to put it all in beautiful writing once we get the content from the archbishop and Mpho, pull content from his speeches, and find the stories to illustrate the big ideas and each of the key points. The whole outline fits on one sheet of paper. On the back side, we list the four steps to forgiving that are going to form the structure of the book. These have been predetermined.

"There's just one more chapter to figure out," says Doug. The whole process has taken less than an hour.

"What's the last chapter?"

"The chapter on self-forgiveness."

I make a face at him.

"What?" he asks, when I sit back in my chair.

"I don't know anything about that," I say.

"Of course you do."

I watch him sketch out six key points for the chapter, and then he hands the outline of the whole book to me.

"You can do this," he says. "All your experience in jail makes you the absolute best person to cowrite this book."

I think about Daddy and Kiki and Officer Lonnie and Cassandra. Doug doesn't know any of my jail experiences, so it's a stretch for him to say that jail made me the best person to help write this book. But I know he's trying to hype me up, and I appreciate it.

We schedule Skype calls with Archbishop Tutu and Mpho. Because of the time difference the calls are late at night. After Kaden goes to bed, I perch my laptop on my tiny kitchen table and try to angle the camera really high so the yellow fridge four feet behind me doesn't show. I take notes while Archbishop Tutu speaks, even though it's all being recorded for transcription.

We talk through the outline and revise in real time. I can't believe Archbishop Tutu is actually in my tiny apartment talking to me.

In seventh grade I had done a social studies report on apartheid for my favorite teacher, Mr. Miller. He encouraged me to write every day. I would sit in his class, hiding behind my Farrah Fawcett bangs, and then go home and write stories about all the history lessons he had taught. I wrote a story where I was a soldier in the Vietnam War who didn't want to fight. I wrote a story that took place during the Armenian genocide. But when we learned about Archbishop Tutu and apartheid, I had written a full essay and created a presentation with poster board and then given an impassioned speech that I was pretty sure would create fairness and equality in South Africa.

Now I'm on a video conference with the man himself, but I try to play it cool.

Archbishop Tutu is kind and loving and wise and funny, and I pay close attention to his quirks of phrasing and his generosity of language. He is a formal speaker whose language is both precise and lofty.

I've agreed to do the book, mostly because I don't really have a choice, this is the job. But then I procrastinate. I don't call it procrastinating, though; I call it deprioritizing the writing part of the book. It's not due to the publisher for a year, so I tuck the outline away for as long as possible and instead write more questions for Archbishop Tutu to answer over Skype, and I research forgiveness stories, and I transcribe other talks and do lots of research into the science of forgiveness. When I finally start writing, the early chapters come together easily because I have so much material to work from, but the deadline for delivery is looming, and it's time to tackle the chapter on self-forgiveness and that's basically all new material for the book.

I pull out the chapter outline and read it over again and then I tell Doug I'm going to a coffee shop to write. The office is small, and Doug talks loudly on the phone, so he wishes me luck and waves me off. "You can do this," he says as I walk out the door. "You can write this chapter."

I get to the coffee shop at 10 a.m. and settle in at a table that's big enough to spread out all my folders and transcripts. I feel important at my big table doing important work, but the blank screen in front of me is terrifying. I give myself an inner pep talk and glance at the clock. I decide I will not leave this coffee shop until the full chapter is written.

I start doing calculations in my head. Twenty-five to thirty pages for the chapter, twelve hours until the coffee shop closes, two to three pages an hour, a page every twenty minutes. It all seems reasonable. I think of Doug's words: *There is no such thing as writer's block—if you are stuck, it just means you don't have enough information.*

I turn it into a game. If I finish three pages before the hour is up,

I get to go on Facebook or play *Candy Crush* until the next hour starts. I race against time and figure I will just get a bad first draft down, and then Doug can edit and make changes. A bad something is better than a great nothing.

I realize I trained for this in seventh grade, and I trained for this in jail. My confidence and energy increase. I don't always meet the one page in twenty minutes but I am close. I write all day and into the night about how you have to be willing to face the harm you've caused someone, be willing to make amends, and accept that a person may choose to end the relationship even if they choose to forgive you. I only stop to go to the bathroom, buy more coffee, and check on Kaden who is being watched by Cody.

The sound of chairs being put away registers as I type the chapter's last line. It's thirty-two pages long. I don't read it over, and instead email it to Doug with disclaimers about how rough it is and how bad it probably is and how we can revise. But inside I feel good. It's ten fifteen and I just wrote an entire chapter of a book in one day.

A few days later, Doug meets me outside the office when I pull up. "Sit down," he says. We sit on the front steps. I can tell I'm in trouble.

"What's wrong?"

Doug looks at me seriously. "Why does something always have to be wrong?"

"Really? Do you even know me?" We both laugh, but I'm still nervous.

"I read the chapter you wrote," he says.

"I know it needs work . . ."

"It's fucking fantastic."

"Really?"

"Really. I mean, do you know what you just did? It's like watching

243

THE MANY LIVES OF MAMA LOVE

Roger Bannister break the four-minute mile. You just wrote a thirty-plus-page chapter in a day. That's not really possible. Only it is possible, and you did it."

"Wow, I can't believe it."

"Well, there was one line I cut—'the hamster wheel of retribution'—that was a little much."

I shrug and laugh. "I thought it was clever, but I'll fix it."

"I already cut it and sent the chapter to Archbishop Tutu."

"What did he say?"

"He said we do a better him than he does." When I don't respond, Doug clarifies: "He loved it, he said to tell you he loved it. We still need to send it to Mpho."

I am stunned and thrilled. "You know," I say, "I was thinking it would be good to test out the forgiveness practices in the book."

"How would we do that?"

"Well, I could do them with a certain group of people who really need to learn about forgiveness and self-forgiveness."

Doug thinks for a few seconds and then nods. "That's a great idea. We can see which practices really resonate with people. What's the group?"

"The Gemma Program. I can volunteer to do a course on forgiveness with the girls in jail."

"Lara, I think that's a really good idea. For them and for you."

Cynthia agrees with the idea as well.

~

When I walk in the first day it feels surreal. Sandy, the social worker who was hired to run Gemma after I was fired, is warm and welcoming. I only recognize one girl from my time in G, but I can't remember her name.

"Hi," I say. "My name is Lara."

"Mama Love," the woman yells and laughs.

I look around the room. "That was my nickname, and I'm a graduate of the Gemma Program." This gets their attention. "I work for a literary agency now, and I'm working on a project called *The Book of Forgiving* with Archbishop Desmond Tutu and Mpho Tutu. Does anyone know who Archbishop Tutu is?"

Only one woman raises her hand—an older woman of about sixty.

"When did you get out?" another woman asks.

"Almost four years ago," I say. "I was the first one out on the work-release program." The women pepper me with questions about how long it took me to get a job, and did I have a home, and was I still on probation.

I answer them all and confirm yes, I'm still on probation.

"Does the guy you're helping with the book know?"

"My boss knows, but Archbishop Tutu doesn't know. But he's an expert on forgiveness so I think he would be okay with it." I am sure this is true, but I'm also sure that I don't want him or Mpho to find out. I don't want any of the authors we work with to find out. I'm afraid of what they would think of me. I'm afraid of them thinking less of me.

I don't say any of this to the Gemma women, but instead tell them about Tutu and apartheid, the Truth and Reconciliation Commission, and how mothers forgave the men who killed their sons.

"The book has a lot of forgiveness exercises, prayers, and meditations that Mpho Tutu wrote, and I'd like to try them out with all of you and have you tell me if they're helpful or not. That will help us decide what to put in the book."

"You mean if we don't like them they won't go in the book?"

"Probably not. They might try to improve them or find better ones. And if you're okay with it, some of the stories you share over the next six weeks might be used in the book. I would change your name, of course."

The older woman raises her hand and asks softly, "If we wanted you to use our name, could you?"

I get choked up at her question because I understand everything she's not saying. "Of course. If you want your name in the book, it will be in the book."

There's only time left for me to read Mpho Tutu's opening prayer about forgiveness called "The Prayer Before the Prayer."

I want to be willing to let go, to forgive.
But dare not ask for the will to forgive,
in case you give it to me
And I am not yet ready.
I am not yet ready for my heart to soften.
I am not yet ready to be vulnerable again.
Not yet ready to see that there is humanity in my tormentor's eyes
Or that the one who hurt me may also have cried
I am not yet ready for the journey.
I am not yet interested in the path
I am at the prayer before the prayer of forgiveness
Grant me the will to want to forgive.
Grant it to me not yet but soon
Can I even form the words?
Forgive me? Dare I even look?
Do I dare to see the hurt I have caused:
I can glimpse all the shattered pieces of that fragile thing
That soul trying to rise on the broken wings of hope
But only out of the corner of my eye.
I am afraid of it.
And if I am afraid to see
How can I not be afraid to say: Forgive me?

Is there a place where we can meet?
You and me
The place in the middle where we straddle the lines
Where you are right and I am right too.
And both of us are wrong and wronged
Can we meet there?
And look for the place where the path begins
The path that ends when we forgive.

Several of the women start to cry, and the moment feels bigger than this little room. After a few moments of silence, I break the tension.

"So that one's a keeper then?"

~

I get the women journals, and for one hour a week for the next six weeks we meet and do the forgiveness exercises. The women are thrilled to be part of a book project, and I understand their thrill. It's the thrill of feeling like you matter. Like you are part of something bigger than your own sad story. The exercises on asking for forgiveness are hard, as is the discussion about how you have to tell the truth about what you did and then hear the truth about the harm you caused others. But the topic of self-forgiveness is the hardest, especially within a punitive system.

The women are hard on themselves, guilty and ashamed and frustrated at the choices they've made in life, and I advise them to forgive themselves so they can move on. I tell them that Archbishop Tutu says that telling the truth, witnessing the harm you've caused, and asking for forgiveness, even if it's not given, is the path to freedom. It's the only way to not be bitter. To not hate yourself so you can have a fighting chance to be something beyond the worst things you've done.

I teach what I'm not brave enough to do myself. Even out of the system, it's hard not to stew in the juices of punishment and feel like it's where I belong.

When the book goes to print, I read the acknowledgments section and see Archbishop Tutu has paid tribute to me as his literary companion through many drafts and he calls me an aptly named genius with a heart of gold.

It feels good to see my name in his book, to show it to my boys. Chapter by chapter, book by book, I am creating a new legacy to pass on to my children. I am the neighbor from hell in the newspaper, but I am also the person in the acknowledgments of the books I help create.

I am officially a ghostwriter, and finishing any chapter feels like being high, only different. The edges are full of confidence, and that makes it nothing like the high of opiates, which were only outlined in glittery fear and false bravado. This feeling will return every time I finish writing a chapter for the next eight years—a feeling I will chase like I used to chase drugs.

~

My phone rings late one night. When I see Darcy's name on the caller ID, I quickly slip out of bed and go into the bathroom so I don't wake Kaden.

I answer the phone with a question. "Are the boys okay?"

"What? Hi."

"Are the boys okay?" I don't know why she's calling me so late, so of course I am assuming bad news.

"Yeah, they're fine."

"Okay, good." I fall silent, and she does too. Over time, we have established a truce of sorts. We took a picture together when Cody graduated high school. We all went to dinner together the night before Dylan went off to study abroad in South Korea. It was easy to fall back

into casual friendliness with Bryan; he doesn't have the attention span to hold a grudge. I am still wary of Darcy, though, and whenever we're all together, I end up feeling bad about myself. I told them about my job at Idea Architects in a voice I didn't like. I sounded hungry for their approval, and they looked at me in a way that made me feel like I was lying. I try to focus on the fact that Bryan and Darcy saved Kaden from foster care with strangers while I was in jail. But I still can't forget all the ways she hurt me when I was hurting.

Darcy takes a deep breath, and I steel myself for another false accusation of some sort. I hate conflict, and especially late-night conflict. I am working on five books at once, and I need what little sleep I can get.

"I had therapy today," she says.

I remain silent as I sit down on the edge of the tub and play with the snorkel and goggles Kaden likes to wear in the bath.

"My therapist says you and I should hang out more."

"What?"

Darcy starts to cry. "You're the only one I can trust in Santa Cruz," she says. "Bryan is cheating on me."

This news does not surprise me. The fact that I am the only one she can trust shocks me.

"I'm so sorry," I say. I don't tell her that I suspected as much when I saw Bryan constantly texting during one of Cody's basketball games. There was a certain look of excitement mixed with chagrin that is Bryan's cheating face.

"But you have lots of friends," I say. "Why does your therapist think I'm the only one you can trust?"

"Because you've been through this before, you know what I'm going through, you're the only one who can understand. Besides, my friends here are his friends too." Darcy is from Boston, so all her real friends are far away.

I don't know what to advise her. "It's hard," I say, "but you'll be okay."

This makes her cry harder. I am in no position to be the therapist for my ex-husband's soon-to-be-ex-wife who I think may have tried to get me sent to prison. "I can't get out of bed," she says. "I'm so depressed."

I tune out while she sets forth the gory details of Bryan's affair. It's not my business, and I'm no scientist, but I bet the research shows that when you marry a cheater, there's a good chance he's going to cheat on you. As a woman, I feel for her. As a person once married to her husband, I feel for her. A petty part of me clutches a bit of schadenfreude, but I set that aside.

"Try to sleep," I say. "I'll call you this weekend."

~

The next day I talk to Ty, who tells me she won't get out of bed. On Sunday, I call her. It's Mother's Day, which is a tough day for her anyway because she couldn't bear children of her own. She doesn't answer. I call Ty again; he says his dad is out, and Darcy is still in bed. I pack up Kaden and we make the short drive over to their house.

I park Kaden with Ty, walk upstairs to her bedroom, and knock.

A weak voice says, "Come in."

She is sitting up in bed. Her eyes are red-rimmed and swollen. I quickly take in a pile of pill bottles and crumpled tissues on the nightstand. She looks like shit. "How are you?" I ask. "I brought you something." I hold out a coffee cup to her. "It's a mocha."

"Thanks," she says.

"Happy Mother's Day." She starts to cry again, and I sit on the bed next to her with my own coffee.

"Look, I know it seems like the world is ending, but you can't just stay in bed. Ty said you've been in here for a couple of days."

"I can't get up," she says. She sounds groggy, and I try to read the labels on her pill bottles without being obvious about it.

"It's a beautiful day," I say. "Let's go for a walk on the beach."

She looks at me blankly, and I'm surprised at my suggestion as well. I was just going to hand her a coffee and then slip out. But she's a mess. I was a mess too. Like recognizes like.

"Come on," I say, "it'll be fun. It's beautiful outside." It's actually kind of cold and foggy but now is not the time for the truth.

I stand up from the bed and hold out my hand. "Let's go," I say. "Let's just go for a walk. And Kaden's downstairs; he really wanted to wish you a Happy Mother's Day." That's another lie, but I'm desperate enough to throw Kaden under this bus. I had to bribe him with the promise of Legos to get him to come with me.

Darcy reaches for my hand. I want to feel the compassion I'm faking, and when she stands up and stumbles a little, I suddenly do. I don't want to be a woman who kicks another woman when she's down. I want to be better than she was to me so she can be better than she was to me.

Kaden doesn't want to walk with us, so we make our way to the beach alone. Darcy stops every few houses to tell me a Bryan story from when they first met, when they once took a walk here, when they were once in love. I just listen and hold space for the betrayal she's feeling. Bryan isn't a bad guy, and a part of me is surprised he lasted this long with the bitterness that's simmered between them for years, but I still support her as she complains about the unfairness of it all and repeats everything she already told me over the phone.

We have just turned around to head back to the house. She's vented all there is to vent for now, so we walk in silence, and it's actually pretty nice. I haven't walked with a friend on the beach in years.

"I met someone," I offer. I'm still wary of trusting her with personal information, but I want to build a bridge, and this is good gossip.

"What? Who? Tell me everything!"

"His name is Sam. He's great, but he's seven years younger than me, so I don't know . . ."

"Bryan is seven years younger than me . . ." she says and then falls silent. We both know how that's turning out.

"I hope he's a nice guy," says Darcy before she starts crying again.

"I hope he is too," I say as I put my arm around her shoulders. Sam does seem like a nice guy; he drops coffee at my doorstep every morning on his way to work. He has two children from a previous marriage whom he dotes on. Since DJ, I've tried dating two other men. The first lied to me about being almost divorced; in fact, he wasn't even separated. The other also turned out to be a liar, and when I broke it off with him, he threatened to call Probation on me. Both were men I met in recovery meetings who were supposed to be practicing the principles of honesty. I had sworn off dating and relationships forever, but then I saw Sam and he saw me. And I liked the person I was in his eyes. I liked that he seemed to love and adore me, but it was still new, and I hadn't yet told him much about the life I was struggling to leave behind.

I told the boys to make Darcy breakfast before we left. When we return, we both climb into her bed, and the boys carry in our breakfast on matching wooden trays. I think about the boys coming to visit me at Blaine on Mother's Day. At the time, I was so happy to spend the day with them, I hadn't realized that my time with them meant Darcy had spent the day alone.

But here we were years later, spending Mother's Day together with all four boys. Sometimes, the path of forgiveness doesn't look anything like we think it will. Sometimes it looks a lot like runny scrambled eggs and overly buttered sourdough toast.

After breakfast, the boys take the trays away and I get up to leave.

"You going to be okay?" I ask.

Darcy nods. "You know," she says, "I never told you or anyone this, but I've had my own struggles . . ."

I think about her anger, her vitriol, her seeming delight at my failure. I think about her leading the mob in the courtroom, and it suddenly all makes sense. Maybe she hated me for all the complicated reasons we hate people who are more like us than we can admit.

Or maybe she never hated me at all.

~

Sam comes over later that evening, after Kaden is asleep. His kids are with their mom, and when I open the door he is standing there in his work boots holding a bouquet of flowers and a bunch of carrots.

I tell him about my day with Darcy.

And then I tell him about my Mother's Day in jail with the boys, my arrest, my time in jail, the newspaper headline, and Doug googling me. He doesn't say a word until I'm done.

"Thanks for telling me all that. I'm sorry you went through it, but I think you're amazing. Your past doesn't matter to me."

"Why?"

"I only care about who you are now. And I can promise you one thing, I will never google you. I don't need to."

How could I not fall in love with a man who refused to google me?

~

A few weeks later, Darcy, Bryan, and I stand awkwardly together for pictures at Ty's high school graduation. At the dinner that night, Darcy gets drunk, and the tension between them overshadows the celebration. I yell at her for making the night about her rather than Ty, and then I immediately apologize.

That dinner is the last time I see Darcy before she and Bryan officially separate and she moves back to Boston.

I send her love and light and wish her well. I don't know what next year's Mother's Day will bring. I know I will gladly share my Mother's Day with the women in jail, with Darcy in her bed, and with whoever comes after her as stepmother to my children.

I forgive Darcy and I hope she forgives me.

chapter 18

A BEAUTIFUL
DAY IN THE
NEIGHBORHOOD

I dea Architects has outgrown Doug's home office, so we relocate across the county and I move out of my chair and into a real desk. I am writing a book with a neurosurgeon, so early every Friday morning I drive to Silicon Valley and meet him at his office before he goes into surgery. On one Friday morning I accompany him to the hospital and change into scrubs so I can be in the operating room while he performs brain surgery. I ask him if I can keep the scrubs and when he says yes, I wear them often over the next two months while I work with him on the book.

In the middle of this new book I'm under deadline for, Sam and I decide to move in together and Doug rents us his house while he moves to a house closer to our new office. Neither Sam nor I want to get married again. Sam's only been married once, but I've been married twice, and I don't think I have a third time in me. I'm not Elizabeth Taylor. Although secretly a part of me at least wants Sam to

want to marry me, plus I am curious about what it would be like to be married for ten years, twenty years, thirty years. But a larger part of me doubts I have it in me to stay married that long. I have never made it to five years before, so maybe I am Elizabeth Taylor.

Kaden and I carefully pack up all his Legos and drive behind the U-Haul to our new home. It's a big change from our four-hundred-square-foot apartment, and I'm excited and nervous. The new home is in a nice neighborhood and near the elementary school that Kaden and Sam's son, Chase, will attend. They are only a year and a half apart, and for the two years that Sam and I have been dating, they've acted like they were at a slumber party whenever they were together. I hope that rapport will continue now that they're sharing a room. I am grateful he will now have siblings close to his age and a house full of company, instead of just me and my hypervigilance. Sam's daughter, Dahlia, will have her own room, and the house has an extra guest room for Dylan, Cody, and Ty to stay in when they want to. It's taken five years, but I finally have a home that can hold all my children. They're all out of high school now and Ty will be off to college soon after traveling post–high school, but we'll have the holidays together. I love being a day-to-day mom again. I love setting the table for dinner, watching a movie together. When I have to sweep the floors and do the dishes I tell myself to be grateful I am doing these things in my own home and not in Blaine Street.

Work keeps me busy, and I often pull one all-nighter a week just to keep up. But apart from the occasional brain surgery with an author, I feel like I have finally found the nice, conventional life I have longed for since my arrest. I didn't appreciate what I had before, so now I relish the domesticity of it all. The comfort, the security, the neighbors who wave to me when I drive by.

~

Ty, Kaden, and I pick up take-out dinner a few days after we move in. It's a celebration, and we're in high spirits. I have just made the turn off the freeway at our exit when flashing blue and red lights appear behind us.

I quickly pull into a parking lot. I know I've done nothing wrong, but the terror is instantaneous. My body remembers my arrest, even if my mind knows not to worry. Ty seems unconcerned, and I glance over my shoulder at Kaden in the back seat. He is staring out the window.

"It will be fine," I say.

Ty moves to take his seat belt off, but I tell him to leave it on.

Because we are in an unincorporated part of the county, a sheriff's deputy has pulled me over. I am grateful I don't recognize the deputy when he walks up to my window. I am grateful it isn't one of the two who arrested me, or one of the deputies who works in the jail. I remind myself that I am just a mom driving home from picking up takeout with her children.

He shines his flashlight at the boys, and then stands next to my rolled-down window without saying a word.

"Hi?" I say, waiting to see why he pulled me over.

"You have a taillight out," he says.

"Oh no, I didn't realize . . ."

"Could I see your driver's license and insurance?"

I dig my license out of my bag and ask Ty to get the registration from the glove box. The deputy shines his flashlight in Ty's face again.

"Is this your son?"

"Yes," I say.

Ty gives him a fake smile. Kaden hasn't said a word.

He takes my license and registration and walks back to his car. A second deputy I hadn't noticed before stands behind my car.

"It will just be a fix-it ticket," I say. "No big deal."

Kaden is staring down at his lap. "You okay, baby guy?" I ask. "There's nothing to worry about." I wonder if he's thinking about the last time he saw me with the police when I told him everything would be okay.

Our dinner is getting cold.

We've been sitting in the car for close to twenty minutes, and the two deputies are outside the car talking when suddenly five more sheriff's cars pull into the parking lot, their sirens blaring and lights flashing. Two of them pull in front of our car, blocking our way forward. The other three line up behind and around the car that pulled us over. Two officers get out of each car and stand at the back of my car. Ty is starting to look nervous now, and Kaden still hasn't uttered a word.

The deputy comes back to the window.

"You're on probation. You don't have any violations, but we've called your probation officer."

"For a burned-out light?"

The only reason I'm still on probation is the fact that I haven't been able to pay the remainder of the restitution back yet.

"We have the right to search you and your car, but we're waiting to hear back from your probation officer."

"You can search my car," I say.

"What?"

"I'm fine if you search my car, you don't have to wait for him to call back."

The deputy seems surprised at this. He walks back to confer with the other ten officers who have assembled to deal with our broken light.

Another deputy walks up to the car and asks us to get out. Ty opens Kaden's door and I grab the bag of Chipotle so at least we can eat.

"Leave everything in the car!"

Apparently they need to search our dinner.

Ty, Kaden, and I sit on a curb in the flashing lights while they pull everything out of the glove box and the trunk. My backpack gets dumped on the hood of the car while three deputies shine their flashlights under the seats, between the seats, across the dash, and inside the car doors. I am scared and embarrassed, but mostly I'm worried about Kaden. He has climbed into my lap and buried his ten-year-old face in my neck. He is shivering even though the night is warm. I rub his back.

"It's okay, Boodle," says Ty, using his favorite nickname for his little brother.

After another twenty minutes, the original deputy walks up and hands me my documents along with a fix-it ticket for the light.

"You know we could impound it for the broken light."

I don't reply and he looks at me like he's waiting for me to thank him. But I feel no gratitude and say nothing. I feel only anger at this man, and all his buddies, and the system he represents that could ruin my happy, hard-won life over a five-dollar taillight.

"Your probation officer said you're good to go. That's quite a record you have."

I don't have to check in with Probation anymore; I just file a monthly report online. So I'd almost forgotten that I can still be sent back to jail for anything at any time. I had thought about homeschooling Kaden earlier in the year but found out I can't because I have a record. I am ghostwriting a book for two Stanford professors, but I can't homeschool my son.

We gather up all our stuff and put the car back together as quickly as possible after the deputies leave. The sirens, the flashing lights, the six sheriff's cars—it all feels like intentional overkill. Do I look that dangerous sitting in a car with my two children and a bag of Chipotle? They knew when they looked me up that I had never violated

probation for five years, but still they acted as if I had just robbed a bank and was driving the getaway car.

"Let's just order pizza," I say as we head home.

~

When I tell Sam what happened, he's angry with the police on my behalf. I try to explain to him how scared I am every day that people will find out about my past, but he doesn't get it. "Who cares?" he asks. "Why does it even matter?" He has never been arrested, never gone to jail, and he can't seem to understand the terror that lives right under the surface of my happy life.

I can't sleep that night. At 2 a.m. I get out of bed and decide to check my email. There's a note from Doug saying our next-door neighbors are upset with him for renting to me without talking to them first.

A friend of another neighbor, someone I know from recovery meetings, gossiped about me, and now all the neighbors know the neighbor from hell has moved next door. "Let's discuss in the morning," writes Doug. "But I told them I'm free to meet on Saturday."

When Sam gets up for work at five, I am sitting at the kitchen table. "What's up?" he asks.

"Bobby told the neighbors across the street about my past and he told another neighbor who told another neighbor. And now Zack and Karen are upset and want a meeting to discuss it with us and Doug."

I start to cry. I should have stayed in my little apartment with Kaden.

"We don't have to defend where we live to anyone."

"Doug wants us to all sit down and talk."

"No way," says Sam. "Fuck the neighbors. You've been in this neighborhood, this house, all day every day for years working with Doug, and they haven't had a problem."

"Until Bobby made sure they knew my past."

"Fucking Bobby," says Sam. "Isn't he supposed to keep things anonymous?"

I just shrug. "Will you go to the meeting with me and Doug?" I ask. "On Saturday?"

Sam is quiet for a moment, and then he says no. In a way I'm relieved. I don't want him to witness my humiliation.

"I disagree with the need to meet on principle, and there's no way I'm going to give them the satisfaction. You do not have to defend your past. Besides, I have to work on Saturday."

I've never been able to make Sam understand the burden I carry. Going to jail, the newspaper headline, probation—it's all a secret I keep from everyone I know except him and Doug and my family. In Sam's mind, the past is past; it has no bearing on our present or future. I appreciate this Tolle-level detachment, but it also makes me feel alone as I face my next hurdle.

The prospect of this meeting makes me fearful and nervous. Doug shows up at the house full of his usual energy and goodwill.

Zack and Karen have set out a fruit plate, and we sit awkwardly at their kitchen table. "Lisa and Will didn't want to come to the meeting," they say, referring to the neighbors across the street who spread the gossip. "Will objects to it. He says you can live where you want to live, and it's not our business. Obviously, we understand his point but disagree that it's not our business. Doug, you should have told us before you rented the house."

Doug smiles. "Well, actually I didn't need to do that. And you've known Lara for years now. It never crossed my mind to tell you. We trust Lara with our home, our business. Besides marrying my wife, the best thing I've ever done is hire Lara."

My eyes fill with tears.

Karen and Zack nod in some kind of agreement with Doug's sentiment, but they still ask to hear my story. I tell them I have many years in

recovery but go silent after that. I don't know what to say. I am suddenly exhausted, and I realize Sam is right, I don't need to defend myself. I shouldn't have to defend myself. Doug steps in and tells them I committed identity theft and went to jail but how responsible I am now.

"Given my job, you can understand my concern," says Zack.

I don't know what he does for a living, and Doug seems to have forgotten as well. We both look at him, puzzled.

"I do cybersecurity," he says. "Obviously, identity theft is a big part of what I fight every day."

I'm not going to steal his identity. I'm too busy working at my job assuming the identities of our authors and writing their books.

"You have my word," says Doug. "There will be no problems whatsoever—Lara is a perfect neighbor."

Karen and Zack seem dubious but say okay, as if they are being magnanimous in letting me live where I live. Before we leave, they both backtrack on the whole meeting and remind us of how committed they are to social justice issues.

I tune them out. I want to go to my new home in my new neighborhood and cry. We say our goodbyes, and Doug emails me the next morning:

> How are you "the morning after . . ."? Hope you are still feeling that the meeting went as well as I did. I hope you will feel at home in the new neighborhood, and I do feel that going through experiences like this and the kind of honesty everyone shared yesterday deepens relationships significantly.

I send a smiley face emoji back, but as I walk Kaden to school on Monday the neighborhood doesn't look as shiny and hopeful as it did the week before.

~

Not long after, Sam and I are sitting in the backyard enjoying a Saturday night at home without the kids. Dylan, Cody, and Ty have taken Kaden on a road trip to Oregon for the week. It's a rare summer night without fog, and I feel content. It's a feeling I'm still not a hundred percent comfortable with but I'm trying.

Sam starts to say something and then stops. He seems nervous, and my contentment leaves as I brace myself for whatever shoe is about to drop.

"What?" I ask. "What's wrong?"

"Nothing's wrong."

I wait him out, thinking suddenly that he's about to break up with me. I start to ponder how I'm going to pay the rent myself, and vow never to get in a relationship again. In an instant, I play out our entire breakup and I'm surprised at how much it hurts, how much I really do love him.

"Will you marry me?"

"You want to marry me?" I ask. "*You* want to get married?"

"I do."

"But why? You said you never wanted to get married again."

"I want to marry you, I love you, can you please just answer the question?" Sam is laughing now.

"I want to marry you, too, so yes, the answer is yes!"

Sam howls at the night sky. I jump up and throw my arms around him. We kiss, and he howls again, and I don't care about the neighbors next door and what they'll think, or how I've failed at marriage in the past. All I know is that I love him and he loves me, and it feels so good to feel chosen.

We make plans to get married the following June and spend the fall and winter planning a big wedding.

One night in March, as we're about to go to sleep, I tell him I can't see our wedding.

"What do you mean?"

"I mean, I know we're making these plans, but I don't see it. I don't see us at this big wedding, and you know how I am . . . If I can't see something happening it never happens."

Sam is quiet for a moment.

"Plus, I hate the word *venue*," I add. "If someone asks about our 'venue' one more time, I'm going to lose it on them. It's a horrible, horrible word."

"Do you want to marry me still?"

"Of course," I say.

"What if we elope?"

We already have a wedding party, and people helping us plan the wedding, and Sam's parents would be devastated. Plus, I want the boys at our wedding. Eloping seems impossible.

Sam sits up in bed. "Let's just do it. The day after tomorrow. We'll take a long weekend. Just us. We can do a party later with the family."

It feels so wrong, but also so right. Planning a wedding in a day feels way easier to me than planning a wedding over a year.

We try to sneak off, but twenty-one people, including Dylan, Cody, Ty, and Sam's parents, decide to elope with us on a day's notice. It's crazy and chaotic and fun and perfect.

On our wedding night Sam and I stand at the window of our hotel room looking out at the lights of Reno, Nevada.

"I hope you know how special this is," I say.

"Of course I know. I love you, Mrs. Lara Love Hardin."

"No," I say. "This is the first time I've gotten married without getting pregnant first. This is a big moment in a girl's life." Sam looks at me in silence for a moment, and then we both laugh.

I have begun a marriage with laughter, and I take this as a good omen.

chapter 19

THE DALAI LAMA HATES ME

Doug decides to sell his house, and Sam and I find a rental home a few blocks from where I used to live with Kaden. It's hard to find a place to rent that has enough room to fit all the kids, takes a dog, and doesn't require a criminal background check.

I barely have time to unpack in our new place before I'm on my way to India to work on *The Book of Joy* with Doug, Archbishop Tutu, the Dalai Lama, and other members of our growing company. We have moved into even bigger offices, and I was excited for the business trip of a lifetime.

No one else at our company knows about my past. None of the many authors I have written books with know about my past. I keep my secret and pray daily that our authors don't find out. I am constantly worried that if people know, it will hurt our reputation as a literary agency and that will somehow torpedo the business. Maybe I am

overreacting, but I don't want to find out. Mostly I am just constantly ashamed, and I also don't want people to see me through the lens of being a felon. Am I smart, or am I just smart for a criminal? Am I a good writer, or am I a good writer for someone who was an addict? I also manage the company's money, and I don't want my honesty and integrity to be questioned. Yes, I keep the secret to protect the business, but I also keep it to protect myself.

Two of the books I have cowritten had become *New York Times* bestsellers—I am Idea Architects' secret weapon, and I guard my secret past like I used to guard my drug addiction. Secrets are a lonely place to live, though, and I can't imagine making new friends. There are too many gaps in my life story that don't lend themselves to long, getting-to-know-you talks. I don't want to feel like I am lying to anyone, even by omission. And I am too ashamed to think about telling the truth. I can't face the horror I imagine crossing the faces of people who might find out my secret. I worry about people judging me because I am constantly in judgment of myself. I work on a book where the authors cite research that shows how having close female friends is a huge predictor of a woman's health and longevity. The more female friends a woman has, the better.

My takeaway from this is that lonely old me is going to suffer a miserable early death if I don't make some friends, but I am afraid to try. So I work day and night to clear my karma, and prove that I am good because I do good work. I'm not really worried about being judged in any afterlife, just in the one I am living.

I'm still on probation because I haven't paid the restitution back in full. I apply for my passport and my visa, not knowing if they'll get approved. I do research on whether foreign governments do background checks on visa applicants; some do and some don't. My visa for the trip to India is denied at first. I had written "Writer" as my

profession, so I reapply and change my profession to "Secretary" and it gets approved.

I don't have time for feminist outrage because the logistics of bringing an entire team to the Dalai Lama's house are all-consuming. I am excited and nervous but mostly excited. I reach out to a friend from my early soccer-mom days who is a devout Buddhist and follower of the Dalai Lama. Over tea, she gives me a crash course on how to behave with monks.

"You're a woman, so they won't shake your hand or touch you," she says.

"That just makes me want to shake their hands so I can pull them into the twenty-first century."

"Please don't."

"His Holiness sees everything," she says. "He has this way of knowing you because he can look right into your soul. Listen carefully when he speaks. He will tell you exactly what you most need to hear."

I don't like the idea of the Dalai Lama mucking around in my soul, rummaging around like a girlfriend going through her boyfriend's drawers when he's not home. Mostly I'm afraid of what he might see in there. I worry that he will blow my cover.

"It's really special that you get to do this," says my old friend, Kate. "Usually it takes a lot of merit to have an opportunity like this."

I shrug, unsure how to address my merit or lack thereof.

"Well, it's my job, and I know it's an amazing opportunity," I say eventually.

"Hmmm . . ." says Kate, looking at me suspiciously like I'm passing counterfeit merit.

We talk about the travel and what India is like, and Kate shares her stories from Dharamsala and elsewhere. Her work as an educator is based on the Dalai Lama's vision for children. I haven't seen her

since my older boys were in a Buddhist preschool with her kids. At the time, we were part of a close-knit group of moms. I'm grateful to her for giving me so much of her time and expertise after all those years.

At the end of our tea, Kate tells me that most of our old friend group is coming over for a game night at her house.

I get excited at the thought of seeing my former best friends. And I love game nights. I realize how much I miss having friends—how much I miss this group of friends in particular and being in a large group of women in general. It's the one thing I miss about jail.

"They'll be here soon," Kate says. I nod enthusiastically and give her a big smile.

She stands and picks up our teacups. "So you'll probably want to get going now. I can't believe it's gotten so late."

"Oh, of course." My face flushes, and I hug her awkwardly.

"One more thing," she says.

"Yeah?"

"Did you ever steal Pali's traveler's checks?"

Pali is her daughter. "N . . . n . . . o," I stammer.

"Okay, then," she says.

~

In the days leading up to the trip, I alternate between worrying about my merit, which I learn is another word for karma, and what the Dalai Lama might see when he looks in my soul. When I'm not worrying about my soul, I also fantasize that when he meets me for the first time he will instantly recognize me as special. He will see me as good. Or he will see me as bad. My fantasy life is very flexible.

~

Andrew, my colleague, and I are flying business class to India and I'm terrified. As he orders champagne, I imagine being arrested or turned back. I'm afraid of what will happen when I show my passport to enter the country. Will the system light up with bells and sirens? I've gotten permission from Probation to leave the country, but I haven't gotten permission from India to enter as a person on probation.

Andrew doesn't know that he's traveling with a felon, and probably wouldn't care if I told him, given how much champagne he's had, but my anxiety gets worse as we proceed across the Pacific.

When we stop to change planes in Hong Kong, I have my first true flash of excitement. Even if I get turned around in India, I am now someone who changes planes in Hong Kong, and that feels like a win for the women in G.

We are meeting up with a film crew in New Delhi and going early to set up for the dialogue between Archbishop Tutu and the Dalai Lama. Doug will be interviewing them along with Thupten Jinpa, the Dalai Lama's longtime translator, and all will be filmed and transcribed into content for the book Doug will write with them and possibly for a film. My job includes all things logistical: scouting with the film crew, coordinating hotels and guests, making sure everything goes as planned, reviewing the questions Doug is going to ask each day, and general crisis management for the entire team.

So far, I am the only one in crisis.

The ultimate goal is to take the outline Doug and I created with Jinpa and get enough content during the week to fill a book.

When we land in Hong Kong for our connecting flight there are two flight agents outside the gate holding signs with my name and Andrew's on them. I panic and turn back to reboard the plane.

"Ms. Love?"

I turn around slowly and nod.

"We have rerouted you to New Delhi. The headwinds caused you to miss your connection so now you will travel to Bangalore, go through immigration, and then transfer to another flight to New Delhi. Follow us, please."

~

While Andrew snores, I spend the flight from Hong Kong to Bangalore wondering what prison is like in India. When we land, the immigration line moves quickly, and my throat goes dry when the officer asks me the purpose of my visit. "Work," I squeak out. I can see him noticing my nerves, but he shrugs and stamps my passport.

~

When the time comes for me to meet the Dalai Lama, I prepare my mind with only good thoughts so he doesn't go looking into the corners of my dark past. My heart is pounding as he makes his way along a reception line of sorts. I am so ready for my big moment, for him to gaze into my eyes and clear the room so we can talk.

When he gets to me, he glances at me and nods slightly.

And that's it.

That night I join Doug and Archbishop Tutu and some dignitaries for dinner in Dharamsala. I sit next to this man who I wrote about in middle school, and as we share delicious Tibetan dumplings called momos he thanks me for the work I did on *The Book of Forgiving*. Doug takes a picture of us sitting together, and later that night he texts it to me.

In the photo Archbishop Tutu and I are holding hands and looking into each other's eyes. Doug has caught us in the middle of laughing about something. I lay in bed too excited for the week ahead to sleep, and I look at myself in the picture.

I look like the shiny, happy person I have always wanted to be. Only this time I'm not pretending. The joy on my face is real.

~

The dialogues go off without a hitch. His Holiness invites us to meditate with him in his private residence. It's an honor to be part of the entourage in his sacred space, and as I sit to his left on the floor and join him in his morning meditation in front of his personal shrine, I feel like I am levitating.

Look at me now, Eckhart Tolle.

As we sit, my eyes meet Doug's. We stare at each other for a moment, and he gives me a smile. He knows how far this room in Dharamsala is from where I've been. I tear up and smile back. I am overcome with gratitude, for Doug, for Archbishop Tutu, for the Dalai Lama, for the strange life that has taken me from G block to this holy space. I did not hustle or cheat or defraud my way into this room—I was invited and welcomed.

What if this is my merit?

I roll the idea around in my head and when Archbishop Tutu leads us in prayer and offers me the Eucharist, I take it. When he bows his head to me and murmurs a blessing, I bow my head, too, and think about the times I prayed in jail. On the floor of the holding room the night of my arrest when I prayed for help, and with the chaplain when I prayed to never do drugs again and to know my path and purpose.

Here, with the Eucharist melting on my tongue, my prayer is simple: *thank you*.

~

I still spend the rest of the week convinced that the most compassionate man in the world doesn't like me, because he never singles me out for attention like he does other members of the crew. Either he hates me, I decide, or maybe he is teaching me a bigger lesson. There is the old part of me that is sure that he hates me, but the new part of me,

the part that grows with every book I work on and every difficult moment I face, thinks it must be a lesson. I am just one of seven billion people living their lives. Making big mistakes over and over. Growing and shrinking and growing again.

In the evenings I walk around the temple grounds, monkeys chattering in the trees, and the lesson becomes clear: It's easier for me to think the Dalai Lama doesn't like me than to face the fact that deep down, despite where I am and who I'm with, I'm still not sure if I like myself.

Spending a week listening to Archbishop Tutu and the Dalai Lama alternate between teasing each other for not acting holy enough, and then crying over the profound suffering that is the human experience, changes me. Every day I walk away with some new nugget about the way I want to live my life—in service to others, accepting that I am always a work in progress, being more compassionate and more forgiving. Living in gratitude. Every day of the dialogues seems like a horoscope—there's something specific relating to my life that I need to hear.

The two holy men see the possibility of joy in every hard moment, and I want to live like that. They listen to each other deeply, and reach out to hold the other's hand when someone tells a difficult story from their life. His Holiness is curious about everyone filming them: the photographer's red hair, the sound guy's tattoos, the cameraman's beard. Even though it's a joke, when the Dalai Lama says he would rather go to hell than heaven because there are more people to help in hell, I start to cry.

They pause midway through each morning so everyone can stop work and drink tea together. The tea isn't great, but the communal pause feels like another profound lesson. These men, who have both carried the fate of countries on their backs, have a lightness I crave. They teach me not to take myself too seriously. When His Holiness

says all people are equal, no one is higher up or better than another, I feel like he is saying this just to me.

Each night, after my walk, I go to my hotel room in Dharamsala in the shadow of His Holiness's temple, and I write down what I saw and how I felt and who I still want to become.

On our last day we do a photo shoot with Archbishop Tutu and His Holiness. Miranda, the photographer, clicks away as, one by one, members of the team receive a special khata, a blessed Tibetan scarf from the Dalai Lama, and pose for pictures.

When it's my turn, I am nervous to be standing between these two men, and a bit flustered. My security badge is tangled up with my khata and both are tangled in my hair.

His Holiness takes my hand, and our eyes meet. His hands are softer than any skin I have ever felt before, softer than any baby I have ever held. Then he holds his hand up to Miranda to stop the shoot.

This is it, I think, *this is my moment.* He has seen my soul. I hold my breath to see what will happen next, and he starts fussing with my hair. Untangling the khata and the security badge and freeing my hair. Smoothing it down, putting me back together again.

Miranda takes photos of it all, and I know I will look at them on the nights when the world questions my merit. When *I* question my merit.

Standing between these two spiritual leaders, it suddenly doesn't matter what people think of me. I am standing in the light, at a temple, in service to something bigger than my insecurities and flaws. Bigger than my past and my mistakes.

Before I walk away, each man holds one of my hands and I tell them both, "Thank you. You have changed my life."

When I turn to leave, His Holiness grabs my hands again and slowly bows and touches his forehead to mine. I close my eyes, and we stay that way for a few seconds, or maybe a lifetime.

chapter 20

MANY
LIVES

Doug spends the next year writing *The Book of Joy* based on the dialogues in Dharamsala, and I work on a relationship book about the eight conversations you should have before you marry someone. I never had any of these conversations before any of my marriages.

I am also writing a book called *Designing Your Life* that publishes on the same day as *The Book of Joy*. Both books hit the *New York Times* bestseller list. I am ecstatic and proud, and all the hard work and sleepless nights feel worth it.

Each literary accolade is like money in the bank to me. A savings account I use as leverage against other parts of my life that are not as successful.

I am still on probation even though it should have ended two years ago. To get me off probation, Elizabeth and I go back to court. She argues with Probation, saying that I had gone above and beyond during my incarceration and on probation and I should be let off and allowed

THE MANY LIVES OF MAMA LOVE

to pay my restitution as I can over time without the threat of going back to jail hanging over my head.

She tells the judge that *Designing Your Life* is number one on the *New York Times* list. I think she is trying to show I have a valid job and also prove I'm a valuable member of society now and will not walk away from my debt.

The judge does not seem that impressed.

I hate sitting on the bench outside the courtroom waiting for the judge's ruling. I feel automatically guilty. I can taste jail in my mouth—rusted metal and locked doors and the bitterness of isolation. Before I was locked up, freedom used to feel like a vague, blurry concept and a given privilege, about as easy to pin down as wind. Now I understand freedom in the way you can only understand something when it's gone. Even out of jail, as long as I'm on probation, I'm still not free.

The judge gives me the choice to either stay on probation until restitution is completely paid or make my restitution payments to a county collection agency and get off probation. The judge wants to make sure I understand that the latter option will ruin my credit.

Elizabeth starts to argue, but the judge stops her. She looks at me and shrugs. There's just no way they are going to let me off probation without some penalty hanging over me.

The choice is roughly equivalent to declaring bankruptcy, and it will keep my credit rating abysmally low for seven years. Choosing between two bad choices is never easy, but I choose door number two. Bad credit seems better than living while holding your breath. Probation has turned my one-year sentence into a seven-year sentence, and now I have to add another seven years of bad credit. But I take this trade-off in order to sleep in peace.

The irony is that probation was originally invented as an alternative to incarceration. In the mid-1800s a man in Boston convinced a judge

to let him keep another drunken man in his care so he could rehabilitate him before sentencing. When the State of New York introduced probation in the early 1900s, one of the magistrate's arguments for creating a probation system was that it could be "punishment without disgrace, and effective without producing embitterment, resentment or demoralization."

Disgrace, embitterment, resentment, and demoralization is just another Monday in the modern world of probation.

And if it was hard for me to navigate all the conflicting requirements and illogical bureaucracy as a white, educated woman with some social support, how difficult was it for others without the same sort of opportunities and privilege? Late at night I sometimes read through the jail arrest logs, so I know when Kiki is back in, and the same for Spider, Vivian, and Nina. The only women I don't see rearrested are the ones who went off to prison.

I send care packages to them through the commissary—chocolate bars and bear claws and ramen. I know the money should go to paying back my own restitution, but this is a different kind of restitution. These strangers saved my life and lifted me up with their friendship when I was at my lowest. I owe them.

Meeting the Dalai Lama and Archbishop Tutu and all the other authors I get to interact with every day makes me feel valuable, but so did these women. The difference is, I could be honest with these women. Living a covert life, whether for good or bad, takes its toll. If I am only as sick as my secrets, well then, I am in hospice.

And I have had enough. Not enough to tell my secrets, but enough that I have decided I need to move away from this place I have lived for the last twenty-five years. I'm going to work my ass off and save enough money to pay my restitution and move far away. I want to go live in Hawaii, on an island thousands of miles away from this community where I no longer belong.

I tell Doug this stretch goal. "I need to save up enough money—Kaden graduates in 2023 and then when he goes off to college I'm going to move to Hawaii. I can work remotely."

"Is that what you really want to do?"

"Yes. I want to build a big family compound for all my boys—a place where they can come home to, a place where if they have families one day they can bring them. And when I die it will be theirs to share and create memories in.

"I'm tired of running away from things," I say. "I want to run toward something. And that something is Hawaii."

"So, if I'm understanding you correctly, you want to run to Hawaii?"

I laugh. "Yes, exactly. Someday I'm going to run all the way to Hawaii."

"If that's what you want, then I support you in doing that, and you have job security for life. I want us to work together until we are a hundred years old. We are peanut butter and jelly. Lennon and McCartney," he says.

"Ride or die," I reply. I'm trying to make Doug more "street" and he flashes me a sideways peace sign in response that makes me laugh.

With every new book I write I get to be a different person, live a different life. I want that same freedom in my real life. I hope I can find it in Hawaii, and I hope I can bear the weight of my secrets until I get there.

~

"Lara, will you tell Bryan about your past?" Doug asks.

I choke on my scrambled eggs and take a sip of water. The number one rule of fight club is I don't tell our authors about my past. Doug is to my right at the small table in a hotel restaurant in Montgomery, Alabama, across from the offices of the Equal Justice Initiative.

Bryan Stevenson, one of the country's leading social justice activists and lawyers, and one of the authors we represent, sits across the table, and we're catching up and having a nice breakfast before meeting Anthony Ray Hinton for the first time. Hinton had spent thirty years on Alabama's death row for a crime he didn't commit. We flew to Alabama at Bryan's request, to meet Mr. Hinton and potentially help him with his book. I want desperately to be his cowriter.

I take a deep breath. Montgomery's air is humid, thick with its history of slavery and oppression and the fight for civil rights. I wasn't prepared to talk about my crimes, my incarceration, my shame, and my work with others in recovery and incarcerated women who are reentering society.

But I understand why Doug has asked me to share my story. While almost a year in Santa Cruz County Jail doesn't compare to thirty years on death row, I know the pain of being alone. I know the sound of a door closing that you have no power to open yourself. I know about being judged. I know Ray before I've even met him, and I know that of all the books I've worked on, this is the book I was meant to do.

And Bryan knows me as a competent member of the literary agency that represents him; he doesn't know the many lives I have led before this breakfast until I finish my story.

He doesn't judge me. He shows compassion and kindness and understanding and says how relieved he will be to have someone working with Ray who has knowledge of the criminal justice system.

And when I meet Ray, we hit it off instantly. He doesn't trust easily, but he trusts me because I have been locked up. He was innocent, and I was guilty, but we share an understanding of captivity that transcends our differences.

We walk side by side behind Bryan and Doug on the sidewalks of Montgomery.

"How much time did you do?" he asks.

"Just a county year," I say, and he knows the reference.

"I'm glad you understand," he says.

"I bet you didn't think a middle-aged white woman would be help-ing tell your story."

Ray laughs. "No, I can't say that I did, but I'm glad it's you."

~

My mother dies a week after I get back from Montgomery. I had moved her to Santa Cruz and taken care of her financially and physically for the past two years while an extremely aggressive form of dementia—Lewy body dementia—changed her into someone unrecognizable. My mother, once so smart and aloof and vain and sad, had become childlike. I had become her mother. And in the last weeks of her life, I had to put aside all our history and be present for her in a way she could never be present for me.

Ray, whose mother died while he was on death row, comforts me long distance in my grief. When I say I don't have the words for grief, for regret, and I worry whether I did the right thing in her last days, he tells me to write about it.

"I did," I say. "I wrote a little each night for the last week of her life."

"Read it to me," he says.

I am embarrassed to read what I have written. It's a jumble of random thoughts and my attempt to make meaning out of something horrific. I need to work on Ray's book proposal, but my mother's death fills me with a feeling of loss that I can't reconcile with our discon-nected relationship. Ray insists it will help me feel better, so I read him what I have written of the past week.

Ray is silent for almost a minute after I finish reading.

"You were there for her," he finally says. "On death row, you die alone. In prison, you die alone. In prison you can't be with the ones

you love as they are dying. You were there. You weren't locked up. You took care of her while she passed; be grateful for that."

Ray is right. It is the first of many lessons he will teach me about gratitude and freedom.

"I walk every day simply because I can," he says.

"I eat dessert first because I don't ever want to be too full to enjoy something sweet and delicious.

"I stand in the rain because you never know when you won't be allowed to feel the rain on your skin. I don't ever worry about the weather."

I listen to him carefully and the week after my mom dies, I write three sample chapters and his entire book proposal in a few days. Doug submits the proposal to editors, and all those interested in publishing Ray's book meet with Doug and Ray in New York City. I stay home and anxiously wait to hear how it all turns out.

Ray gets a fantastic book deal and before we start writing the book, Doug has me listen to all the meetings he recorded in New York about the book so I can hear the different editors' ideas for the structure of the book. There are lots of great ideas, but I'm most attuned to the line Doug says to every editor in every meeting when they ask who is going to be helping Ray write the book.

"Do you know how hard it is to find an MFA who has been incarcerated?" Doug asks every editor after telling them I will be the coauthor.

"I didn't know that about Lara," says one editor. "How wonderful . . ."

My biggest secret, my greatest shame, has become a selling point. And that changes everything.

Over the next year Ray and I spend lots of time working together on *The Sun Does Shine*. We mix our pain together, and we pour it on the page, and we become family. He trusts me with his story, and I trust him with mine.

I learn so much about hope and gratitude and faith and friendship from Ray, and I pour everything I have in me into his story. When I write about how alone he felt on death row it helps me touch how alone I felt in jail, and some days I am on my office floor crying because through Ray I am able to tap so deeply into grief and loss that I'm not sure who I am crying for or who I am crying as, but it doesn't matter. Other days I am so full of the goodness of Ray's soul that the writing comes quickly and lightly. This innocent man who spent thirty years on death row teaches me as much about forgiveness as Archbishop Tutu. They both suffered and they both let it ennoble them rather than embitter them.

"I forgive," Ray says, "because I'm not giving the State of Alabama one more second of my life."

I try to adopt this worldview and apply it to myself. Bryan and Ray know about my past, so I bravely tell another author I work with before I work with her, and she doesn't run away from me screaming.

I take these baby steps, and then I pause to see if the world will come crashing down. When it doesn't, I take a deep breath and contemplate my next step.

For my birthday, I decide to try something I've always wanted to do but was too terrified to try: improv. I think of myself as an introvert so being unscripted on a stage feels like a nightmare, but there's an equal part of me that loves to entertain and make people laugh.

I show up for a drop-in adult improv class on a Saturday morning. It's an eclectic mix of ages and personality types, and as nervous and terrified as I am, it is fun. It's been so long since I played, since I acted silly, since I lived in the moment without carefully scripting all my interactions with others. This tribe of misfits and theater geeks and artists and writers welcomes me warmly. They invite me out to lunch after class. And so every Saturday morning, I put aside work and fear

and hypervigilance, and I stand on a stage saying ridiculous things and laughing for two hours.

I have found my tribe, my people, and not one of them knows about my past.

When improv becomes the gateway drug to a stand-up comedy class, my new tribe comes to watch me perform my routine.

Alone on a small stage I say, "So this one time when I was in prison . . ." and I do a routine about my felonies and how someone gets a prison nickname and how a woman made a tiny candy shiv out of a Jolly Rancher.

Afterward my new friends come up to me and say, "Is that true? Were you in prison with thirty-two felonies?"

Because I have learned to be in the moment from improv class, I reply immediately in the time-honored improv style. "Yes, and . . . it was jail, not prison."

There is silence at first, but before I can even get mortified, my new friend Eileen says, "Cool." The others follow with similar responses, and we all go to lunch where I am not the center of conversation. And my definition of freedom gets bigger.

I thought what I craved was approval and praise, but it's simpler than that. I craved acceptance. For all the different versions of me I have been, and all the many lives I have lived.

~

I am riding the comedy wave with my tribe, and it's such smooth sailing that when a local Rotary Club asks me to come speak to them about my work, I readily say yes. They don't mention my past, and I am excited to talk about our literary agency and the impact our books are having in the world. Our team has grown so much that with our foreign rights coagents, staff, and the collaborative writers I have hired

and trained, we number close to thirty staff now. Ty is working full time for our company as well, and Cody is creating videos for us, so my success is also their success. The work is nonstop, and I go to the office on a Saturday morning.

I am getting a contract out of Doug's inbox when I see the email. It's from: one@victimoflaralove.com.

I open the email and read:

SHAME ON YOU FOR PUTTING THIS VILE PERSON IN CHARGE OF FINANCIAL THINGS. THE COURT HAD BANNED HER FROM BEING IN THAT KIND OF FUNCTION AND YOU ARE BOTH VIOLATING THAT. I WILL BE CONTACT-ING THE D.A. AND COURTS.

The sender has included a link to the *Sentinel* article—I guess in case Doug didn't know about my past.

The panic attack hits me right away. I can't control my breathing, and my office seems to have tilted. I want to run but I can't feel my limbs. All I can think is I'm going back to jail, and so is Doug.

I call him, and when he answers I am hysterical and incomprehensible. "Someone sent you . . . in your email . . . trouble . . . jail . . ."

"Take a breath," says Doug. "Are you hurt? Are the kids okay? Sam?"

"Yes, but someone sent an anonymous email."

"Where are you?" asks Doug. I can't control my crying, and I can hear the fear in his voice, but it's like I'm listening from underwater. Everything is muffled and removed.

"Of . . . fff . . . ice," I stammer.

"Stay right there," he says. "I'm on my way."

I sit on the couch under shelves of all the books we've created and realize none of it matters. None of it changes a thing.

Doug charges into the office like he's going to battle, and I start crying all over again. "I'm sorry," I say. "I'm so sorry."

"There's nothing to be sorry for. You're not going to jail. I'm not going to jail."

I hear what he's saying, and I know he's being logical, but all I can think of is that my worst fear has come true: My reputation has ruined his reputation. Doug, who has never broken a law in his life, done a drug, been anything but kind and good, is now being threatened with jail.

"Let's go for a walk," he says.

I blindly follow him out of the office, and we walk away from the downtown area of Santa Cruz. I don't feel safe outside. I don't feel safe inside. As we walk, I keep looking over my shoulder, sure that the police are going to pull up any moment and take us both away.

When Doug stops in front of the bank where we do business, I follow him inside without question. If he wants to get a little banking done while I'm having a meltdown, who am I to judge?

We approach Gustavo, who handles our accounts, and Doug greets him warmly. "Listen," he says. "I want to add Lara as a signer on all our business accounts."

Gustavo looks at me and I know I look like hell, but I smile weakly.

This is Doug's way of showing me how much he trusts me. "I meant to do this a long time ago," he says. "I just never found a moment where we were both free at the same time. Today is the perfect day."

The paperwork appears in front of me and I sign.

Back at the office, Doug makes sure I am okay before he leaves. "This is nothing to be worried about," he says. "The person who sent that email is a coward. If someone was concerned, they could just call me."

I nod. I know he's right, and I'm a bit embarrassed that I thought we would both go to jail. When he leaves, I call Eileen. Besides being my new best friend, she used to work for the NSA. I tell her about

the email, and she goes to work trying to trace it with some computer magic. The closest she gets is an address. I look it up online, and it is a business park with multiple offices.

I leave the office and drive to the address. If someone is threatening me, I want to know who it is. I slowly drive by each business in the lot. A sign shop, an accounting office, a boat supply company. I google each business trying to find out the owner's name. Is it one of my old neighbors? I don't recognize any of the businesses. I don't know any of their owners or employees.

I try to think about what could have triggered this email seven years into my job at Idea Architects, nine years after my arrest. And then it hits me. I agreed to give a public talk about my work as a ghost-writer. I search out the Rotary Club that invited me and see that they have just announced me as a speaker. For years I have lived under the radar, and then I forgot. The person who sent this email must be a member of the Rotary Club. I call the woman who set up the speaking event and leave her a voicemail.

"I'm so sorry," I say, "but I won't be able to speak at your event after all. Something's come up."

Logically I know I can't go back to jail now that I'm off probation, but this message about my past triggers me. This hatred from the community triggers me. For every two steps forward, I take one step back. Or maybe it's the other way around.

The only difference now is I don't have to walk alone. I have Bryan Stevenson and Ray Hinton and Eileen and Doug. I have Sam and my children. I have my comedy friends. They love me, they trust me, and I try to tell myself that it's enough to keep me safe.

REAL POWER

I've had lots of imaginary conversations with Oprah Winfrey.

I used to watch her talk show every afternoon. I laughed when she laughed, cried when she cried, and imagined myself sitting on a couch with her. Reading was escape, and so was Oprah.

Ray and I are at Book Passage in Corte Madera, California. I've come to see him while he is on his book tour. The moms whose game night I couldn't join at Kate's house before I met the Dalai Lama have now invited me to join their book club. I gave them all my advance reader copies, the early versions of the book reserved for reviewers, and they're also in the audience here, clutching their early copies. The bookstore's owner is distressed at seeing the review copies in their hands. "You're not supposed to have those," she says to them.

I step in and point to my name on the cover under Ray's. "It's okay," I say. "Those are my copies, and these folks will still buy the hardback version tonight." Dylan and Eileen are also with me, and it

feels like a great event. Ray is on fire as he shares his story, and there's not a dry eye in the house.

After the event, we only have a little time to catch up before he's whisked off to another event in a different city.

I am in the office the next day when Ray calls.

"Hellooooo," I say. "That was such a great event last . . ."

"Lara!" He's whispering.

"What?" I ask. "Are you okay?"

He clears his throat. "I'm hiding in the bathroom at my hotel. They are setting up for an interview outside the door so I have to be quiet."

I'm still confused. "What's wrong?"

"Nothing's wrong. She called me, Lara."

"Who called you?"

"Oprah! Oprah Winfrey just called me. She told me it was Oprah, and at first I didn't believe her."

"Really?" I ask dubiously. Ray is known for playing jokes, so I don't know if he's teasing or not.

"She picked the book, Lara. She picked *The Sun Does Shine* for her book club. I'm not supposed to tell anyone, but of course I'm calling you right away. This is our book. But you can't tell anyone, you can't tell anyone."

"Not even Doug?"

"Not yet. She told me I can't tell anyone."

I want to say "oh my God" or "holy fucking shitballs," but Ray is a man of faith who never curses, so instead I just scream.

"I'm so happy for you, Ray! So many people are going to read your story now. This is absolutely amazing!"

"I have to go do this interview, but I will call you tonight."

I want to laugh and cry and scream. This is the first Oprah pick for our agency. The first book where my name appears on the cover as a coauthor. This is Ray, one of my dearest friends, and a man who has

experienced more injustice than just about anyone I know. I want to dance and shout and tell everyone the news, but I can't.

I sit with the news for three hours. I can't concentrate on work, and all I want to do is call Doug. I want to tell him as a friend. I want to tell him as his business partner. And I want to tell him because he's Ray's agent, and he should know. But Ray trusts me, and I gave him my word.

Mostly I just want somebody to celebrate with.

I am just about to give in and tell Doug when a flurry of emails come in from Ray's editor and the publicity and marketing people at his publisher. Oprah has officially picked the book, and we all have to sign nondisclosure agreements and keep it secret for a couple of months.

I call Doug immediately. "Did you see your email?" I ask.

"No, what?"

"Read your email and call me back," I say and hang up. I realize then that he might think it's another threatening letter so I quickly text him: IT'S GOOD NEWS!

He calls back within seconds and we scream into the phone. I call Ray back and tell him that Bryan, the publisher, and Doug have all been informed.

When the publisher explains to us that it could be months before the official announcement because they have to order enough paper to meet the demand for books once the news is out, the significance of this news sets in.

I'm invited to go to New York City with Ray for the live television announcement on *CBS This Morning*, hosted by Gayle King. Despite growing up in Boston, despite working in publishing, I have never been to New York before. I can't tell anyone why I'm going so I just say it's for work. Dylan is in New York on a business trip, so we spend two days together before he has to leave.

Ray, his best friend Lester, and I are all staying at the same hotel. Doug is also joining us at CBS but is staying with his family. We all meet for breakfast before the car arrives to take us to the studio. Our editor, George Witte, meets us there and we all walk in together.

The entire morning feels surreal, but it's real. And it's fucking fantastic.

Ray is going to be live on air with Gayle King and Oprah, and I'll be in the glass-walled greenroom on set where Lester, Doug, George, and I can all watch the action in real time. Ray is calm as can be while my heart pounds. Once we get settled, Lester and I are sitting next to each other on the couch facing the set when I look up and see Oprah looking in at us. Behind her looms an image of the book's cover that takes up the entire wall. The title, Ray's name, and then my name below his.

Oprah gives a little wave. I wave back.

I stare at her in real life and feel vindicated, because in my mind anything Oprah approves of the culture approves of. And Oprah approves of me.

Ray is doing so well with his interview that they keep him on for an extra segment. He comes back to the greenroom and we hug, and I tell him he absolutely killed it. Before he can reply, Gayle and Oprah walk in.

Ray introduces me to Oprah. Tells her I am his writer.

"Hi," she says and gives me a big smile.

"Hi!" I have nothing more eloquent to say in her presence.

"You did a great job," she says. "You are an incredible writer."

And that's it. I can die now. My life is complete.

"Do you want to take pictures?" she asks. Gayle and Oprah, both in yellow, flank me on either side and Doug snaps away with his phone. I am smiling so huge I must look like my head will burst.

It's all a whirlwind because Gayle has to get back on the air for

her next segment, and Oprah has to go be Oprah. We're just about to leave when an assistant to Oprah comes in and invites Doug and me to lunch with Oprah and Gayle and Ray and Lester.

I am about to be someone who lunches with Oprah. We have an hour to kill before lunch so the four of us wait in the lobby. I have dozens of messages and emails from people who see the show. The news is out.

The restaurant we are going to clears the back half because it's Oprah. The manager takes me through first.

"Is this table okay?" he asks nervously.

I look around the room not knowing exactly what I'm looking for. In jail, you never want to sit with your back to the door. Oprah is the ultimate shot caller, so I pick a table to the side, so she can see all the entrances and exits.

At lunch I am seated to her left, and when the waiter comes to take our order, Oprah points to Ray and asks the waiter if he knows who he is.

"No, sorry."

"You will," says Oprah. "You want to know him. And you will."

She orders champagne for the table, and we toast to Ray.

"I'm going to go stand on Fifth Avenue and hand this book out to every person who walks by," she says. "It's going to be a bestseller!"

The lunch is lively, and everyone is in a great mood. Doug and Gayle and Ray and Lester are engaged in some conversation that I'm not tracking because I am sitting next to Oprah.

She has been making little side comments to me on the bigger conversations all throughout lunch. I hang on every word—the ultimate fangirl.

She tells me she loves the book, and that her team didn't want her to pick it because she had just picked a book about someone incarcerated.

"But you know what I said?" she asks.

"No, what?"

"I said, 'Do you see your name on this company? No, you don't. That's my name, and this is the book we are going to do.' And they read it, and I was right." She leans toward me and whispers, "That's power, Lara, that is real power."

I recall telling Daddy that real power is quiet power. And I smile at Oprah as she toasts the table, and I think maybe real power isn't always quiet. Maybe real power is saying things out loud and owning your own story like you own a company or a network or a magazine. Real power is putting your name on things. Real power is about using your power to shine a light on other people so they can find their own power.

A crowd has begun to gather outside the restaurant. I listen as Oprah schools me about power, Doug about movie deals, and Ray about managing his money and what to do when cousins of cousins come out and want him to pay their bills because he is famous. With each person she has a way of speaking their exact language. It's a gift. A powerful gift that gives her the kind of power Daddy couldn't even imagine.

I look around this table, this restaurant in New York City, this unlikely lunch party, and realize that I have no idea what I want to do next. Life is strange and heartbreaking and wonderful, and it can change on you in an instant.

I have been so many different people in my life—wife, mother, real estate agent, Little League coach, school board member, lover, fighter, addict, felon. I have done good things, and I have done bad things.

I have been so many different people in the books I've ghostwritten, and worn so many different hats in my job, just to keep myself busy and striving.

And during all of it, there was always this desperate undercurrent

of me trying to prove to the world that I'm valuable and worthy, more good than bad.

I realize suddenly that I'm tired of pretending I am anything other than who I am. People may love me or hate me, praise me or criticize me, reward me or punish me. All I can be is who I am now, and then work hard to become the person I most want to be. I'm tired of hustling for an approval even the great and powerful Oprah can't really give me. I know what I'm looking for can only be found on the inside, and it's going to be my job to keep finding it over and over.

By the time we finish lunch, *The Sun Does Shine* has become the number one best-selling book on Amazon. Ray and I take this in on the car ride back to the hotel, both of us sitting side by side in silence at first.

"We did it," he says.

"We did it, Ray, we really did it."

And then we look into each other's eyes and laugh and I start to cry. Neither of us has the words to convey how this feels. We were both somewhere else and now we're here. Together. He leans toward me and I meet him halfway across the seat and we embrace.

Ray was once a condemned man on death row, and I was once in jail with a sheet wrapped around my neck. Now we are both number one bestsellers.

~

Twenty-four hours later I am back home, doing laundry, sweeping dog hair off the floor. Lunch with Oprah already feels far away. The entire flight home I replayed the lunch and Oprah's words.

I know I have a lot more inner work to do. I thought I had to convince the whole world that I am more than the worst thing I have done, the worst person I have been, but really I just have to convince myself.

Now that I have brushed up against Oprah, old friends I haven't spoken to since before my arrest call me and gush. People want to get together. People want to have lunch. People want to know how I am.

It all feels hollow, though. I don't want a community to welcome me just because Oprah made me valuable again in their eyes. I don't want any friendships that are shallow or conditional. I want real relationships. Real friends. Real community. And, I realize, I don't want to divorce Santa Cruz. I want to stay and make it work. Hawaii is a beautiful place to visit, but I don't want to banish myself to an island.

~

Soon after I return from New York, Sam, Chase, Kaden, and I go to Hawaii for a vacation. I didn't want to live there anymore, but I did want to visit. We go straight to the beach from the airport, and Kaden and Chase are boogie boarding while Sam and I watch from the sand. The swell picks up out of nowhere, and suddenly the waves are huge, and the sets are relentless. Chase rides his board in, but Kaden is struggling. The waves are crashing over him and pulling him farther from shore. It is like one of my natural-disaster nightmares I've had since my arrest—where my boys are being pulled away from me and I can't reach them. Only this is real. As if in slow motion, I see the lifeguard jump out of his tower and run into the ocean, with Sam running right behind him. Everyone on the beach stands up to watch. Another swimmer is trying to reach him as well.

Three powerful swimmers who all know the ocean are trying to save him while I can only stand on the beach and watch. Only I can't watch. I can't even breathe. I turn away, turn my back on the ocean and on Kaden.

I am a coward. I am weak. I am afraid.

I only look away for a few seconds before I force myself to turn

back and stand witness to my youngest son's struggle to survive. Sam, the lifeguard, and the other man have hold of Kaden but they're all fighting the waves to get to shore. At least he isn't alone. I stand on the sand in the sun and face him and will them all to come in safely.

The old me would have hid my fear from him, but when he makes it onto the beach I run to him. I wrap my arms around him and burst into tears. "Are you okay? I'm so glad you are okay. I was so scared. Oh my God."

He is shaking and he hugs me back, but then quickly lets go. "I'm fine. I'm okay."

"I couldn't watch," I say. "I was so scared, and I turned away because I couldn't watch. I'm so sorry I did that."

I start to cry even harder, and as a crowd gathers around us, he gets frustrated. "It's okay," he says. "Let's just go! God!"

I'm embarrassing him even more than a public beach rescue.

I quickly gather our things from the beach and we walk to our rental car. Sam opens the back for us and puts the boogie boards in, and then he and Chase get in the car.

Kaden and I stand at the open trunk and I fold him in my arms again. He rests his head on my shoulder.

"I love you," he says. "I was so scared."

"I'm sorry, baby guy. I was so scared too. I love you so much."

We hold each other like that, sandy and afraid, but together. "It's okay," I say. "You're okay. We're okay."

I have been watching Kaden for signs of trauma ever since his year away from me. When he was in first grade, he told me he had a secret he couldn't tell me and I panicked, thinking it was something horrific, some abuse from his nights in foster care before Bryan and Darcy had

taken him. I begged Dylan, Cody, and Ty to try to get the information out of him and tried to steel myself for the bad news. It turned out he had kissed a girl on the cheek.

Every day I inspected him for any places where I had broken him, and year after year, even though I didn't find any outward signs, I was prepared for his trauma to manifest in some big way.

Just when I start to think that we've escaped unscathed, almost overnight, he is hit with crippling anxiety. He suddenly thinks he is going to be kidnapped. He is afraid to be home alone, afraid to sleep without a flashlight aimed at his door, afraid even to walk downstairs and get water on his own. He stops hanging out with friends, he doesn't go outside, and his fears overwhelm him.

I immediately take him to therapy, to an anxiety coach, to EMDR treatments. I buy him herbal stress remedies. I try everything, and still he is afraid. I don't know if it is just puberty hormones, a phase, or if it's the beginning of mental health issues he will struggle with for a lifetime. This anxiety is real and tangible and stronger than something that can just be cured through a mother's love and attention. It's something unseen and unknown, and nothing I try seems to help. I feel guilty and powerless. I want him to feel safe, and no matter what I say or do, he simply doesn't.

We talk about his anxiety often, and he keeps telling me we need to move. We're still renting the only home that hadn't required a background check when we left Doug's house, and finding another such rental seems impossible. But Kaden is insistent. He starts to email me real estate listings.

"We can't buy a house," I say.

"Why not?"

"We don't have the money you need to put down on a house. Homes are so expensive here, it's impossible."

When I tell Doug about Kaden's anxiety and his wanting to move, Doug is sympathetic.

"Maybe you should listen to him."

"I can't afford to buy a house. I have nowhere near the kind of down payment money I would need."

"You could borrow the money against your profit share in the business."

"Seriously?"

"Seriously."

Sam and I make a list of everything we want in our dream house. Bedrooms for the kids, an office for me, outdoor space for the dogs, a workshop for Sam. We describe this imaginary place to each other and ask Kaden, Chase, and Dahlia what they imagine in their dream home.

A week later a friend of a friend tells me about the house she is selling. It is on seven acres and has everything on our list. This is right before Halloween, and by Thanksgiving we are set to close escrow.

I have never owned a home, and when Sam and I go to sign the paperwork, I realize that this thirty-year mortgage isn't just a whole new level of financial commitment, it's also me committing to being a stable, income-earning, non-drug-using, stay-out-of-jail, gainfully employed type of person for the next thirty years. I'm going to be someone's permanent neighbor. This is going to be my permanent home. It feels so much bigger than just a new house—there's a weight to it that I take on.

A week after we move in, I can't find Kaden anywhere in the house and I panic.

"Sam, Kaden's gone!"

"He went for a walk with the dogs."

"What do you mean?" I am incredulous.

"I mean, he's walking. Outside. With the dogs."

After nine months of his not being able to go downstairs alone, I can't believe it. I am waiting for him when he gets back.

"How was your walk?" I ask.

"Awesome."

"How did you sleep last night?"

"Great!"

"How's the anxiety, then?" I sound anxious when I ask this, so I say it again more nonchalantly, and he laughs.

"I told you we just needed to move. I'm fine. Stop freaking out all the time. Jeez."

It is such a normal fourteen-year-old thing to say that I laugh, and when he rolls his eyes I laugh harder.

~

At Christmastime all the boys and their friends converge on the new house. We are sitting around the dining room table laughing and I think about being in G and imagining a home with sunlight and happy faces. It's taken a decade but this, I realize, is that home. And it didn't just help Kaden's anxiety—it helped heal mine as well.

As long as I keep showing up every day in my life, no one can take this home away from me. There is no other shoe that is going to drop. I have all my boys with me, and this home is all I have ever wanted—safety, sanctuary, and joy. All I've ever really wanted is a place to call home, and now I have it.

Kaden and I are both growing up. And for the first time, I really believe we are each going to be okay.

chapter 22

THE WORST
THING I
HAVE EVER
DONE

I 've obviously lost my mind.

It was easy when I was high on Oprah and New York City to de-cide to own my story and stop caring what other people think, but it's another thing to step out on a stage and actually rat myself out. Plus, I've had no time to prepare. We've had an author in town all week, so I've had no time to rehearse or memorize what I'm going to say or how I'm going to say it. The theme of this TEDx is hope.

I hope I don't throw up.

I was also hoping Doug would talk me out of it at the last second. "A lot of our authors still don't know my past. People might be upset."

"Lara, I will say what I've always said. If people don't want to work with us because of your past, we don't want to work with those people."

"I know, but . . ."

"Look, if you're not ready, you can back out. A bad TED Talk is worse than no TED Talk."

This gets my competitive edge up, as he knows it will.

"I can do it," I say. "I just need a couple of hours to practice what I want to say so I don't embarrass myself while I'm humiliating myself."

Doug laughs.

A year earlier I had gone to see a shaman and she told me she needed to do a soul retrieval. "What does that mean?" I asked.

"Sometimes a part of our soul fractures off. It can happen in early childhood or during trauma. I can go in and retrieve it."

I still didn't completely understand, but if I had left pieces of my soul lying around I wanted to pick them up. I was ready to be whole.

During the ceremony or procedure or whatever it was that had me lying on a table while she shook rattles over me, she told me that before I was born into this life, my soul made a contract.

"What was the contract?"

"I'm not sure exactly what this means, but maybe it will resonate with you."

"Okay," I say. "What contract did I make?"

She looks at me and gives a little shrug. "Your contract was to be on a stage as no one."

"What does that mean? Is that a good thing or a bad thing?"

"Your contract is what you agree you're here in this lifetime to learn—it's always something hard."

"Well, can I break it?"

"Once you've learned what you've needed to learn, you don't need to break it. You've fulfilled the obligations of that contract. It can end."

I think about the secrets I had been keeping, my ghostwriting, my addiction, my lying, my loneliness—all the things that had kept me feeling removed from myself, from life.

I was done being on a stage as no one, I was done living in shame,

and I was done living under the shadow of the worst person I had been. I was ready to be on a stage as me.

So for almost fourteen minutes I stand on a stage and tell everyone who wanted to listen exactly what I was so afraid they would find out.

I was once the neighbor from hell.

And then I tell them about some other people I have been.

I ask everyone in the audience to think about the worst thing *they* had ever done, and then I ask them to tell it to the person to their right. The audience gasps, and that feeling behind the gasp is exactly what shame feels like.

I am done living in shame.

I talk about how high the barriers are to rejoining society after incarceration, and how much harder it becomes under the weight of gossip and judgment. I am telling myself what I most need to hear.

That I'm human, and humans make mistakes.

~

I no longer live in fear of the "Neighbor from Hell" headline. I own it and say yes, that's who I was for a moment, for a season of my life, but it's not who I have always been nor who I have become. That headline has no power over me anymore.

It won't shut me up or shut me down.

For the first time in over a decade, I google myself. The headline doesn't immediately pop up. It's still there. It will always be there. But now you have to click through a few pages in the search results, and this feels right.

For the first time since my arrest, I drive past my old house. Around the cul-de-sac where neighbors and friends stood gawking as I was taken away in handcuffs.

My former front yard is full of plastic toddler toys. The fence DJ and I built is sagging, but it still stands. As I drive through my old

neighborhood, I wait for my heart to race and my chest to constrict. I'm on the lookout for an angry mob. I watch for the shame and fear to flood my body.

They don't.

In the end, it's just another house in another neighborhood. And behind every front door is a family made up of people with their own struggles, their own secrets, and their own fear and shame that someday those secrets will be found out.

So yes, I was once the neighbor from hell. I have also been a dozen different people in a dozen different books. I have lived many lives and will hopefully live many more. But for now I am just myself.

I have done lots of good in my life, and I have also done lots of bad. One doesn't negate the other. And the truth is, I don't believe the worst thing I have ever done is found in the stealing or lying or drug abuse. The worst thing I've ever done is build an identity out of the worst thing I've ever done. I've condemned others for not being able to see beyond my past when I was the one who couldn't see beyond my past.

There's no doubt that our "justice" system is broken. There's no doubt that as a society we ask people to pay far beyond what their criminal sentences ask of them. It's a truth we all need to examine. Because how we take care of broken people matters. Fundamentally, I believe, it determines our own humanity.

And we don't just sentence someone to a year or five years or ten years—we turn every sentence into a life sentence.

Every sentence is a life sentence.

~

I believe the best thing that ever happened to me was going to jail. I am a better mother, a better friend, a better worker, and a better writer because of my experiences.

I've been a liar and a truth-teller, selfish and selfless. I've been smart and stupid. I have hated myself and learned to love myself. I have hustled for my self-worth—looking for it in the things I owned, in other people's love and approval—but I have come to accept it as fundamental regardless of what I do or don't do.

There is freedom in owning all the parts of me—the good, the bad, the ugly, and the beautiful. I made the conscious choice to create an identity out of the worst things ever said about me, and now I choose differently.

It was always my choice.

~

I eventually become co-CEO of Idea Architects, but then in 2022 I leave to start my own literary agency. I name it True Literary because I want to create something wholly true to me, to my vision for books and stories that will make the world a better and kinder place for everyone. It sounds a little cheesy, but I think, as the Dalai Lama would say, it's my dharma—that I'm finally living my soul's purpose.

I think often about what Oprah told me about real power—and my takeaway was that it's not only having your name on the door but using your power to shine a light on other people. I will always have a soft spot for the underdog, the ones living at the margins of life, the addicts, the criminals, and anyone who wants to transform their suffering by using their own stories to inspire others. I'm grateful for all the people who lifted me up while I was at my lowest, and I try to pay it forward wherever and whenever I can.

~

My older boys are all grown and out of college. Kaden will be graduating and heading off to college soon, and his memories of being taken from home have faded. I no longer overcompensate for what

happened, and he no longer tests me to make sure I will stay. The single year we were apart no longer defines our relationship or haunts my sleep.

DJ eventually found his way out of drugs. He is an ultra-endurance runner and a good father.

Sam and I have been married for close to a decade, and each year that passes I settle more and more into the unfamiliar space of being vulnerable. Talking to him after a hard day, asking for help with a problem I'm struggling with, working through a disagreement—all of it still feels like learning a foreign language, but with practice it gets easier. I guess the third time really is the charm.

My home is chaotic and loud and full of children and animals and love.

My addiction to escape is in remission, but I stay vigilant in case it shows up again. For now, there is no other place I'd rather be than where I am.

There is no other person I'd rather be than who I am.

And no other life I'd rather live than the beautiful mess of a life I'm living.

acknowledgments

Buckle up because this is going to be a lot. For as much as I like to think of myself as a loner, there are so many people from my many lives who I need to acknowledge.

First, I have to thank my agent, my friend, my partner in crime (not literally, people), my first champion, and the person who opened up a brave new world of wonder and opportunity and words to me when I was at my lowest—Doug Abrams. If "thank you" is the most powerful prayer there is, then I offer it up to you, Doug. Thank you, a million times thank you! *Peanut Butter Meet Jelly.*

I also must thank my other agent, my more fashionable and chic twin, my work bestie, my Wordle foe, and one of the most brilliant and badass women I know in business and in life—Rachel Neumann. I want to be you when I grow up. Thank you for supporting me through this process, even when I was crying in parking lots, and for the many times you were just simply there—a calm presence when I was anything but.

Doug and Rachel make everyone they meet better humans. You should meet them!

I also want to thank everyone at Idea Architects for being the best hype team for me as a boss and as an author; Janelle Julian, Mariah Sanford, Ty Love (see dedication), Bella Roberts, Sarah Rainone, Mark Hitz, Jordan Jacks, Alyssa Knickerbocker, Kelsey Sheronas, Julia Shefcik, Staci Bruce, Stacie Sheftel, Kelly Miner, Andrew Mumm, Michael Matkin, and all the collaborative writers I got to train and

work with over the years. I miss you. I love you. I am grateful for every single thing each one of you taught me over twelve years.

Eamon Dolan, my brilliant, kind, ruthless, savvy editor at Simon & Schuster, thank you for pushing me out of my comfort zone when I needed it, reassuring me when I needed that, and teaching me what the phrase "vague bombast" means. I'm still going to send you that T-shirt! We chose each other, and this book is better for those choices. You make me smarter every single time I talk to you. Eamon has his own book coming out—and you all want to read it!

Thank you to everyone at Simon & Schuster who believed in me and in this book—Jonathan Karp, Priscilla Painton, Tzipora Baitch, Lewelin Polanco, Beth Maglione, Sara Kitchen, Bri Scharfenberg, Alyssa diPierro, Omesha Edwards, and Julia Prosser. There are so many people working behind the scenes in production and sales and publicity and marketing, and while I may not know all your names, I appreciate you, I hope to meet you, and you are the bridge between author and reader and there should be monuments in your likeness.

A big thank-you also to Joseph Papa of Joseph Papa PR for taking me on (even though I'm not a celebrity) and being my publicity champion!

In the UK I want to thank Caspian Dennis and Sandy Violette at Abner Stein, and Camilla Ferrier, Jemma McDonagh, Brittany Poulin, Saliann, and everyone else at the Marsh Agency. You are all my UK family, whether you signed up for that or not.

I also want to thank my UK publisher and editors: Claudia Connal (miss you), Jake Lingwood, and the amazing Mala Sanghera-Warren. There are also a ton of people behind the scenes at Hachette/Octopus Publishing Group launching my book into the UK, and I am grateful for all of you and hope to meet you in person.

Thank you to Scott Budnick, Ameet, Gabby, Katie, Lauren,

ACKNOWLEDGMENTS

Saul, and the entire One Community team for reading about my trauma and thinking this would make some great TV comedy. Obviously. Thank you to Amy Welsh-Hanning and Mallory Edens for believing in this project and lending your passion, expertise, and humor. And a big thank-you to Sylvie Rabineau and Elizabeth Wachtel, my film/TV agents at WME for being both brilliant and bighearted. Hollywood needs more people like you and like all the people I've mentioned.

It wasn't easy to write this book and I'm grateful to all the friends, authors, early readers, late-night talkers, guides, and cheerleaders who helped me along the way. Eileen Burke-Woodward, Heidi Rielly, Bill Rielly, Clifford Henderson, Dixie Cox, Erica Smith Jiminez, Lori Cressy, Lisa Smith (thank you for finally letting me into a book club), Noel Diop, Evy Poumpouras, Silvia Vasquez-Lavado, Jane Chen, Emma Nadler, Crystal Hefner, Benjamin Gilmer, Mark Daley, Karen Sparks, Ren Ligon, Ben McBride, Eldra Jackson, Aaron Shulman, Robert Waldinger, Ethan Kross, Jim Doty, Dave Evans, Bill Burnett, Cynthia Chase, Cassandra Byard, Tracy Van Hoy, Irene Tsouprake Holombo, Peggy Callahan, Boo Prince, Alexandra Metzler, Chris Metzler, DNA, Kristy Gateley, Carly O'Brien, Oliver Midgley, Anaya Saipresert, and so many more. I could write a whole other book with the names of people who have been there for me when I was finally brave enough to share my story. Thank you for helping me find the humor in the tragedy and the meaning out of the mess.

A special thank-you to Bryan Stevenson and my dear friend Anthony Ray Hinton. You are both an inspiration to me always!

Before I began my writing journey, I took another kind of journey to Soltara in Costa Rica with twenty perfect strangers. I love you all, and we shared a weeklong psychic battle few could comprehend

(what is behind door 2?). Megan, Mike, Luke, Tariq, Will, Liz, Weslie, Bronson, Rachel, Banay, Irene, Phil, George, Anthony, Kazu, Bree, Beth, Alan, and Catherine × 2.

Thank you to Kenton Bell for the coaching, the laughter, the guidance, and reminding me that everything I need, I already have. Still waiting for that Zap!

And finally (finally), I have to thank my family (buckle up again). I want to acknowledge my new family (thank you, DNA testing—this is a story for the next book): my father, Dave Lawrence; my sister, Shelley Welander; my two new brothers, Kevin and Craig Lawrence; and my brother-in-law, Cam. My seven nephews and nieces that I never knew I had: Copper, Ever, Jasper, Ella, Grace, Sofia, and Mackenzie. We have become a family late in life, but you have given me the greatest gift of my adult life: family. We recognized each other from the jump, and my heart is full with each one of you.

To the children I gave birth to, Dylan, Cody, Ty, and Kaden, I love you always and forever and it's you all who put the "Mama" in Mama Love. You are all such amazing young men, despite the messiness of my many lives, and thank you for your grace and forgiveness and unconditional love. To the children I have been lucky enough to play the role of stepmother for, Hailey, Logan, Chase, and Dahlia—thank you for letting me be the bonus parent in your life as you've grown. I love you all fiercely.

Finally, to Sam, my third-time's-a-charm husband who shows me every day just how magical and exhilarating steady love and support can be. You make me feel safe. You make me feel loved. You adore me at my quirkiest, and support every single crazy idea I've ever had. You have no idea what a gift you are just by being next to me. I can't believe I've made it married so long, and I can't wait to see what the next thirty-plus years have in store for us!

ACKNOWLEDGMENTS

Thank you to the women in G and the women in Blaine who shared this journey, you know who you are . . .

To learn more about how to help incarcerated and formerly incarcerated women, please visit: www.thegemmaproject.org